6.76 - B+T   5-67   (Sweeringen)

THE IDEOLOGICAL
REVOLUTION IN
THE MIDDLE EAST

THE IDEOLOGICAL REVOLUTION IN THE MIDDLE EAST

LEONARD BINDER

DEPARTMENT OF POLITICAL SCIENCE
UNIVERSITY OF CHICAGO

JOHN WILEY & SONS, INC.
NEW YORK · LONDON · SYDNEY

To my father

PREFACE

Over a number of years, the study of ideological change in the Middle East has been the major topic of interest to me. In fact, I think it is fair to say that most of those concerned with Middle East politics have been primarily concerned with the ideological problem. This concern, as will be seen in the following chapters, is shared with Middle Eastern intellectuals. That which draws both foreign scholar and native graduate to the same problem is the common realization that some form of Islamic religious belief dominated political life in the Middle East until recently. The questions we have asked have not been one in phrasing, but they have been the same in purpose. We would ask whether Islam has lost its former influence entirely; and we would ask whether changed material circumstances are at the root of the changes which have occurred.

Although our starting point is quite parochial, eventually it must be acknowledged that our answers relate to the most general issues of the study of ideology. In essence, *the* central question of this field of study is whether or not Truth, as it relates to social organization and political institutions, exists and can be known independently of a given socio-historical situation. This central question seems difficult enough without adding the complication involved in the attempt at the objective study of alien cultures. Relativism and parochialism are the two dangers which threaten our enterprise. The solution which is suggested in the following pages is not revolutionary. It views ideological change as a dynamic process in which the reasoning of the mind is primary, but wherein it is, nevertheless, part of a system. That system is composed of material circumstances in part, but it is also composed of received ideas of the Good, of reasonable and pragmatic considerations, and of arbitrary notions of personal and group identity. Obviously, the task which this book approaches is rendered somewhat simpler by starting from a given situation. That situation is the assumption of the earlier prevalence of something called mediaeval Islam. It is for this reason that we concentrate on ideological change, and not on the origin and nature of ideology itself. Because we do not assume primeval man as our starting point, we do not need a pure theory of ideology.

This book is in no sense meant to be a history of ideological change, but rather is an attempt at an explanation of the process of ideological change in a geographical area which can be delimited for scholarly purposes because of the cultural unity prevailing therein. In the first two chapters the ideological connections between nationalism and politics and between Islam and politics are examined. In Chapter 3, the characteristic manner in which Islamic philosophy dealt with irreconcilable opposites is discussed within the context of Muhammad Abduh's attempt to reconcile reason, religion, and politics. But the philosophical approach dealt with in Chapter 3 is insufficient for an understanding of what now appears to be the full victory of nationalism. For that we must grasp the manner in which subjective sentiments were freed of religious domination. That is the burden of Chapter 4. Chapter 5 discusses the impact of the resultant ideological compromise on the formation of political communities in the Middle East. It does so on the assumption that the political community is conventional and not natural, but seeks to understand that conventional character in terms of social processes in which ideology plays only a partially determinative role. Chapter 6 offers a detailed analysis of the influential ideological synthesis of the Ba'th Party. Chapters 7 and 8 describe the growth and application of similar doctrines in Egypt. Finally, Chapter 9 discusses the effect of the ideological revolution in the Middle East upon its international politics.

That this book represents the product of many years' work makes it all the more difficult to acknowledge adequately the sources from which I have learned and the institutions which have made these investigations possible. The subject of nationalism is most prominent here, so it is fitting to mention explicitly the name of one of my teachers, Professor Rupert Emerson of Harvard University, who has devoted his career to its study. I have, additionally, drawn heavily upon the work of others. If it appears in places that I have been overcritical, let it not be thought that I have not learned much from all those works cited. The numerous citations will doubtlessly disturb many readers, but they do represent the meanest form of acknowledging a huge debt, while serving as a guide to those who would pursue the matter further. A number of people have read parts of the manuscript, and the book is better for their criticism. Among these people I would particularly like to mention my colleagues Morton Kaplan and Morris Janowitz. David Apter and Jeremy Azrael have read and criticized individual chapters.

The Ford Foundation, the Rockefeller Foundation, and the Social Science Research Council have all aided my work at one stage or another. Were it not for their confidence, I would not have been able to accomplish these studies. None of these people or institutions are in any way responsible for the opinions expressed or for the interpretations offered in this book.

Most of the material in this book has appeared or will appear in print in other places and contexts and in similar form. Permission to republish has been granted and is herewith gratefully acknowledged. Part of Chapter 1 appeared under the title "Prolegomena to the Comparative Study of Middle East Governments," in the *American Political Science Review* of September 1957. Part of Chapter 2 appeared under the title "Problems of Islamic Political Thought in the Light of Recent Developments in Pakistan," in the *Journal of Politics* of November 1958. Chapter 4 is to appear in the fifth Free Press annual, *Ideology*, which is being edited by David Apter. Chapter 6 appeared under the title "Radical-Reform Nationalism in Syria and Egypt," in the *Muslim World* for April and July 1959. Chapters 7 and 8 appeared in *The Revolution in World Politics*, edited by Morton Kaplan and published by John Wiley and Sons in 1962. Chapter 9 appeared in *World Politics* for April 1958.

A final word of gratitude is due my wife and my daughter for their assistance with the manuscript and with the index.

Leonard Binder

Chicago, Illinois
March 1964

CONTENTS

1

INTRODUCTION: POLITICAL
CHANGE AND THE NATION-STATE

I

Nationalism has not resulted in uniform political arrangements wherever it has been accepted, but the rise of modern nationalism has invariably coincided with significant political change. It would be an exaggeration, of course, to hold that all of the political changes of the last century and a half are due only to nationalism. There were profound material and social transformations which coincided with the rise of nationalism. If nationalism was a response to these conditions, then it was not cause but effect. Whether cause or effect, the categories of nationalist thought do not really comprehend with the changes wrought by the industrial revolution but deal with other questions, such as the source of legitimation and the increasing political awareness of the masses. If nationalist thought is a reaction to material conditions, that reaction is not specific to those conditions except as programmatic consequences were added to the concept of nationalism. On the other hand, the rise of nationalist thought is to be correlated with the two historical developments the justification of which is perhaps the only solid content of nationalism: the politicization of the masses and the derivation of political legitimacy from the real or purported will of the masses. In this sense, at least, nationalism is coincident with and inseparable from political change. This conclusion holds regardless of whether nationalism is associated with radical or with conservative ends.

As a minimum nationalism involved an ideological adaptation of traditional institutions to new social and economic conditions. This is what occurred in Germany, in part in Italy, in France during the latter part of the nineteenth century, and even in England after 1870. Nationalism brought about even more significant changes regarding the legitimacy of boundaries in Germany, Italy, Scandinavia, Austria-Hungary, and the Ottoman Empire in Europe.

With regard to the politicization of the masses, this was accomplished only gradually. There is wide agreement that early nationalism was the ideology of the rising bourgeoisie, and the growing class of intellectuals and "clerks." Later nationalism served to integrate the working class and to a lesser extent part of the agriculturists into the political community—often enough in coalition with the haute bourgeoisie or aristocracy rather than on a class basis.

There can be even less question about the politically revolutionary character of nationalism in non-European countries. Occasionally we find nationalist symbols employed to sustain the entrenched position of a traditional elite, but even such efforts involve a new concept of legitimacy which vitiates the possibility of political success unless there exists a truly traditionally legitimate ruler who can be identified with the entire territory in question. The more traditional the ruler, the more likely it is that he can succeed in assimilating himself to "the glories of the past"— a constantly recurring category of romantic nationalist thought.

Even such a traditional ruler must make increasingly significant concessions to the bureaucracy, the military, and the new commercial classes. In the most favorably situated countries with long-established traditional rulers, the throne is shaky because of the incongruence of nationalist ideas and traditional concepts of legitimacy. It will suffice merely to enumerate a few of these: Morocco, where there is powerful opposition demanding a reduction of royal power; Ethiopia, which has had its first but unsuccessful nationalist coup; Thailand, where the king is subordinate to an ambivalently modernizing elite; Iran, which had its Musaddiq and still has a National Front. Cases which have already been decided against the traditional ruler are those of Turkey and Egypt, to which it appears one may now add the Yemen. The problems of the Sardauna of Sokoto and the Kabaka of Buganda are still in the future, but not hard to perceive, particularly since these rulers are not associated with the whole of the territory of the new states in which they now find themselves. In most of these cases it will readily be noticed that there was either no colonial rule or a relatively short or indirect colonial experience. Elsewhere colonial rule itself destroyed traditional institutions, or integrated so many traditional communities as to render none of them capable of laying claim to a new territorial sovereignty.

Outside of Europe nationalism has had much the same impact on traditional political institutions as in Europe, but its policy and programmatic consequences have been more uniform outside of Europe. There is no conservative nationalism worthy of comparison with the European variety of the twentieth century. Revolutionary groups have been of a similar social class in all the underdeveloped areas, despite significant variations in terms of original position in the traditional class structure. Frequently, in the areas formerly blessed with a high and a written cultural tradition, ideological atavisms are perpetuated in contemporary nationalist writing. Still, the disparity in power and economic and administrative capacity between these countries and those of western Europe is so great that nationalist policy is invariably committed to rapid development and the mobilization of resources, and decidedly unrelated to any of the romantic symbols, traditional atavisms, imaginary histories, and other elements which together make up nationalist ideologies. Of course, these writings are regularly adapted to the specific circumstances of the country concerned, but they also reflect more specifically those political ideals imbibed during the colonial period which have become identified with the modern, the efficient, and the good—insofar as these do not clash directly with mobilization needs.

II

For our purposes, the impact of the West took three major institutional forms: the new division of labor within the military, government concern with economic development and financial stability, and the anonymity of government itself. The net effect of these influences has been to enhance the importance, while transforming the function, of the military and administrative classes. New industrial and commercial classes have developed, and the old corporative groupings have begun to break down. Finally, the old imperial governmental forms have been demolished and replaced by new institutions which have been defined in secular legal terms.

Of course, there are parts of the Middle East where this process has not yet taken place, but it is hard to believe that even the remote fastnesses of tradition can withstand the onslaught of twentieth century forms. Even Afghanistan has accepted foreign technical and financial aid toward agricultural development; and its government has in recent years embarked upon a program of fostering Pakhtun nationalism both in the schools and among the tribes along Pakistan's northwest frontier. The Yemen is presently drawn toward modernization through the revolution of non-Zaidis who have been supported directly by Egyptian troops and indirectly by the peacemaking efforts of the U.S. The king of the Libyan Federation has suffered foreign air bases to be constructed on his soil, and the development of a major petroleum industry portends many far-reaching social and economic changes. It seems inevitable that all must tread the same path of transformation, at least in some approximation of these three Western influences.

The acceptance of Western military organization, including the citizen army, and of Western administrative organization, including the merit system, and of Western industrial organization, including state capitalism, does not commit the Middle East on the central question of the nature of legitimate government. Many of the changes involved in the acceptance of these ideas and institutions were accomplished by the traditional sultans; others were imposed by external pressure; and some were the work of the military and administrative elites themselves. The principle of the anonymity of the state, and of its adjunct, the rule of law in the form of systematized, positive codes, has not yet been fully accepted. The military and civil services seem to favor such a change, but the industrial and commercial elites are at least ambivalent. To the urban lower classes this kind of government is incomprehensible, and devoid of that element of human charity which is often the only positive aspect of Middle Eastern government. The peasant has already suffered grievous loss by the application of Western ideas of contract to his agricultural borrowing.

Without settling the question of legitimacy, Western governmental institutions have been established throughout most of the Middle East. The reasons and historical circumstances behind each incident vary, but generally speaking parliaments have come into being to limit a sultan or to begin the process of the devolution of Western imperial power. It is a matter of more than passing significance that parliamentary institutions, already accepted in the West, were simply transferred wholly grown to the Middle East. They were, and remain, artificial legalisms and a continuing temptation to go outside the law. The two bases for the establishment of parliaments imply two not necessarily coordinate theories of legitimacy. The first of these is that associated with the idea of democracy institutionalized and modified in a representative assembly. The second is associated with the somewhat vaguer idea of national self-determination. The ambivalence with which representative institutions are regarded in the Middle East is not due to a simple misunderstanding of these Western inventions, nor merely due to the theoretical ambiguity which attends them; it is more significantly due to the ambivalence of contemporary Western democratic thought itself.

III

The dominant tendency of contemporary democratic theory suggests that a) not every state is suited for democracy; b) democracy is not necessarily the best form of government; c) democracy is not to be associated with any ultimate values; d) it is only a practical arrangement of institutions; and e) it can never come into being, even given all the necessary prerequisites, unless people consciously and deliberately establish these institutions. Is it, then, any wonder that contemporary Western statements of democratic theory repel Middle Easterners?

That geography and culture are prime determinants of institutions is to be found in the work of Ibn Khaldun and in Bodin, though also more familiarly in Montesquieu, Rousseau, and John Stuart Mill. Similar views are reflected by quite modern writers on democracy, such as A. D. Lindsay and J. Roland Pennock, who point out that not every nation is fit for democracy. The value implications of this last view run quite contrary to the cultural relativism which permeates much of anthropology and area studies in general today. The extreme relativist might assert that it is not only kinship systems which are to be evaluated in terms of the relevant cultural context, but also political systems. But even this approach seems to conceal a condescending attitude, for it is mostly limited to small primitive societies. When once we get to "transitional" or "emergent" nation-states, which, themselves, comprehend vocal minorities clamoring for modernization, we soon find the test of Western liberal democracy being applied. A suggestion more significant than moral relativism has arisen out of the study of primitive societies, and that is the view that in diverse societies different institutions may perform the same function. Some would say that the outward manifestation of the function is no more than a cultural accident, and it is this outward manifestation that is often associated with what are known as formal political institutions.

We need not go so far as to insist that institutions are mere epiphenomena; we need only go as far as democratic theorists do themselves, to ask whether democracy, as defined by them, is a valid scientific category capable of being differentiated from other types of political system within the framework of an empirically relevant general theory. Granted that we can find these institutions wherever they exist and that we can devise tests to find out to what extent they do what they are supposed to do; are we not simply discovering symptoms rather than causes? If we have a theory of symptoms and none of causes, how can we be sure that these symptoms are meaningful?

One cannot avoid the admission that the transition to democracy (in its usual institutional sense) must be achieved by deliberate constitutional engineering. In other words, man-made laws are a necessary but not a sufficient condition of democracy when democracy is so defined as to include popular control of policy makers through periodic elections, civil rights, and isonomy.[1] Some would hold that this approach is not wholly tautological, for, following the Aristotelian view of the relationship between education, habit, and virtue, it can be shown that democratic institutions have been acquired by some non-European states after a period of political tutelage. The experience of other countries, and that would include most of the Middle East, has not confirmed this pattern; so that political transition by means of cultivating the symptoms known as democratic institutions is a hit-or-miss proposition. This is the view of Henry Mayo, whose arguments for the value and purposes of democracy as a method of determining policy apply only to those societies capable of sustaining democratic institutions. He rightly points out that we know next to nothing about the prerequisites of democracy.[2] Given the degree of social change in the present, all that the "new nations" can do is to keep trying until they hit the jackpot.

There is something admirable and yet more disturbing about Mayo's treatment of democracy. He is not concerned with alternative theories of democracy. For him, democracy is a particular method and institutional arrangement for resolving conflicts and determining policies binding on a whole society. One admires his effort to avoid claiming any ultimate or absolute value for this method, and also his searching for a universal definition of the political. Mayo further admits that many of his "democratic values" can be and have been realized under other kinds of government. What is disturbing is the bland assertion that the institutions described are the only ones relevant to democratic theory.

One ventures into the realm of speculation in trying to discover why contemporary Western expositions of democracy ignore or deplore the alternative theoretical trend which stresses community, the general will, and the positive role of government. The obvious answer which comes to mind is that these are ideological apologies for existing political institutions. As for most ideologies in this Mannheimian sense, the exponents of Western democracy are foxes rather than hedgehogs, casuists rather than true advocates, Pharisees rather than Essenes. Absent is the glorious vision of a truly united community, wherein each individual submits to government and still retains his freedom by morally willing the policies which are for the good of all.

The dilemma of modern democratic thought is seen in Professor Pennock's *Liberal Democracy*.[3] While he is concerned primarily to show that democracy can work under the conditions of modern industrialism and international tension, he draws upon some of the findings of the psychologists to show that the values and interests of individuals are not wholly self-regarding. The work is one of reconciling and compromise, however, for the democracy which works under the altered conditions of modern times is itself altered from the ideal of Rousseau, and the psychology which permits social cooperation is not the rational one of Hobbes and the Utilitarians but the irrational psychology of Freud.

The practice of democracy has fallen short of its early promise, and the theoretical foundations of "pure democracy" have been shaken near to dust. What we have now are defenses of rationalizations of democracy, or one might better say conventionalizations, for by convention it is agreed that a popular election is somehow the equivalent of popular government, or that a majority vote is the evidence of the will of the whole community. As an ideology, this conventionalization works fairly well, and given moral support the political systems which it characterizes work satisfactorily. It may even become possible, following Mayo, that democratic ideology can be shifted from its institutional biases as a more adequate theory of politics develops. But for the time being, there seems to be no adequate answer to the criticism that modern democratic thought lacks the appeal which is born of religious conviction or utopian idealism. This defect is all the more enhanced when searching critiques of democratic theory such as that of Professor Dahl show that in actual operation, democratic institutions are conventionalizations of conventions.[4]

Neither political leaders nor political theorists in the Middle East are concerned to apologize for the actual working of democratic institutions in their countries. They are concerned with why these idealized institutions, where they exist, have not worked so as to render operational the utopian vision of a harmonious and progressive society. It is they, rather more than we, relatively speaking, who have become concerned with the prerequisites of democracy and the methods of calling it into being. Above all, they have shown greater interest in the positive role of government in this transition. By the positive role of government here we do not mean mere recognition of the expanded scope of government in the industrial age, nor the limited role of government action envisioned by T. H. Green, Bosanquet, and even A. D. Lindsay. Green's idea of the government's obligation to promote the moral personality of individuals comes closest, but Lindsay's genetic analysis poses the real issue. If so many unique ideas and events contributed to the growth of the modern democratic state over so many centuries, how can a similar result be attained by the differently situated societies of today? For Middle Eastern leaders and theorists, the question is "How can one change a culture and a society?" Their name for these changes is revolution, and its instrument is government.

The Middle Eastern idea of revolution is stated in terms of a social, cultural, and psychological regeneration; but it also entails giving power to the many by means of what is usually referred to as an awakening. Perhaps this is a concern with the prerequisites of democracy as we know it; creating the fundamental agreement so that smaller disagreements may be tolerated. For the time being, however, popular control of government, individual rights, and isonomy find little or no place in Middle Eastern theories of democracy. The epithets of plebiscitary democracy and totalitarian democracy come immediately to mind, but these ideas do not accord with the limited resources at the disposal of Middle Eastern governments, nor with their actual lack of strict hierarchical control. For the present, at any rate, these governments and their justifiers can rightly claim a hearing, for we have no proven alternative, only the weak suggestion that democratic institutions are firmly established by practice.

There was a time when aspiring Middle Eastern elites sought constitutionalism rather than utopian democracy. The dates 1879 for Egypt, 1876 for Turkey, and 1906 for Iran mark the salience of constitutional limitations upon traditional despotism in the programs of the liberal reformers. The failure or frustration of each of these movements opened the way to the more radical demand for democracy.

It is not at all clear that the reformers understood by constitutionalism and democracy what we understand by those terms. What is clear, however, is that even the earlier constitutional movement was stimulated by the encroachments of Western imperialism. It is not surprising, therefore, that the notion of popular freedom was confused with that of national freedom. The twin ideas of nationalism and democracy grew and reinforced one another in the Middle East to the extent that they presently dominate the political thinking of the educated classes. The possibility that there might be some incompatibility between the two is flatly rejected as a typical bit of Western sophistry. It is urged that Western imperialism is itself proof of the absence of democracy in the West. The West, it is argued, has not attained the democratic goal of perfectly harmonizing the needs of the individual and the claims of the community. It is this perfect harmony that is now being sought through nationalism and through a groping, stumbling experimentation with new forms of political organization. The sum of the process is a transfer of legitimacy in institutional terms, in ideological terms, and finally in policy terms.

IV

Of the centrality of the transfer of legitimacy, there can be little doubt; but what is doubtful is the relationship between the ideological aspect of this transfer and its institutional and political aspects. It is not difficult to discern the change from an Islamic political perspective toward a nationalist-democratic preference in matters of political legitimacy in the Middle East. This transformation has been paralleled elsewhere among the newly independent states, with significant differences born of the inevitable retention of certain traditional ideas in all cases. It may also be possible to note the proliferation of modernizing oligarchies heavily dependent upon the support of new military forces among these new states. Similarly, policy legitimacy is often associated with the goals of development, mobilization of national resources and sentiments, and the reestablishment of the ancient and largely fictitious glories of an anachronistically defined nation.

These gross similarities do not establish the logical interdependence of these three referents of legitimacy. Suffice it to point out that most of these ideas, institutions, and policy orientations have been borrowed from European sources, where their application led to quite different outcomes. Of the historical necessity of their interrelationship it is, at this early stage, more difficult to speak. Nevertheless, existing evidence suggests that there is enough diversity in the understanding and working of all three among the new states to permit the prediction that the apparent uniformities which presently prevail will succumb to those very historical and situational factors which have seemingly brought about the common pattern of development.

Situational differences will not alone determine the diverse developments among the new states. The preference for utopian democracy above constitutional democracy, the extremely high value placed upon national solidarity, and the near compulsive need to eradicate the indignities of the colonial experience are significant and suggestive. These factors point to the importance of the subjective rather than the philosophical in the political thinking of the intellectuals in the new states. In the fumbling, belated evocation of the subjective, drawing in part upon traditional cultural elements but also upon recent colonial experience, these intellectuals have, perhaps, followed in the footsteps of obscurantist and traditional movements of protest against Westernization. Despite the pressures which led to the rejection of the dominant Western interpretation of Western ideas, those same ideas were not abandoned but used in conjunction with traditional symbols. The consequence of this shift, in the Middle East rather more than anywhere else, has been the politicization of the now more popularly recruited military and civil services. This ideological shift has also opened the possibility, for the first time in Islamic history since the mission of the Prophet Muhammad, of the close integration of the people and their government. The latter eventuality is a goal much sought by contemporary political leaders, and the use of traditional symbols is a price which they are willing to pay. Indeed, some Middle Eastern leaders do not even consider this a payment at all. Foreign observers must also admit that the use of such symbols entails a transcendental and not merely historical-ideological limitation upon legitimacy.

But what is the significance of ideological change upon institutions and policy? At first sight the question appears ridiculous because, in common sense terms, we all know that ideological change will have a profound effect upon both. If, however, we ask whether it is possible to predict institutional and policy consequences from known ideological perspectives, the question becomes more serious. The difficulty or even impossibility of accomplishing the latter task is at the root of the very idea of ideology, or at least of ideology as mere justification. By definition, ideology as justification must come after institutions exist and after policies have been determined.

Of course, ideology is not merely justification *ex post facto*. The effectiveness of ideological appeals to legitimacy depends upon the distribution of existing values and notions of reality. Hence the effect of ideological perspectives is reciprocal, determining institutions and policies as well as justifying them. This brings us back to our common sense beginning, which can be sustained by retrospective analysis only. No safe predictions can be made.

In our brief discussion of contemporary democratic theory the disparity between its ideological justification and its institutional manifestations in the West have been referred to. A similar, but more comprehensive, demonstration of the same point has been made for the institutional consequences of nationalism.[5] Both expressions of the problem of the relationship between ideology and institutions are themselves related. The rise of nationalism is intimately connected with the continued difficulty in using "democratic" ideology to justify "democratic" institutions.

In a sense, the tension in contemporary democratic theory is the result of the attempt to justify seventeenth century British constitutional reforms in terms of late eighteenth century French democratic theory. The juxtaposition of the two is the consequence of the appearance of the peculiarly modern problem of the relationship between the individual and the state. It may be surprising that the problem of the relationship between the individual and the state is described as a peculiarly modern problem, for is not this problem one of the "great issues"? Yet in mediaeval times, whether in Europe or in the Islamic East, the individual was properly a religious and not a political category of concern. Subjective identity, too, was not political identity as nationalism holds that it must be. The unity of individual and communal political spheres was a characteristic of only the most perfect theocratic societies, the ancient Hebrew, the early Islamic, and perhaps the Greek city-state. The social and economic changes which led the rising bourgeoisie to demand the reaffirmation of the independent sphere of the individual also undermined the exclusive social basis of the state.

The consequent political change was described by Marx as rendering the state merely superstructure—as the instrument of the class interests of the bourgeoisie.[6] The more profound revolutionary consequence is, however, that the state should represent the interests of anyone but itself. There may always be an analytically definable ruling class, but when that class is no longer a functionally specific oligarchy and acknowledged as such by common sense observation, then surely a profound change has occurred.

Once it is understood that the state is not the exclusive prerogative of a clearly defined group, an entirely new set of questions is opened. The real purport of these political changes is not simply whose interests are to be represented by the state—that is the class struggle. The far more significant issue running through the whole of modern political thought is the proper relationship of individual and collectivity. The ideas and constitutional devices of those who sought to defend individual rights were insufficient to fill the gap left by the breakdown of mediaeval aristocratic oligarchy. Once the monopoly of the state by the aristocracy was broken, the aristocracy itself penetrated by the middle classes, and utilitarian principles substituted for particularistic ones as the basis for access to the state; there could be no absolute limitation of citizenship in class terms. To put the point in another way: political modernization in Europe has meant the decline of the structural differentiation of the ruling class. The ruling class must now be defined in terms of its nongovernmental characteristics. The social dualism which, it is held, was a constant feature of Western civilization, was not a political problem until social class was no longer the basis of political functional specification. Once this change took place, it became necessary to reconcile the political and nonpolitical roles of the individual. For it was not the class that came to rule, but individual members of an ill-defined, amorphous group of rural notables and urban merchants known as the middle class. The major form which the intellectual reconciliation of the diverse roles, political and nonpolitical, of the individual took was nationalism.

This analysis will not permit us to predict specific institutional consequences from particular ideological premises. Nevertheless, it can help us to understand the goals of much institutional and policy experimentation in a very general way. It will also help us to understand the kind of political change which nationalism entails.

In the present work, we shall be less interested in institutional consequences than in ideological change. The one inescapable institutional consequence of the ideological revolution in the Middle East that will concern us is the nation-state. In other words, we shall be concerned with the intellectual processes by which the central basis of legitimacy was changed from the Islamic to the nationalist. Nationalism, itself, does not necessarily represent a terminal point either ideologically or institutionally. In this sense, it is more clearly impossible to make institutional predictions. But if we settle for a term ending with the foreseeable future, and if we remain at the highly general level of the institutional legitimacy of the whole political system, it is possible to suggest that the product of the ideological revolution in the

Middle East will be continued pressure for the establishment of nation-states.

As has been indicated, this tentative conclusion is not as simple as it looks. It rather entails the opening of a host of questions, none of which have been adequately resolved for any Middle Eastern state. These questions involve the relationship between Islam and the state, the relationship between democracy and nationalism, the relationship between traditionalist populism and modernizing elitism, the tension between the individual and the state, and the tension between the requirements of subjective political identifications and the rational requirements of the conventionally limited political community.

V

Presumably, nationalist theory prescribes that subjective political identifications shall set the limits of the political community, in personal if not in territorial terms. Certain aspects of this problem will concern us in a later chapter, but for the present it will suffice to note that the practical requirements of running a modern state far outrun the need for subjective sentiments of loyalty. Moreover, the kind of political change which we have associated with the increasing salience of the issue of the political role of the individual citizen does not take account of the ways in which boundaries between political systems are set, maintained, or changed. If traditionally rooted subjective sentiments set historically transcendental limitations on the formation of nation-states, historical and practical requirements set no less firm limitations. It is with the application of these generalizations to the Middle East that this introduction will be concluded.

The establishment of nation-states throughout the Middle East entails the final breakdown of mediaeval society and the deemphasis of the heretofore all-important religious distinctions. Wherever traditional institutions obtain, the newly rising middle classes will have to transform or overthrow them. The privileges and obligations of citizenship will have to be much more widespread. The obligation of the government in terms of popular health, welfare, and education, and in the creation of economic opportunity, will have to be fulfilled in more than mere declaratory fashion. Communication must improve to the point where the individual's horizon spreads beyond his immediate community, and appropriate national myths will have to be evolved to keep the individual's allegiance within the territorial bounds of the nation-state. The nation-state must also have sufficient power, and its leaders sufficient skill, to maintain its independence under all foreseeable circumstances short of a third world war.

Given certain prerequisites, all these things may be achieved in an orderly political environment capable of adjusting to and controlling a sustained economic development of an appropriate magnitude. The absence of optimum political and economic conditions, which we know to exist, will hamper and possibly permit the perversion of the development of nation-states. But even under optimum conditions certain difficulties may appear which cannot be overcome. These difficulties arise primarily from the manner in which the contemporary Middle East is politically demarcated.

Paradoxical though it may be, the primary legal and political sphere of the nation-state is territorial. Language, history, and religion may be the stuff of nationalism, but the nation-state remains heir to the territorial sovereignty of the monarchic states of premodern Europe. The territorial divisions of the Middle East were devised by European powers to meet their own needs and aspirations. Boundaries do not coincide with the areas of strongest potential national feeling in many cases, and yet they mark the limits of governmental effort toward the creation of nation-states. Arbitrary territorial divisions have not always hampered the development of nation-states elsewhere, when they were not evolved in a period of conscious nationalism. But arbitrary territorial divisions have created states which must be economically and militarily dependent on their neighbors.

The population-land ratio will also have much to do with the successful creation of nation-states in the Middle East. Economic development may be severely disturbed by either too low or too high a ratio. Underpopulation may make the maintenance of external security difficult, while the maldistribution of population and the existence of large tribal groups hinder social integration.

Religious minorities, whether heterodox Muslims or non-Muslims, and linguistic minorities are other obvious obstacles to the creation of nation-states.

The unequal distribution of natural resources in the area will tend to encourage more rapid development in some states, and may be an insurmountable obstacle to development in others. The more advanced state may then attract the loyalties and cooperation of its neighbor's citizens.[7] Wide stretches of desert throughout the area will remain a barrier to rapid and efficient transport and communication. Territorial nationalism will have to compete with Pan-Islam and Pan-Arabism, which survive in the area in the guise of competing nationalist ideologies. Finally, there is always the possibility that intra-area conflict or external subversion may bring the effort to establish nation-states within the territorial states of the Middle East to an untimely end.

VI

The preceding observations enable us now to make a preliminary classification of the countries of the Middle East into three groupings in terms of their satisfaction of the prerequisites of the nation-state. The first grouping, comprising Turkey, Egypt, and Iran, comes very close to satisfying the conditions. The second grouping, comprising the states of the Fertile Crescent, is furthest away from fulfilling these conditions. The third grouping, comprising Saudi Arabia, Libya, the Yemen, and possibly Afghanistan, still retains elements of an earlier legitimacy.

The population of Turkey is largely homogeneous, with the Kurds forming the only significant minority. The Kurdish "problem" has been managed by a twofold process of repression and assimilation; and since both Turks and Kurds are Sunnis, there has been no religious extension of political issues between them. For the present Turkey is somewhat underpopulated, but the trend is toward rapid growth. At the same time, with the support of American foreign aid programs, the improvement of communications and the provision of state capital for economic development has been steady over the last decade. In the forty years since

Ataturk's victory over the Greeks, nationalism has spread through the educational system, which has been modernized and expanded. The alphabet reform speeded the spread of literacy, which, in turn, has been fed by a new nationalist literary movement. A new national myth has been created by skipping back over the Islamic period to the legendary reports concerning the Turks of Central Asia. The dominant political elite has its roots in the Westernized official classes of the Ottoman Empire, but they have found in the Turkish nation an adequate compensation for the loss of a reactionary Sultan and an unmanageable empire.

Egypt is also a country of homogeneous population. The Copts number barely 7 per cent of the population and are Arabic speaking. There are only a few, unimportant nomadic tribes in Egypt. The country is predominantly agricultural, and the overwhelming majority of the population is concentrated along the Nile. Among the consequences of this concentration are ease of communication and the necessity, realized by all, of centralized control. Egypt is, however, limited in agricultural resources, and suffers from a very adverse arable land-population ratio. The national myth of Egypt has been based upon the glories of the Pharaonic civilization almost as much as upon Arabic symbols. Even under Islam, Egypt long enjoyed an independent administration, and its ties to the Ottoman Empire were loose to the point of insubordination. Given a stable political order and the skill and finances to overcome its population problem, there is little doubt that Egypt can emerge in the recognizable form of a Western nation-state. Even if no transitional political system can long persist, but if economic development proceeds, one might expect the same results.

Iran suffers from maldistribution of population, poor internal communications, and the decentralizing effects of large and powerful tribal groups. On the other hand, Iran is most favorably endowed for development as a nation-state. It has a large territory and a growing population, tremendous resources of petroleum, and adequate resources of other minerals. The ideological, historical, and literary bases of Iranian nationalism are stronger than those of many a European state. Iran is a Shi'i state, and yet is ruled by a Shah who calls himself *Pahlavi*, referring to the rulers of ancient Parthia. Modern Iran has been an independent, unified empire for over four centuries. Like Turkey, it has a unique national language, and one which can boast of an exceptional poetic achievement crowned by a national epic which may be heard from the lips of many an illiterate Iranian. Had the government of Iran the will and the ability to invest the proceeds of its petroleum sales properly, it could most probably effect the social integration lacking in that country. The problem of Iran is, however, much greater than that of either Turkey or Egypt when seen from the standpoint of existing linguistic and racial heterogeneity. On the other hand, the tribal and linguistic minorities may be swept up in a new, vigorous nationalism, since there are few external attractions for them. The only seriously competing nationalism is that of Soviet Azerbaijan, but here the USSR overplayed its hand in 1946, and this is not forgotten or forgiven. In any case, once economic development gets under way, the peasant classes should become far more important than the tribes.

The Lebanon, in the Fertile Crescent, is an Arab state but not a nation-state. The precarious balance of Christians and Muslims in the population is institutionalized in the division of political offices and in the distribution of parliamentary constituencies. Though the Lebanese standard of living is higher than that of Syria, its economic position is precarious also. Its major sources of income are from the transit trade, the tourist trade, foreign receipts from emigrants, and an overworked agriculture. Its attempt to boast an historical connection with ancient Phoenicia is belied by the prevalence of Arabic sentiment and the rigidity of confessional politics. The historical basis of its separate existence is French intervention on behalf of the Christians of the Levant. There is little likelihood that the Lebanon will ever become either a nation-state or an Islamic state; but there is the danger that it may be incorporated in a Greater Syria.

The Hashemite Kingdom of Jordan was created in 1922 by the British government for reasons of British policy. Until recently it was ruled as a traditional sultanate, but with the annexation of Cis-Jordan the Kingdom acquired a new majority. This new majority was far more advanced than the sparse population of Trans-Jordan, and also politically frustrated. The only nationalism popular in Jordan is Pan-Arabism. Jordan, itself, was sustained economically by subventions from the British government which it later sought to replace by similar grants from Egypt, Syria, and Saudi Arabia. This arrangement failed and now Jordan has become a client of the United States. The patronage of the greatest world power is bound to prolong the existence of even this most artificial of states, but sheer power does not suffice for every purpose. Recent events suggest that Jordanian independence cannot withstand the growth of nationalism within its own borders.

Syria and Iraq are alike in many ways. They are separated in the south by the Syrian desert, and they are joined in the north by the potentially rich agricultural area of the upper Euphrates. Both are underpopulated. Both have powerful nationalist and Pan-Arab movements. Both have important minority problems, but in both the Sunni Muslims are politically dominant. They share the problem of settling nomadic tribesmen, but Iraq's share is greater. Iraq has great resources of petroleum, and Syria accommodates two Iraq petroleum pipelines at a considerable income. Both Syria and Iraq can look forward to a substantial expansion of their agricultural land area.

At the present time both Iraq and Syria are ruled by relatively insecure combinations of Ba'th Party leaders and military officers. The Ba'th ideology of Arab unity draws them together, as does their common opposition to Egyptian domination. But there are important factors keeping them apart. To the extent that their national myths differ, Syria emphasizes the Umayyad Caliphate of Damascus, and Iraq emphasizes the Abbasid Caliphate; but the distinction is not crucial. The greatest obstacle to unity is doubtlessly Iraq's Kurdish minority, but the existence of two sets of political, military, and administrative elites is in itself no small difficulty.

Should the two states combine in the near future, a stable Sunni electoral majority would be created, the income from Iraqi petroleum could be shared and development thus equalized, the problem of transdesert communication and the settlement of the tribes could be jointly dealt with, and the military security of both would be enhanced. Should they remain divided, it is difficult to imagine the ideological basis for separation, and even more difficult to conceive of a widely accepted legitimacy being granted these governments. At present neither Iraq nor Syria can claim complete nationalism. Possibly because of the prevalence of heterodoxy, neither country has a powerful fundamentalist movement, so that the prospect of the creation of an Islamic state in the Fertile Crescent seems remote. The governments of Syria and Iraq may stumble for a long time before losing their opportunity of creating an Arab nation-state in the Fertile Crescent.

In the third grouping of states, still dominated by traditional political forces, one can only speculate as to the timing and source of political change. In Saudi Arabia one looks to the growing group of Westernized administrators not belonging to the royal house, and to the employees of the Arabian-American Oil Company; in Libya one looks, perhaps, to the federal parliament; in the Yemen one looks to the non-Zaidi revolutionaries and the Yemeni emigrants; in Afghanistan one looks to a handful of military and administrative officials. It is possible, if unlikely, however, that political change will come about peacefully in these countries; if so, they may avoid the growth of nationalism and hit upon some intermediate form. In all likelihood, developments in other parts of the Middle East will be so far advanced by the time these traditional governments are weakened that the nation-state will be the only logical solution.

NOTES

1. Henry B. Mayo, An Introduction to Democratic Theory (New York, 1960), Ch. 1.
2. Ibid., esp. p. 293.
3. J. Roland Pennock, Liberal Democracy: Its Merits and Prospects (New York, 1950).
4. Robert A. Dahl, A Preface to Democratic Theory (Chicago, 1956).
5. See Rupert Emerson, From Empire to Nation (Cambridge, 1960).
6. Karl Marx, The German Ideology (New York, 1939), p. 59.
7. See K. W. Deutsch, The Political Community at the International Level (New York, 1954), p. 44.

2

RELIGIO-POLITICAL ALTERNATIVES

I

There is hardly any subject of relevance to the Middle East these days which is not sensitive. Still, the two general areas of religion and politics are perhaps more sensitive than most. The difficulty in dealing with these two arises not alone because of their controversiality, but also out of the fact that considerable changes are occurring in both spheres. Hence we find problems on two levels: the first level might be described as the normative one, where differences exist as to what the political and religious arrangements of the Middle East ought to be; and the second might be called the academic—one wishes we could say scientific—where there is disagreement about the nature of conditions actually obtaining. I want to avoid the first level of controversy, if I can, in order to deal with the latter.

I have always been fascinated by the suggestion that Middle Eastern politics had to be different from Western politics because of the factor of Islam. In its simplest form, the assertion is made that church and state were never distinguished in Islam as they

were in Western Christianity; hence it follows that Middle Eastern politics cannot be understood without first understanding Islam. This dictum seems not unreasonable, though its antithesis,
i.e., that one may study Western politics without understanding
Christianity may not be as reasonable. There are however, a number of practical difficulties that have arisen as a result of this view.
The basis of one of these difficulties we shall call the phlogiston
thesis, and another the Sir William Muir syndrome. The phlogiston
thesis continually recurs in the form of any number of unfalsifiable
propositions about the peculiar political force of Islam. I would
not take the position that everything political can be resolved into
specific categories of observed social behavior, but neither would
I hold that religious ideas or even divine revelation can enter into
the universe of political discourse unmediated by social activity.
The Sir William Muir syndrome appears where the all too frequent occurrence of manipulative and opportunistic political behavior is attributed to Islam, thus distinguishing instable Middle
Eastern political systems from the nice neat constitutional de-
mocracies of the West.[1]

Both kinds of difficulty arise from the attempt to attribute specific political acts to a theological ideal, without concern for in-
tervening and, indeed, parallel variables. Once we have indicated
that we have not the wherewithal to solve the normative controversy, we must further admit that no adduction of instances of
good or bad political behavior can prove that the revelation on
which Islam is based is either true or false. I would further hold
that the political scientist is not properly interested in that question at all.

But still the fascination is there; how can Islam and politics be
meaningfully studied? The answer to this question involves some
refinement of the naïve notions with which we began. Once we
stop looking for the Islamic essence, it dawns on us that there
are many views about the nature of Islam. Which one shall we
pursue?

As might be expected, the prerequisite of productive inquiry is
an adequate classificatory system. It may be objected that formal
classification may tend to gloss over important original efforts, but
at this stage of our inquiry that is a sacrifice we must make.

II

A recent attempt at describing the "Crisis of the Intelligentsia in the Middle East"[2] divides them for purposes of analysis into three groups: the traditionalists, the quasi-Westernized quasi-traditionalists (called the "old nationalists"), and the contemporary Westernized intelligentsia. While the analytical framework is essentially chronological, and therefore related to the degree of exposure to Western influences,[3] the author remarks that traditionalism remains capable of recruiting young intellectuals, "and so makes possible the formation of organized traditionalist movements."[4] It is rare, and therefore praiseworthy, that anyone should note that the traditional ulama have managed to renew and replenish their numbers despite the impact of the West. On the other hand, the notion of an organized traditionalist movement seems to be a contradiction *in adjecto*. Apparently such reference is to movements like the Muslim Brethren in Egypt or the Jama'at-i-Islami in Pakistan, and takes no cognizance of the attacks on the traditional ulama in the propaganda of such groups.[5] The author similarly lumps together Saudi-Arabia and prerevolutionary Yemen by citing "the traditionalism of their respective socio-religious systems of Wahhabism and Zaidism";[6] the first dating from the eighteenth century and the second from the ninth century, as though nothing had happened in Islam during the interim. The attribution of the "attitudes of mistrust and hostility in the Arab masses" toward the West to the influence of the traditionalists[7] (rather than the nationalists) is significant, however, in pointing to the rapport which persists between the ulama and the majority of the Muslim population.

The difference between the "old nationalists" and the contemporary intelligentsia seems little more than chronological. The former compromised by opposing the West on the "political-military plane" but tolerated Western influence on the "intellectual and general cultural plane."[8] The latter are cultural hybrids whose doubts lead them typically to "withdrawal and detachment from responsibility."[9] The problem of the contemporary intelligentsia is defined as the need to "oppose the West politically" while embracing its "humanistic tradition and modern technology." [10] This position seems peculiarly close to that of the old nationalists, while the term itself denotes the younger generation's determination to replace their elders in implementing a policy which accepts Western influences in the spheres of politics, armaments, and economic development while it opposes such influences on the cultural plane. The present writer is not impressed with the tendency of contemporary intellectuals to withdraw from responsibility.

In discussing "Arab Nationalism and Islam," [11] S. A. Morrison cites the need for Arab nationalism to define its attitude toward the West, primarily as a result of Western imperialism. Morrison also found three classes of response, all of which tend to combine Islam and Arab nationalism to the exclusion of Christian-Arab nationalist sentiment. The first group would reject the spiritual, cultural, and ethical influences of the West, but not its material achievements.[12] This group would return to orthodoxy and a revived Islam. Here, once again, no important distinction is made between orthodox and "revived" Islam, and it is assumed that orthodox Islam is now "dead." The attitude of this first group is the result of dismay at the policy of the great powers. Since Morrison gives us no literary sources for this view, we are compelled to assume that a revived orthodoxy refers once again to the Muslim Brethren, or the school of Rashid Rida. If this is the case, it is probably incorrect to see their reaction as a result of the international policies of the great powers. Their rejection of Western intellectual influences and supposed acceptance of Western technology is more likely the misguided effort of a (traditional?) lower middle class to prevent the social and economic changes which are rendering them progressively less able to compete. It would seem that those who have been most dismayed at the policies of the powers have been most anxious to reform Islamic law and to reduce the influence of the orthodox ulama.

The second group, believing it possible to "distinguish within Western civilization between those strands which are originally Hellenistic and those which are essentially Christian," would reject the latter while weaving in the former and reviving Islamic religious consciousness.[13] The third group, though attracted by

Western materialism and secularism, nevertheless holds to Islam as a center of political and cultural unity. It is to be noted that neither of these groups coincides with those discussed above. The apparent overlaping of these two groups does lead to tactical political alliances, but they will be found to fit, more or less, into our categories of the "romantics" and the "secularists" respectively.[14] Even a secularist cannot deny the entire political and cultural heritage of the Middle East.

In discussing the Westernization of ideas in *Syria and Lebanon*,[15] Albert Hourani states that small groups of extremists would rather reject all aspects of the West or become so completely Westernized as to deny their spiritual heritage, but most Muslims would find a middle way.[16] The majority is then divided into two main tendencies: the revivalists and the secularists. The revivalists are of three types: those who would emphasize political activity, especially on the international plane; those who emphasize a fundamentalist reform of religion; and those who emphasize a "revision of Islamic jurisprudence." [17] The first group is associated with the views of Jamal al-Din al-Afghani,[18] the founder of Pan-Islamism; the second with the Wahhabism of Saudi-Arabia; and the third with the modernism of Muhammad Abduh.[19] The secularists are divided into two groups: those who would separate "church" and state, and end the regulation of society by Islamic law and doctrine; and those who would make the welfare of the individual the "norm of social organization." [20] The latter are called "social secularists." Hourani states frankly that these are all "ideal types" and that most Arab thinkers hold a number of these views in combination.[21] It would also seem that none of these views adequately describes the reaction of the traditional ulama to the impact of Western ideas.

Sir Hamilton Gibb, in his *Modern Trends in Islam*,[22] canvasses the field of Islamic modernism with a keen sense of the break in the historical continuity of the Islamic social and religious heritage. He finds that the impact of Western ideas may be characterized in the main as the acceptance of contemporary Western romanticism by certain classes of educated Muslims.[23] This romanticism, described as a revolt against reason and objective standards, is congenial to the "intuitive bent of the Arab and Muslim mind." [24] Thus Islamic modernism is represented as a form of romanticism which, after the end of the Ottoman "Caliphate" and the Pan-Islamism attached thereto, was manifested in three political tendencies.[25] The first approach was that of the "pure modernists" who would institutionalize the legal doctrine of consensus (of the Islamic Community as a source of religious law) in a modern legislative assembly. The second approach, attributed to the more secular-minded, is that of nationalism either of the Pan-Arabic variety or within the geographical framework of existing Middle Eastern states. The third approach is called the "revival of Mahdism" which would purify and reunite the Muslim world by the sword.

Each of these tendencies is criticized as being incompatible with the religious heritage of Islam.[26] The consensus-modernists are criticized for their willingness to restrict *ijma* to something less than the "religious conscience of the people as a whole" and, perhaps less justifiably, for restricting this refined version of the Caliphate, i.e., Islamic government, to spiritual matters only. The Nationalists are criticized for setting up a competing principle alongside that of Islam, one that can only lead to the separation of "church" and state. It is pointed out that the ulama have not been vigorous in their condemnation of nationalism because they have not fully understood it, and because their traditional tendency is to acquiesce in non-Islamic government so long as it formally recognizes Islamic law and does not interfere with Islamic social institutions. The alternative to such acquiescence, the "violent assertion of the supremacy of the sacred law," is characteristic of Mahdism. Mahdism, therefore, has a certain doctrinal appeal to the ulama, but it also characterizes the response of the Muslim masses to the nationalist appeals of the Westernized intellectuals. It might also be suggested that this kind of response has affected the terms in which Western-educated "secularist" Muslims have couched their nationalism; and it is in this phenomenon that we may find the connection between Islam and Middle Eastern nationalism.

Sir Hamilton asserts that it is the ulama who are the true exponents of the Islamic religious heritage, and he suggests that a healthy reform which will avoid a "cultural catastrophe" [27] can only come about through their agency.[28] The challenge of these three forms of romantic modernism will, it is thought, lead the ulama to revise their conception of the history of Islam, and their attitude toward reform and change as a consequence. In his *Modern Islam in India*,[29] W. C. Smith has made a unique effort at classifying the various attitudes of Muslims in that country before partition. Here, also, the analysis is chronological; but the author's chronological sense was affected by his belief in the "ameliorative evolution" of human society.[30] Smith has related the different stages of Islamic modernism to the social and economic development of the Muslim middle class in India, and has further related these tendencies to the political development of Muslim India. Unfortunately, a number of interesting problems are not squarely faced: the development of parallel doctrinal tendencies under differing social and economic conditions in other parts of the Middle East;[31] the difference between the Indian middle classes and those of Western industrialized countries; and the differences between landowners and the middle classes,[32] properly so called. Despite certain scientific accoutrements, the author was an ethical socialist; and he seems to have felt that ethical socialism was the highest ideal toward which Islam or any other religion might aspire.[33] The scientific character of his socialism emerges in his preoccupation with the "next phase," which leads him to judge Islamic modernism primarily in terms of the acceptability of change to each tendency.[34]

The first stage of Islamic modernism in India was an effort to demonstrate that Islam was not very different from Christianity.[35] The adherents of this tendency were the merchants, civil servants, and professionals who both admired British culture and benefited from British rule. This group rejected the authoritarian legal structure of Islam and the folk-religion practices which had accrued to Islam over the centuries. The second stage was that of a more aggressive apologetic, which claimed for Islam all of the cultural achievements of the West.[36] The adherents of this tendency were members of a now enlarged middle class which found the expansion of economic opportunity hampered by British imperial rule. The third stage rejects Western capitalist society, but this tendency has bifurcated into a "progressive" and a "reactionary" branch.[37] Indeed, until the prospect of Pakistan became a reality, it seemed to Smith that the reactionary attitude had superseded the progressive.[38] The latter aimed at something like socialism, and it definitely lacked in religiosity. The former would return to the pure and rigidly logical Islam of the authoritative law books. The reason for the transmutation of the progressive tendency lies in the apprehension of that same middle class lest the masses gain power and destroy the institution of private property.[39] These fears arose out of the widespread character of the social crisis preceding the partition of India. Looking forward to the creation of Pakistan, Smith expressed some hope of a revived "progressive" trend, despite the reactionary leadership of the Muslim League.

While the author based his analysis on the concept of "ameliorative evolution," it may be possible to equate his categories with those of Sir Hamilton Gibb if we assume that they are all continuing tendencies. Thus the admirers of Western culture and Western religion are the secular nationalists who would separate "church" and state. The agressive apologists are the romantic, consensus-modernists who empasize Islamic legal reform and the exercise of independent judgment in interpreting the law (ijtihad). The "reactionaries" are, of course, the Mahdists. If this kind of reconciliation is correct, then we must be wary of lumping all the modernists together by "historical" stages. For example, Smith treats the work of Maudoodi with both the Westernized apologists and the reactionaries, and thereby associates him with the upper-middle-class leadership of the Muslim League, which Maudoodi has consistently opposed.[40] Nu'mani is treated as a modernist, whereas Gibb sees him as a bright star in the clouded firmament of orthodoxy.[41] Smith similarly fails to distinguish between the "nationalism" of the upper middle class and the Mahdism of the masses.[42] Finally, the experience of independent Pakistan has not revealed a struggle between progressives and reactionaries, but rather a struggle among three competing elites: the landowners of West Pakistan, the middle class of central India (refugees) in combination with the middle class of West Pakistan, and the middle class of East Pakistan. The so-called progressives are little in evidence.

In a more recent work dealing with ideological development

throughout the Islamic world, Smith has not greatly changed his categories.[43] The emphasis on "ameliorative evolution" is eliminated, though the treatment remains essentially historical. Consequently, it is difficult to discern whether the variety of tendencies described are consecutive or contemporary. These tendencies are as follows: (a) Movements of protest against internal deterioration and external encroachment.[44] The earliest of these stressed the strict adherence to a purified Islamic law, rather than reason or emotion, in explaining Islam.[45] Later manifestations stress Mahdism, or fundamentalism plus xenophobia.[46] (b) Liberalism stemming from either or both philosophy and Sufism.[47] This trend is further subdivided into the liberalism of the Westernized elite and the reformism of the traditionally learned.[48] During the last twenty-five years, liberalism has declined in Muslim lands and its place has been largely taken by nationalism.[49] (c) Nationalism in the Middle East is both inspired by the West and directed against the West. The Westernized elite leads such movements, but they have been, at times, surprised by the "Islamic upsurge" they have let loose among the masses.[50] This is similar to Gibb's views on the "Mahdist" response of the masses to nationalist (secular) appeals. (d) There has been an increasing tendency in recent years toward movements of "vitalistic dynamism."[51] These, I think, can also be equated with lower-class Mahdist-nationalism, though possibly also, as Smith suggests, with lower-middle-class fundamentalism. (e) The apologetic movement is here treated as a literary manifestation common to all ideological tendencies, and aimed at defense against attack, against unbelief, or against Westernization.[52]

The movements of protest and dynamism are successive stages of Mahdism or fundamentalism. Again, the liberals are the romantic consensus-modernists, and the nationalists are the secularists.

Despite the obvious variety of emphasis and some omissions and slight divergences, it is clear that all of these classificatory systems attempt to describe identical phenomena. Dr. Sharabi would like to see a pattern of direct development from traditionalism to modernism, so he treats fundamentalism as a vestige of conservatism and secularism as a perverse reaction to the social and political crisis of the Middle East. Mr. Morrison, who has been connected with missionary enterprise in the Middle East, stresses the fact that all nationalistic groups associate Islam with their nationalism in some way; and he therefore minimizes somewhat the various attitudes toward Islam itself. The last three systems agree that there exists a secularist group, a romantic or consensus-modernist group, and a fundamentalist or Mahdist group. Sir Hamilton Gibb alone has stressed the importance and the potential contribution of the traditional ulama.

III

If we examine theological and legal thought in Islam as it came down to the present day, we find that, despite some opposition, there has been one central tendency which has maintained itself to this day. This traditional Islam is the mainstream of Islam in history and in politics. It may be, as the modernists and fundamentalists hold, that that tradition is a distortion of the true Islam, but the fact remains that traditional Islam has been dominant in the Middle East, and even now divergent views are distinguished by their opposition to tradition.

Traditional Islam, while not as singular as the Islam of the Qur'an, was much the same in all Muslim lands. There were different schools of law, different customary accretions to Islamic beliefs and different religious practices throughout the wide territory where Islam held sway; and all of these might be called traditional. There was also a sharp difference of view on the nature of the legitimate political order between the Sunnis and the Shi'ites. Consequently, the degree of unity which has been maintained, even the survival of older interpretations to the point of their forthright restatement in these times, bears explanation. There can be little doubt that this explanation is to be found in the organization and tradition of the ulama. These people, the learned men of Islam, have managed to this day to preserve their status as the proprietors of the symbols of Islam. Their exclusive right to interpret Islam has only recently come into dispute. They have also managed to preserve the mediaeval statement of Islam in all its essentials. Insofar as one can speak of the interests of an institution as formless as this one, the interests of the ulama are inevitably bound up with the fate of traditional Islam.

Traditional Islam, then, is the Islam of the ulama, and the study of the political role of the ulama comes close to being a study of the relation between traditional Islam and politics. This is an approximation, for one cannot exclude from the total picture those traditionally pious Muslims who are influenced by and who in turn influence the ulama. It is, however, clear that no group or collection of people is so closely identified with traditional Islam as are the ulama.

Shi'ite Islam differs from Sunni Islam on the matter of the succession to the early caliphate after the death of the Prophet Muhammad. The doctrinal points and proofs have been presented in detail in the work of Dwight Donaldson [53] and more concisely in a modern restatement for Western readers by Professor Mahmud Shahabi.[54] The essence of the Shi'ite position is that the Prophet designated his son-in-law, Ali, as his successor, but that others less well qualified managed to usurp the office of caliph. The third Caliph was so incapable of restraining his corrupt relatives that his incompetence brought about a violent protest in which the Caliph was killed. Ali is generally acknowledged to have been the fourth Caliph, but his caliphate was contested throughout his short tenure. After Ali's assassination, the Umayyad Caliphate became firmly established, and those who sought to reassert the rights of Ali were suppressed. The most celebrated of these efforts was that of Ali's second son, Husain, who was martyred with his small band of supporters at Kerbela in what is now southern Iraq. According to the Shi'ites, the Umayyad Caliphate and its successor, the Abbasid, were never legitimate, the only legitimate authority of the Islamic Community being that of the Imams. All of the Imams were direct descendants of Ali and of the Prophet through his daughter Fatima. There were twelve Imams including Ali. The twelfth Imam has hidden himself from this world, to return at the appointed time. After his disappearance there began the period of the lesser occultation in which the Imam was represented by a series of four deputies. This period is also known as that of the specific agency, that is, the specific agency of these deputies for the Imam. After the death of the fourth deputy there began the great occultation and the general agency, that is, the agency of all of the learned men or ulama for the hidden Imam. This agency is further sustained by a tradition attributed to the Imam Ja'far al-Sadiq, who said that all those who might act as judges over the Muslims and interpret the law had their appointment *ex ante* from him. Since the Imam Ja'far is looked upon as the founder of Shi'ite jurisprudence and the twelve-Imam Shi'ism of Iran is also referred to as Ja'fari Shi'ism, this tradition is doubly significant in establishing the authority of the ulama.

The Shi'ite ulama, acting as the general agency until the hidden Imam reveals himself, perform the function of the Imam. The Imam is not a prophet, for the Shi'ites, too, adhere strictly to the doctrine that Muhammad was the last of the prophets and that his revelation perfected all earlier ones. The function of the Imam is to interpret the law of the Qur'an and to apply it, even develop it, as new situations arise. Since the Imamate passed, with one exception, by heredity through the eldest male offspring in the line of Ali, it follows that a certain charismatic quality is attached to that office. This quality was further enhanced by the assertions made against the Sunni apologists of the Abbasid Caliphate that the Shi'ite Imam was not only eligible under the Sunni rules of the caliphate, but that he was the best of those qualified and impeccable besides. The infallibility of the Imam is as firmly asserted and in practice unequivocally adhered to. The ulama who act in the name of the Imam do not share all of this charisma by any means, but some of it does accrue to them. They are not considered infallible nor impeccable, and the most careful ulama may sign themselves as criminal and wrongdoer in the humble recognition that they may have judged incorrectly.

The Sunni ulama enjoy no similar charismatic quality. Neither the Umayyad nor the Abbasid Caliphs claimed the legal authority of the Shi'ite Imams. The early Abbasid era knew a moderate form of inquisition; still, a courtier's very early suggestion that the Abbasid Caliphs assume the right to settle doctrinal disputes never came to anything. Only a little later we find Sunni apologists asserting that the caliph need not be the best of those qualified for the job, nor even the most learned. Al-Baqillani was of the opinion that the consensus of the learned should guide the caliph and even depose him if he stubbornly refused to follow the law. Al-Ghazali merely asserted that the caliph could legitimize his position by taking the advice of the ulama.

Under these circumstances we find that the Shi'ite ulama derive their legitimacy largely from the Imam, while the Sunni ulama can lend a measure of legitimacy to the caliph. For centuries, now, we have had neither an Imam nor a caliph; and in practical terms both bodies of ulama have had to contend with political authorities who established themselves without benefit of religious procedure. Both have tried to play the role assigned to the ulama by al-Ghazali. Consequently, a single tradition of the formal relations of the ulama and the Sultan or Shah has come to prevail. On the other hand, there is no question but what the doctrinal authority of the Shi'ite ulama is both more concrete and more prestigious than that of the Sunni ulama. The Shi'ite ulama perform the function of the Imam in his absence. The Sunni ulama do not perform the function of the caliph, but rather assist the Muslim Community to do that which is incumbent upon all. There is no religious office connected with the function of the Sunni ulama.

All Muslims believe that the good is that which God wills and the evil that which God forbids. Man's whole duty is to comply with the will of God, for which reason God revealed His will to man through the prophets. After the last revelation, the Sunnis hold that man can be rightly guided if he follows the explicit commands of the Qur'an, if he follows the traditions reporting the sayings and doings of the Prophet himself, if he follows the consensus of the Community which by the higher authority of tradition will never be in error, or if he deduces new applications by strict analogy to known rules. The Shi'ite ulama believe that more is necessary if man is to be rightly guided. Man must have some immediate inspired exponent of the law, or he will inevitably go astray. The Imams are meant by God for this purpose. In the absence of the hidden Imam, the ulama must provide for the divine guidance of the Community. The Shi'ite ulama, however, claim no charismatic quality or inspiration for themselves. In fact, they claim no more than the long years of study which is the qualification of the Sunni ulama. This failing is accounted for by the differences in the *usul*, or science of the roots of the law of the Shi'ites.

The four roots of Sunni law are the Qur'an, the *hadith*, the consensus of the Community, and analogical deduction. In this system, there is no room for independent judgment, or *ijtihad*, and reason is to be used within the narrow confines of strict analogy. Independent judgment according to the spirit of the explicit law was the prerogative of the early founders of the four orthodox schools alone. The ulama of subsequent ages must accept their authority according to their choice of school. Acceptance of such authority is know as *taqlid* and its corollary is the closure of the gate of *ijtihad*. The four sources of Shi'ite law are the Qur'an, *hadith* of the Prophet and the Imams, consensus of the Imams rather than of the Community, and reason. Reason is not the equivalent of *ijtihad*, for certain judgments will be found to be logically necessary. For the rest, however, *ijtihad* in one form or another is the expression of this principle. Once again we find the Shi'ite ulama enjoying authority superior to that of the Sunni ulama, in that they are either speaking with the infallibility of the Imams or rendering judgments with an authenticity parallel to that of the founders of the Sunni schools.

Evidently, Shi'ite usul were slow in developing. Professor Shahabi explains this late development as the result of the fact that such a science was unnecessary until after the lesser occultation.[55] Before this, either the Imams or their deputies interpreted the law. The period of the lesser occultation lasted from A.D. 869 to 940. Donaldson points out that the Sunni collections of traditions, or *hadith*, were compiled about one generation before those of the Shi'ites. The Shi'ite collections were made during the domination of the caliphate by the Shi'ite Buwaiyhids—which period coincides with the beginning of the great occultation. It is these collections of *hadith* to which Professor Shahabi refers as the first works on jurisprudence, but in point of fact it would seem that the first major works devoted to the science of jurisprudence were those of Allama Hilli, who died in A.D. 1325. Shahabi admits that Hilli went beyond his illustrious grandfather, Shaikh Tusi, in admitting *ijtihad*, or independent judgment. However the study of *usul* may have developed in this period, it was not yet accorded the importance of the study of *hadith* at the end of the Safavid period, when the second Majlisi, who died in A.D. 1699, was the outstanding theologian. Furthermore, Shahabi indicates that the *usulis* overcame the opposition of the *akhbaris*, or those who preferred *hadith*, in Kerbela as late as the beginning of the nineteenth century; and we can guess that the *usulis* did not establish themselves and their views until the latter part of that century. The late leader of the Shi'ite ulama of Iran was reputed to have followed a jurisprudential method akin to that of Shaikh Tusi, so that he was by no means a convinced and thorough *usuli*.

What conclusions can we draw from this controversy between those who preferred to rely on the traditions reporting the judgments of the infallible Imams and those who preferred to supply the ulama with a jurisprudential theory that would permit them to make new interpretations as might the living but hidden Imam? This entire subject has not been sufficiently studied, but I believe it tenable that even today many of the Shi'ite ulama fear losing the authority of the Imams should they venture far beyond their explicitly recorded statements. The *usulis*, on the other hand, are far more aware of the pressures of recent social and political change and fear worse the relegation of Islamic law to a relatively minor position. At the present time no influential *alim* rejects the *usuli* position in its entirety; but, in any case, the *akhbari* position assures the ulama of the infallible authority of the Imams, whereas the *usuli* position affords the ulama a method of approximating that authority while adapting Islamic law to new situations.

Historical circumstances as well as both doctrine and jurisprudential theory have served to enhance the position of the Shi'ite ulama. Prior to the establishment of the Safavid empire in A.D. 1500, there was no extensive or long-lasting twelver-Shi'ite sovereignty established anywhere in Islam. The other branches of Shi'ism, such as the Zaidis in Yemen, the Isma'ilis, or the Fatimid Caliphate of mediaeval Egypt, all enjoyed the immediate presence of a living Imam which reduced the status of the ulama. The early Safavids also claimed the Imamate, according to Professors Minorsky and Lambton, but the former has presented some evidence to show that this view was accepted only by an elite tribal formation.[56] Professor Lambton offers a good deal of evidence to show that under the late Safavids and throughout the Qajar period, the twelver ulama predominated and were able to suppress to some extent the Sufi or mystic tendencies which made such extreme claims by the early Safavids possible.[57] In any event, it is obvious that the Shi'ite ulama were well established and identified with the Imam long before there was a secular political leader who needed to justify his office by reference to Shi'ite doctrines. For the Sunni ulama the opposite was the case.

What is the more remarkable about the position of the Shi'ite ulama is that they have not been challenged in their religious authority in any manner approximating that in which the Sunni of neighboring countries have been. Nearly all modernist movements are critical of the Sunni ulama and their traditional Islam. Nearly all of them reject *taqlid* and would alter the application of the doctrine of consensus. Above all, they would take from the ulama the exclusive right to interpret Islamic law, and incidentally usurp their proprietorship over the symbols of Islam. Nationalist and secularist movements have joined with the chorus of modernists, apologists, fundamentalists, and romantics in denouncing the pretensions of the ulama. "The doctrine of *taqlid*," they assert, "has stultified science and the arts in the East." "There is no priesthood in Islam," they remind the ulama. "The distorted interpretations of the ulama have withheld from Muslim women the equality which is justly theirs," and so on. In more practical terms, the influence of the ulama has declined, their educational functions have been restricted, and their judicial functions have been all but eliminated. Ulama control over and income from pious endownments have been reduced and their prestige has fallen among the urban classes. They have become increasingly dependent upon the government of the day.

It is erroneous to believe that the Sunni ulama wish to reestablish the government of the pious caliphs. Their ideal remains the mediaeval pious sultanate, in which the ruler recognized and cooperated with the ulama to the extent that Muslim personal-status law was maintained, religious endowments respected, and outward official piety upheld. Under this sort of government the tradition of Islamic learning could be maintained, and, given the limited scope of government, the ideal of an Islamic society, more or less God-fearing, was realized. Consequently, there is no real unity among so-called traditional groups such as the Muslim Brethren (which would reestablish the early Arab caliphate) and the ulama.

Because orderly community life within a permissive political framework is an unequivocal prerequisite of the traditional function of the ulama, they have little tendency toward open agitation. Since a benevolent government is necessary to the achievement of their goals, the ulama have little incentive to cooperate continuously with other traditional groups against the government. Just as the ulama join with traditional groups in opposition on occasion, so may they join with certain Westernized or lower-middle-class groups. In so doing the ulama have no sense of stepping outside of their traditional role. For the ulama, a president, cabinet, or parliament is merely a complex form of the mediaeval sultanate; and for the clique of the Westernized, the ulama are another client group to be manipulated as circumstances require.

The political role of the ulama is further complicated by the fact that the Islamic institution is not a hierarchically organized, monolithic group. Generally speaking the organizational divisions among the ulama depend upon legal schools, institutions of learning, discipleship and acceptance of the authority of particular teachers, and the ability of certain ulama to distribute piously contributed largesse to their followers.

Leadership within these divisions of the ulama also depends upon a number of factors. The primary basis of leadership is learning, but other criteria such as a teaching position in one of the important theological academies, designation by and apprenticeship to an acknowledged leader, or appointment to an official position or being shown special favor by the government are all important. The latter point is especially significant, because the ulama insist on the importance of a benevolently disposed government and because they identify recognition of their institution with the establishment of Islam. Insofar as these two may be distinguished, a further broad distinction is sometimes made between political ulama and religious ulama, i.e., those who stress recognition of the institution by such appointments and those who stress the establishment of Islam by legal means.

While all ulama are agreed on the importance of the establishment of Islam, the "religious" ulama are deeply aware of the dangers of too close an involvement with the political institution. Indeed, the position of the "religious" ulama is highly ambivalent. On the one hand they recognize that favorable attitudes on the part of the political leaders will further their cause, but on the other they realize that too close an association with the political authorities may corrupt the religious institution. This ambivalence has contributed to the lack of political effectiveness of the ulama, but there are other reasons for their political weakness, also. In the first place, the "religious" ulama depend upon the favor of a Westernized elite which is out of sympathy with the goals of the ulama. In the second place, when they do cooperate with the government, there are always a good many ulama, both religious and political, who are ever ready to condemn them for cooperating with an un-Islamic government. In addition, the political ulama, despite their lesser influence in the long run, are always ready to outbid the more responsible ulama in dealing with the politicians. In the third place, the Westernized political leadership sometimes makes legislative incursions into the residual legal domain of the ulama. And in the fourth place, new fundamentalist groups accuse the ulama of failing to perform their religious role and aspire to usurp their exclusive right of interpreting Islamic law.

Because they are willing to work with any government that recognizes the establishment of Islam, and because they recognize, at least tacitly, a distinction between religious and political roles, the ulama can accomodate themselves to modern nationalism. It may be, as Gibb suggests, that they do not realize the implications of nationalism as a rival legitimizing principle, but it must also be remembered that Islam did not so much legitimize mediaeval government as did that government legitimize itself by recognizing Islam. The ulama are willing to live with the dualism of an Islamic society ruled over by a benevolent, yet secular, government. Nationalists and fundamentalists reject this dualistic pattern. Nationalists may permit the ulama to understand modern politics in terms of their traditional orientation, but they, too, are ambivalent. Classical nationalism like classical Islam is monistic in its theory of the state. The *modus vivendi* which has been worked out in a pragmatic manner is only possible because of the glossing over of the dualistic flaw in the thinking of both the nationalists and the ulama. It is this glossing over which is rejected by the fundamentalists. In their rejection of the dualism of society and government the fundamentalists become modern despite their verbal predilection for the reestablishment of the classical caliphate. Some fundamentalist groups are willing to accept the "fact" of nationalism, but it is for them a fact from which no important political conclusions may be drawn.

IV

The general similarity of the fundamentalist doctrine as put forward by the Wahhabis, the Sanusis, the Ikhwan al-Muslimun, the Ikhwa al-Islamiyya, the Fidayan-i-Islam, the Jama'at-i-Islami, and the Masjumi is fairly obvious. Yet, there are important dissimilarities among these groups. The Wahhabis and Sanusis have a tribal, nomadic, social base; and their puritanical doctrines served to unite and strengthen relatively weak and backward groups. Though originally two geographically and socially peripheral movements, these two have since contributed to the creation and maintenance of two highly traditional political systems. One might classify both as "early" fundamentalism, and they are relatively untainted by Western ideas. Whereas these two early fundamentalist movements were directed at the shortcomings of the Ottoman imperial system, the Muslim Brethren of Egypt and the Fidayan of Iran opposed Westernized regimes. The Brethren approached the magnitude of a mass movement and appealed to many groups, but found its beginnings among lower-middle-class artisans and bazaar people. The Fidayan were always a very small group of devotees, most of whom were students of theology. The interesting factor in these two organizations is that both condoned nationalism. The Jama'at-i-Islami of Pakistan and the Ikhwa of northern Iraq both opposed nationalism. The Jama'at appealed to lower-middle-class groups, but especially those with some Western education, and for a time made deep inroads among college students. The appeal of the Jama'at to educated Muslims, who were in a minority within the Indian intelligentsia of prepartition days, was matched by the appeal of the Ikhwa to educated Iraqi Turks. Apparently the Masjumi shows greater similarity to the Jama'at and the Ikhwa except for the fact that it is nationalist.

Evidently, all these organizations which we have designated by the general name fundamentalist may be further subdivided; or perhaps closer examination may reveal that they have little in common from the point of view of their class appeal or their views on so central a political idea as nationalism. On the other hand, we find works by Maududi being circulated by the Ikhwan and Masjumi pamphlets being read by members of the Jama'at. Maududi was not unknown to the Ikhwa also. There is, however, no evidence of intellectual contact between these formally organized groups and the communal-brotherhood groups of the Wahhabis and the Sanusis; though the Jama'at does respect the Wahhabis in a somewhat idealized way. Consequently, we may find in the attitudes of the leading members of these groups some *prima facie* evidence for establishing a single classification for all of them. These members act as though all of these fundamentalist groups are on the same path.

The asserted sameness of these groups appears to be related to their basic doctrines, from which we must remove nationalism for the moment. The elements of this common doctrine might be summed up as follows: 1) current Islamic practice has strayed from the true path; 2) most of the ulama have too readily acquiesced in contemporary laxness; 3) worldly oriented governments have been the prime causes for the weakness of Islam; 4) the process of the corruption of Islam has been going on for many centuries, so that one must go back to some original pure foundation; 5) the legal bonds of *ijma* (consensus), of the closure of *ijtihad* (independent judgment), and of *taqlid* (the acceptance of earlier authority) prevent the ulama from carrying out the task of purification; 6) *ijma* must be restricted to the proven consensi of the first generation of Muslims, and *ijtihad* must be opened to those who are qualified by virtue of knowledge and piety; and the authority of the founders of the schools must be limited to respectful consideration in *ijtihad*; 7) the Qur'an, in its obvious meaning, must serve as the foundation of all judgment; 8) the moral, economic, and intellectual decline of Muslims is due to the corruption of Islam; 9) to remedy the situation a veritable spiritual revolution is needed; 10) while the beginning of this revolution is with a small group of enlightened devotees, its ultimate success depends upon eliminating bad influences from the environment and providing for beneficial influences through pious government. The fundamentalist state will declare the sovereignty of God as the foundation of the legitimacy of its government. The sovereignty of God is not merely nominal, for God has revealed His will through His Prophet. The law of the state will be based upon the Qur'an and the traditions of the Prophet, but it will reject the later consensi of the legal schools. The head of the state will have power to interpret the sacred law in applying it to new situations. It is possible that legislation on some points by an assembly will be permitted. The head of state and the assembly will be elected, but there will be only one party, or perhaps none at all. Candidates will not canvass for election, but they will be elected on the basis of their knowledge of the law, their piety, their respectability, and their *modern* knowledge. The composition of the assembly may reflect economic interests, but probably not geographical areas. The law will be a respecter of persons in regard to religious differences. Only Muslims will be able to hold policy-making positions, but non-Muslims will be permitted to live in accordance with their own personal-status law. Private property will be safeguarded, but exceptionally large accumulations of wealth will be prohibited. Women will be excluded from public life, and secluded in the home whenever possible. The major domestic duty of the government will be to foster the good and suppress evil in encouraging the growth of a truly Muslim society.

In general, this doctrine is anti-Western and anti-imperialist, but it is also anticommunist. The most outstanding feature of the doctrine is its logical character, which serves erroneously as the means of coping with the rationalist attack on religion. It includes definite political aspirations, but minimizes the problems of administration, economic development, and military security. Nationalism is condoned as an antiforeign sentiment except where Muslims are a religious minority (prepartition India) or where the adherents are a national minority (northern Iraq). Nationalism seemed even more acceptable to the Fidayan because of the relatively isolated position of Shi'ite Iran. In Saudi Arabia and Libya, the opposition to the ulama has declined with the creation of a body of ulama loyal to the ideals of "early" fundamentalism. Most suggestive, however, is the fact that little interest is shown in altering specific rulings of the traditional ulama. Mysticism, saint worship, and superstitions are severely attacked, but not purdah, nor punishing thievery by amputation, nor punishing apostasy by death.

We must be interested in the fact that such similar expressions of fundamentalist thought occur at widely separated places at approximately the same time. One possible explanation of this occurrence is that we are dealing with a single religious community with an extensive if inefficient system of communication. One can further note a widespread concern throughout the Muslim world with the problem of the "decline of Islam," with the doctrinal attacks of missionaries and scholars, with the adaptability of Islam to "modern conditions," and with the general challenge of science and rationalism to religion. While more specific notions were communicated throughout the Islamic world, we can do no more than point to a few seminal writers such as Amir Ali, Muhammad Abduh and Rashid Rida, or the great agitator, Sayyid Jamal al-Din al-Afghani, in attempting to establish concrete lines of influence. Historically, however, the pressures of Western countries, limited Westernizing policies of traditional governments, and outright imperialism correlate well with the appearance of late fundamentalism.

The class basis of fundamentalism is even more difficult to ascertain. In Pakistan, the Jama'at boasted of no more than a thousand members, though it had many supporters. Members of the Jama'at were drawn from what might be called the lower middle class, while its supporters came from such diverse groups as students and bazaar merchants. Insofar as support in the form of finances came from traditionally oriented merchants, we may ascribe the cause to the same sort of confusion which leads many Western observers to class fundamentalist groups along with traditionalists and the ulama. There is something more in common between members of the lower middle class and students. In our definition of the lower middle class we would insist upon some measure of formal education through the medium of either English or Urdu. For most members of the Jama'at, this formal education has been supplemented by self-education. Literacy is a *sine qua non*. Occupationally, the typical member of this class would be a clerk or secondary-school teacher. Higher civil service positions or responsible positions in private business or professional pursuits are closed to them for want of either enough education, enough education of the right kind, or the appropriate social connections. The parents of these persons would probably come from traditionally oriented groups such as the ulama, small landowners, petty merchants, and even master craftsmen. Some parents might have been petty government officials or officials of the unreformed administration of the princely states. Those students that were attracted to the support of the Jama'at were similarly those whose prospects were limited either because of the general cheapening of the B.A., because they failed to master English well enough, or because of the intense competition for better-paying and more prestigious government positions, or because of their relatively uninfluential lower-middle-class parentage. Financially these persons are unable to maintain a fully Western life pattern. Their homes are small and will usually contain a number of more distant relatives. Purdah is usually observed, often as a line of least resistance rather than of firm belief.

Nevertheless, certainly not all of these classes of people are members of the Jama'at nor even supporters thereof. Hence, attraction to fundamentalism is but one alternative open to persons in the social predicament described. Some additional explanation must be brought to bear upon this issue. We know that "joining" is not a significant cultural or sociological factor in underdeveloped countries. Furthermore, the Jama'at insisted upon "conversion" rather than mere declaration of membership. The candidate was kept on probation for a year or longer. His devotion to the organization had to be established beyond any question.

In the Jama'at's student group, the conditions of membership were less stringent, and the number of adherents was not inconsiderable. Still, the Jama'at never set out to establish any number of front groups. The wide popularity enjoyed by the Muslim Brethren in Egypt may be an indication of the potential of such groups if the restrictions on membership are removed or if appeals are made to lower-class groups like artisans. Consequently, if we are to lay any basis for comparison, we must limit ourselves here to describing the characteristics of the inner circle of militants.

In describing the characteristics of a small core of adherents, who might without grave injustice be called fanatical believers, we must look for some common psychological factors. The inner circle of members is an *ecclesiola in ecclesia*, a group of the elect, puritanical, ascetic, and devoted. The leader enjoys an exceptional charismatic influence, approximating the position of the leader in the "Freudian" group. The individual member believes of himself that he is progressive, scientific, pious, tolerant, and virtuous. Above all, the individual member has eliminated all ambivalence.

These individuals are marginal to the reference groups which they aspire to join. They cannot feel secure with the more highly Westernized, and their shortcomings in this regard are turned into advantages by the idea that true Islam is the most modern and scientific ideology. For the rest, traditional values are insisted upon most violently when they are everywhere being brought into question. Black-and-white distinctions are everywhere made between things that are Islamic and those that are not. But a fundamental insecurity is revealed in the necessity of citing Western authors to prove that Islam has contributed to world civilization and to demonstrate the corruption of Western society and culture. One must be guarded here from too easy stereotyping, for it is also possible for individuals to be attracted who have for other reasons a heavy commitment to orthopraxy but need a modern scientific restatement of Islam to justify themselves. In this regard it may be pertinent to note the very good relations of fathers and sons in the few cases observed.

Even should our hazardous psychological suggestions prove relevant, it cannot be held that all persons filling the description will join a fundamentalist group. Aside from the accidents of time, place, and occasions, there may be an irreducible minimum of incalculable religious conviction or logical conviction. This conclusion appears when we consider that the same social, psychological, and cultural configuration seems to present itself in explaining the membership of other groups like the Khaksars,[58] the Ahraris,[59] and maybe Misr al-Fatat [60] or the Ba'th and other irrational lower-middle-class organizations. Regardless of whether all fundamentalist groups fit precisely into a single mold, that they may be a type of manifestation of a general response to the stresses of instability and change in the Middle East and Asia strongly suggests where we shall find the political element. It is not to be found in the essential nature of Islam, for Islam is as various as the Muslims would have it.

Nevertheless, the fundamentalist doctrine is an Islamic doctrine. That is to say, it is more akin to the position of the traditionalists than to the position of any other group described, in the sense that they are not concerned with the place of Islam in some wider framework, but see Islam as setting the framework within which all questions social, economic, and political are to be resolved. It is for this reason that we have designated the traditional ulama position and that of the fundamentalists as providing alternatives to the nationalist principle of legitimacy.

We have seen, however, that both the ulama and the fundamentalists (wherever it was politically feasible) were willing to accept nationalism. They are agreed with most modern Middle Eastern nationalists in believing nationalism to be objectively determined by language, history, and territory. They differ with the nationalists about the subjective sentiments and attitudes which ought to be the consequence of such objective circumstances. Their subjective identifications are primarily Islamic, but in a more truly religious sense they hold that the subjective is within the sphere of the soul and that the soul must be governed by religious belief. Mere outward verbalization of dogma means nothing; true belief requires the internalization of dogma so that belief becomes an acquired habit of the soul and the mind.

NOTES

1. Aside from the implicit anti-Islamic prejudice in his work, all students of the Middle East are deeply indebted to Muir for such works as *The Caliphate: Its Rise, Decline, and Fall; The Mamluke or Slave Dynasty of Egypt;* and *The Life of Mahomet.*
2. Hisham Sharabi, "The Crisis of the Intelligentsia in the Middle East," *The Muslim World,* **XLVII** (July 1957), p. 187.
3. See M. Berger, *Bureaucracy and Society in Modern Egypt* (Princeton, 1957), p. 222ff, for an attempt to derive certain conclusions from length of exposure to Western influences (and vice versa).
4. Sharabi, *op. cit.,* p. 188.
5. See H. A. R. Gibb, *Modern Trends in Islam* (Chicago, 1947), p. 122.
6. Sharabi, *loc. cit.*
7. *Idem.*
8. *Idem.*
9. *Ibid.,* p. 190.
10. *Ibid.,* p. 192.
11. S. A. Morrison, "Arab Nationalism and Islam," *The Middle East Journal,* **II** (April 1948), p. 152.
12. *Ibid.,* p. 153.
13. *Idem.*
14. See below.
15. A. H. Hourani, *Syria and Lebanon: A Political Essay* (London, 1946), p. 73 ff.
16. *Ibid.,* p. 73.
17. *Ibid.,* pp. 75–76.
18. See E. G. Browne, *The Persian Revolution, 1905–1909* (Cambridge, 1910), Ch. 1.
19. See C. C. Adams, *Islam and Modernism in Egypt* (London, 1933).
20. Hourani, *op. cit.,* pp. 81–82.
21. *Ibid.,* p. 75.
22. H. A. R. Gibb, *op. cit.*
23. *Ibid.,* pp. 106–112.
24. *Ibid.,* p. 110.
25. *Ibid.,* p. 112.
26. *Ibid.,* p. 113 ff.
27. *Ibid.,* p. 128, note 8; the phrase is that of Karl Mannheim.
28. *Ibid.,* p. 122.
29. W. C. Smith, *Modern Islam in India* (London, 1946), revised edition; in the following analysis the past tense is used wherever convenient in order to indicate that the author may have changed some of the views here discussed.

30. *Ibid.*, p. 306.
31. Reference is made to conditions more favorable to the development of a capitalist middle class in Egypt, *ibid.*, p. 165; however, see Gibb, *op. cit.*, p. 56.
32. See Smith, *op. cit.*, p. 309, "Definition of Terms": upper class and middle class.
33. *Ibid.*, pp. 9, 125–127.
34. *Ibid.*, pp. 86, 99, *et passim.*
35. *Ibid.*, pp. 11, 14 ff.
36. *Ibid.*, pp. 12, 47 ff.
37. *Ibid.*, pp. 12, 13, 98 ff., 132 ff.
38. *Ibid.*, p. 13, 154, 193, *et passim.*
39. *Ibid.*, p. 13.
40. *Ibid.*, pp. 70, 149 ff.
41. *Ibid.*, p. 42; Gibb, *op. cit.*, p. 56. This is a case of loose classification rather than misinterpretation, for Gibb seems to have derived his information from Smith; but loose classification seems to have contributed to Smith's failure to foresee the enhanced role of the traditional ulama in Pakistan.
42. Smith, *op. cit.*, p. 269.
43. W. C. Smith, *Islam in Modern History* (Princeton, 1957).
44. *Ibid.*, pp. 41, 47.
45. *Ibid.*, p. 42.
46. *Ibid.*, p. 52.
47. *Ibid.*, p. 55.
48. *Ibid.*, pp. 61, 64.
49. *Ibid.*, p. 72–73.
50. *Ibid.*, p. 75.
51. *Ibid.*, p. 89.
52. *Ibid.*, p. 86.
53. D. Donaldson, *The Shi'ite Religion* (London, 1933).
54. M. Shahabi, in K. Morgan, ed., *Islam, The Straight Path* (New York, 1958).
55. M. Shahabi, *Taqrirat-i-Usul* (Teheran, 1335 A.H.), p. xxxviii.
56. V. Minorsky, ed., *Tadhkirat al-Muluk* (London, 1943).
57. A. K. S. Lambton, "Quis Custodiet Custodes," *Studia Islamica*, 1956, nos. v and vi.
58. See W. C. Smith, *Modern Islam in India*, p. 235.
59. *Ibid.*, p. 224.
60. See M. Colombe, *L'Evolution de L'Egypte, 1924–1950* (Paris, 1951), p. 142.

3

THE UNEASY SYNTHESIS OF

RELIGION AND POLITICS IN ISLAM

"Although we are apt to think of Islam as a religion, it was probable that the Prophet thought of it rather as a nation." With these words did D. S. Margoliouth commence his discussion of the Islamic state in his small classic, *Mohammedanism*.[1] If we examine the sentence carefully we may discern its suggestion of the paradox that is always attendant upon the juxtaposition of the eternal and the terrestrial, of the spiritual and the political, of reason and revelation in Islam. There is no clear contrapositioning of the two principles as may be found in St. Augustine.

If we know Islam today as a religion, but the Prophet thought of it as a nation, is the consequence then that Islam became a religion after it was a nation? The question is obviously absurd. Nevertheless, it helps us to get at Margoliouth's meaning. Let us offer the following, somewhat bold, interpretation: we may, if we choose, see Islam as a religious system; and, alternatively, we may look upon it as a political system. The next question is all too obvious: what is the relationship between these two views? Insofar as this question concerns the relationship between religion and

49

politics in Islam, it may be supposed that the answer lies in a close examination of Islamic history.[2]

If, however, we are concerned to discover the relationship between the concept "religion" and the concept "politics" in Islamic thought, our enterprise is of a different sort. In the latter case, the question is about the relationship between two totalistic conceptualizations of historical reality. The answers which this sort of question must yield will tell us either where Islamic religion fits into the political scheme of things in Islamic history, or where politics fits into the religious scheme of things. The method of abstraction and selective perspective which qualifies this question precludes the comprehensive treatment of opposites in a single and coherent discourse. At least this is the case in Islamic thought. The superficial exaggeration by which religion and politics are rendered a unity in Islam represents a profound misunderstanding of a tension which was a continuous stimulus to theological and philosophical thought in Islam.

Is there really no unified treatment of religion and politics in Islamic thought? An absolute answer to this question would require a far more comprehensive knowledge of Islamic thought than that of which we can dispose, and it would lead us far beyond our present purpose. It can, however, be demonstrated that there are examples, outstanding in themselves, of the failure to treat the two in unified and comprehensive fashion. Consider the immense cultural gap between al-Ghazali's *Ihya* and Nizam al-Mulk's *Siaset-Nameh*.[3] The first takes a religious perspective and the second a political perspective, but both fail to treat adequately of the opposing principle which is to be reconciled. The intrinsic importance and influence of these two works tells us more than any detailed analysis of lesser contributions to the mainstream of Islamic thought.

Surely, there was no more encyclopedic attempt at the reconciliation of all branches of knowledge and all spheres of human existence than that of Ibn Khaldun in the *Prolegomena*. Yet his method is essentially that of the *iqsam al-'ulum* of the philosophers. It is to the credit of Ibn Khaldun's effort, despite the fact that he gathered no immediate following among Muslims, that Western scholarship has debated the degree of his commitment to orthodoxy on the one hand and to the philosophical school on the other.[4] Whether we examine his treatment of religious matters in Book III or in Book VI of the *Prolegomena*, or try to understand either treatment in the light of the other, we are left with an uncomfortable sense of the difficulty of presenting Ibn Khaldun's views on the relationship between religion and politics in Islam in anything approaching a succinct formula.

This difficulty is only in part due to the complexity of the original text and our dim understanding of its cultural context; the rest of the difficulty is due to the fact that Ibn Khaldun, like other Muslim thinkers, attempted to accomplish the purpose of reconciliation through the device of juxtaposition. Now the framework of juxtaposition may be an analytical typology of the sciences (i.e., *iqsam al-'ulum*) or it may be through an analytical typology of the possible kinds of regime. However we may examine the result of this expository device, it never has the form of establishing the essential unity of the political and the religious nor even of the philosophical and the religious.

At the risk of oversimplifying our problem, it may be suggested that the paradox of the historical unity of religion and politics and the philosophical duality of the two concepts in Islam is related to two circumstances, the first of which is historical and the second rather more theological. The historical circumstance which gave rise to ideological concern over the relationship between religion and politics is that, as orthodox thought developed, the ulama held ever more strongly that the sphere of politics was to be dominated by the sphere of religion—even while, in fact, the sphere of politics came ever more strongly to dominate the sphere of religion. At the very least, this enormous generalization is true as regards the institutions of the caliphate and the sultanate. The theological circumstance is more difficult to express, but it is the very heart of the problem. The point is that Islamic theology cannot accept the idea of tension between religion and politics. Islam is at once a religion and a nation, to paraphrase Margoliouth, and there should be no difference in what we see regardless of which perspective we take. In other words, Islam is not only monotheistic but also strives toward an absolute monism in theology. Note, further, that the line between theology and philosophy in

Islam was not clearly drawn, as both Ibn Khaldun and Muhammad Abduh have told us. Is there not at least some hint of this in the adoption of the term *'ilm al-tawhid* (science of unity) as the technical name for the subject matter of *kalam* (dialectical theology)? *Kalam* itself is more method (i.e., applied logic) than subject matter, but even then the common explanation for the origin of this term is that the first theological discussions were concerned with the divine attributes, particularly the attribute of speech, i.e., *kalam*.

Lest this point be misunderstood, we hasten to add that we find wholly acceptable the view of Pètrement that monotheism *cum* dualism is not only a possible configuration of a particular theologico-philosophical tradition, but that it represents perhaps a more sophisticated philosophical development. Surely, Christianity is an outstanding example of the theological coexistence of monotheism and philosophical dualism. It is in this regard that Islam, and incidentally Judaism, are to be most distinguished from Christianity in philosophical terms. It is in this regard that much of contemporary Islamic apologetics is to be understood. Monotheism and monism do not necessarily go together, but they happen to be found together in Islam. Rather than repeat the relevant argument here, it may be sufficient to quote Pètrement's emphatic conclusion and permit those interested to pursue the matter in the admirably brief and lucid original: "Il n'ya pas de dualisme parfait, pas de monisme parfait, mais seulement des degrés de dualisme et monisme. . . . De même que le dualisme n'est pas nécessairement un dithéisme, de même le dithéisme n'est pas nécessairement un dualisme . . . il faut distinguer ces deux séries: monisme, dualisme, pluralisme d'une part, est d'autre part monothéisme, dithéisme, polythéisme; elles ne sont pas équivalentes. Dans la première, il s'agit de principes, dans la seconde, de dieux." [5]

According to the same author, Islam stands between ancient Judaism and Christianity along the continuum between monism and dualism. Pètrement finds the difference between ancient Judaism and Islam in this regard to be based upon the greater emphasis in the Qur'an upon the world to come and upon the gnostic influences incorporated into Islam. [6] But Judaism did "reintroduce God in the idea of a judgment in the afterlife," [7] and Judaic philosophy had a Philo. Let us look at what Kaufmann calls the basic idea of Israelite religion, i.e., ancient Judaism, and see if it is really distinguished from Islamic monotheism. "The basic idea of Israelite religion is that God is supreme over all. There is no realm above or beside him to limit his absolute sovereignty. He is utterly distinct from, and other than, the world. . . . He is, in short, non-mythological." [8] In contrast, all pagan religions contain "the idea that there exists a realm of being prior to the gods and above them, upon which the gods depend, and whose decrees they must obey." [9] Kaufmann holds that this conception of monotheism is common to Judaism, Islam, and Christianity. It will have been noted, however, that there is an important dualistic implication in Kaufmann's emphasis upon the otherness of God. It is doubtful that he meant this otherness in Pètrement's sense of a contrary principle, because the burden of his interpretation points rather to the unknowability of God, or for ancient Israelite religion the lack of any attempt to speculate about God as He really is. Nevertheless, this theologico-philosophical issue is ever there, waiting to be taken up by exponents of any of the three monotheistic religions. The issue was, of course, taken up in all three religions; but such considerations became much more a part of the mainstream of Christian theology than of Islamic or Judaic. At the very least it may be said that Christian theologians did not find a largely dualistic conception of reality uncomfortable, while Islamic theologians did.

It is noteworthy that, in offering an example of Islamic dualism, Pètrement cites Massignon's *al-Hallaj*.[10] Does this not reveal at least part of the reason for the tension between Sufism and orthodoxy? for the orthodox misunderstanding of Sufism as polytheism? for the palpably unacceptable device whereby Sufism and orthodoxy were reconciled by interpreting the former as merely sincere faith and inner conviction? Insofar as the otherness of God was understood in Islam as implying a principle of the spirit as distinct from the worldly principle of matter, this was the concern of Sufi speculation, and of nonorthodox philosophy. We are here concerned with major emphases and not matters of detail, however important those details might be in themselves. The major emphasis is expounded by Pètrement—but in a footnote: "Dans le

Coran, Dieu est consideré avant tout comme Créateur, et par suite le monde n'est pas separé de la divinité." [11] This emphasis was not lost with the development of Islamic theology, it was rather strengthened through the doctrines of Islamic atomism, occasionalism, and the perpetual recreation of the universe. Dualism in Islam was therefore restricted to a marginal existence in the secondary or defeated traditions of Sufism, of the philosophers, and of the Persian influenced *katibs*.

In proper dualist fashion, we have separated the two realms of the historical and the philosophical. It may be readily admitted that, historically, Islamic institutions have exhibited dualistic aspects, for example, the coexistence of the caliphate and what is called the sultanate. For orthodox thought, however, we have decreed a persistent attraction to monism. The question to which we now address ourselves is whether there are any consequences, either necessary or probable, of an historical nature that flow from philosophical or prephilosophical monism. In introducing the question, part of the answer has already been given. On the other hand, it is not at all clear that the caliphate and the sultanate stood for the two separate principles of religion and politics. In fact there is much in the literature on the caliphate which insists on its essentially political nature. We shall return to the consideration of this problem, but let us first consider one interesting argument holding that there are historical consequences of a significant kind which flow from either philosophical monism or philosophical dualism. This is the argument of Frederick Watkins, and it is, perhaps, best presented in his own words in few short quotations:

> The characteristic feature of Far Eastern thought is a tendency to avoid sharp logical distinctions, and to emphasize the underlying identity of apparently irreconcilable phenomena. In this it represents the normal needs of a society held together by ethical rather than legal bonds. . . . The only method for resolving social conflict, without the use of force, is to resort to a process of arbitration and compromise.
>
> Western thought, on the other hand, has always been litigious in character. Ever since the time of the ancient Greeks it has been dominated by the feeling that logic is the basic weapon for the

discovery of truth. To classify reality in terms of a system of clearly defined categories is the essence of the logical process.

With the possible exception of the concept of law 'itself, the concept of social dualism has done more than anything else to determine the specific character of Western Civilization.[12]

For Watkins, then, the political tradition of the West out of which has emerged modern liberalism is the antithesis of the monistic tendency of the East. We have used the words "monistic tendency" rather than "monism" because Watkins writes of "apparently irreconcilable phenomena." It would appear from his terminology that the monistic East is not unaware of the opposition of the principles of such irreconcilable phenomena, but that it is unwilling or philosophically unable to cope with such opposition. While many questions may be raised regarding Watkins' major thesis, it would appear that there is much insight in his characterization of Eastern thought. Let us first try to dispose of the problem of his major thesis, after which we will return to a consideration of the tendency of Eastern thought.

Watkins argues that the dualism of church and state and later of society and polity in Western thought explain the emergence of the Western liberal tradition. The argument thus stated in simple form is irrefutable because both the liberal tradition and ideas setting off the natural order of society and the conventional order of the state from one another are, in a sense, historical facts. There is also, doubtlessly, some significant causal relationship between the two; but the two "facts" are not mutually explanatory as sufficient, sole cause and specific effect. In order to establish the importance of this argument we should have to be convinced of two things. The first point is that the attachment to social dualism in the West must be strong enough to overcome any set of historical circumstances, however uncongenial to the liberal tradition. The case in point is the rise of premodern absolutism in Europe. The second point must be that the resistance to the supremacy of the state be demonstrably related to social dualism, or even religious dualism, rather than to some ideologically defined single or monistic source of right. If neither of these points can be demonstrated, that is, if there were social forces congenial to the mitigation of absolutism and if both the origin of the state and the origin of political right were referred to a single natural law, then a dualistic frame of thought is not a necessary precondition of democratic liberalism. All that can be shown is that, given political conditions thought to be inconsistent with natural law, the cultural fact of the existence of dualistic frames in theology and philosophy provided the ideational form within which ideological attacks on absolutism were cast.

It is not our present task to work out the question of the validity of Watkins' thesis. We have carried this consideration of his views only far enough to raise certain questions regarding Islamic political thought. The first of these questions is whether the prevalence of Islamic belief precludes the possibility of the growth of a liberal tradition in Islamic lands. As indicated above, it is probable that historical circumstances and ideas on the origin of political legitimacy are more significant that ideational forms. Nevertheless, we note that political liberalism has not been an indigenous growth in any Muslim country, and not a few attempts to transplant Western liberalism earlier in the present century have dismally failed. Countering this sorry history we have the arguments of many a Muslim apologist that Islam is essentially democratic, as borne out by its egalitarianism, its urging that deliberation and the taking of counsel precede decision making, its emphasis upon consensus, and its unequivocal insistence that the ruler is under the law. It is argued that the failure of liberalism in Muslim lands is attributable to historical circumstances and not to the tendency of Islamic thought toward despotism. The argument of Muslim apologists is essentially correct; but the granting of this point leads to our second question.

Given the appearance of historical situations which did not accord with Islamic ideas of legitimacy, how did orthodox Muslim thinkers respond? The major effort of orthodox Muslim thinkers was directed at justifying rather than attacking such situations. When they did not justify directly, they sought to justify the exclusion of the consideration of political matters in their works. It is likely that this consistent tendency of orthodox political thought was a result of the fact that the only likely alternative to illegitimate government was heterodox government, a greater evil. The consistent effort of orthodox thinkers was to harmonize orthodox religion and government—any government. Turning back to the subject of the caliphate and the sultanate, we may say that the caliphate represented legitimate Islamic government, in the sense that such government was clearly subordinated in every way to Islamic law. The sultanate represented a contrary principle, that is, the accommodation of Islamic law to the necessary condition of political society. It is notorious, however, that orthodox thinkers did not devise new terms for dealing with the sultanate. By and large they used the same philosophical frames, merely dropping the legal rules relating specifically to the caliphate and at times adding the term "necessity" to their philosophical vocabulary.

It might be argued, therefore, that historical circumstances prevented Muslims from opposing illegitimate government. As a consequence, orthodox thought emphasized the harmonizing of religion and politics, a tendency which was sustained and strengthened by its monistic cast of thought. If this argument is valid, we should expect to find such problems discussed in terms which establish the essential identity of Islam and the state; but we do not. The fact of the matter is that there is a single formula for treating of religion and politics which is accepted by all schools of Islamic thought, but which is least well developed by the orthodox; and that formula is eminently dualistic.

The formula is a most familiar one. It asserts that religion and politics or government are brothers, or twins. What is not so readily recognized is that this is a dualistic formula and not the same as the assertion that they are identical. The origin of this cultural theme, as is also well known, is Persian. Nor is it only accidental that it is Persian, for it was an integral part of Persian dualist thought. It was not Muslims but Zoroastrians who held that:

Religion is royalty, and royalty is the Religion, but this is only an ideal state of affairs, and the aphorism in any case needs qualifying. . . . Because this world is still subject to the malign influence of Ahriman and the demons, spirit and matter are not as closely associated as they were in the beginning and will be in the end; yet, even so, they collaborate harmoniously; they complement rather than oppose each other. The interconnexion between the two worlds was fully explained to Yezdegird I by one Aturpat son of Zartusht, and these are the correspondences he established:

Matter	Spirit
Body	Soul
Wealth	Virtue
Honour	Righteous effort
Kingship	Religion
Generosity	Knowledge [13]

Not only was this formula alien to the spirit of orthodox Islamic thought, but it remained precisely a formula, receiving no significant amplification. In essence, those who used the formula were no more willing to face the question of illegitimate government than were those who ignored the question entirely. Yet, use of the formula itself offers the satisfying delusion that the problem has somehow been resolved. But a dualistic formulation is never a resolution; it poses the problem: "Ainsi s'explique enfin que le dualisme ne soit qu'une metaphysique imparfaite, limitée. . . ." [14] Why did it receive no amplification? We can only speculate about the answer. There was no obviously suitable alternative to justifying illegitimate government, nor was there any orthodox philosophical formula for dealing with illegitimate government. Though unsatisfactory, it would appear that the dualistic formula adopted from Zoroastrianism permitted the justification of illegitimate government in non-Islamic terms; but since the dualistic formula is itself alien to the frame of orthodox thought, it was never developed into a powerful philosophical tool for dealing with the intractabilities of the real world. Usually, whenever the formula is employed, the connection between religion and politics in Islam is not explained, it is swept under the rug.

While it is evident that Islamic political thought does not deny the dualism of religion and politics, the general structure of Islamic thought is not dualistic in the sense that Zoroastrianism was. One of the central problems of Zoroastrianism was the reconciliation of opposites. Muslim thinkers did not bother either to reconcile or to establish clearly the institutional boundaries of the two. The difference in emphasis may be illustrated by contrasting the ancient Greek notion of the harmonization of opposites with

Aristotle's classification of contrarieties. The first notion is available to me as Philo's second law of nature: "Not only are things divided into opposites, but the opposites are also equal, and, because they are equal, an equilibrium is established between them and they become harmonized." [15] Though Philo has taken his theory of opposites from Heraclitus, that theory receives no direct attention from Aristotle in the *Metaphysics*. Aristotle, who is seen by Pètrement as a reconciler of Plato's dualisms, is content to enumerate diverse types of contrariety in logical order: contradictories, relative opposites, privative opposites, and contraries.[16] That contraries need not be reconciled is a corollary of the view that all created things are limited and imperfect. Presumably, a similar view might characterize religion as a social institution. But this view, which is not uncongenial to Islamic monism, was not pursued by orthodox theologians. It was the Muslim philosophers, instead, particularly Ibn Khaldun, who worked out the institutional limitations of religion and politics. Their method was, as we have seen, *iqsam*, or logical classification, which shall have to be understood as a form of reconciliation, without harmonization.

These philosophical influences were of no assistance to orthodox Muslim theologians. These potentialities of philosophy were rejected along with the more suspect philosophical assertion that man could know the true nature of being. Orthodox Muslims relied, instead, upon the Persian formula. It is, however, of great interest to note that the institutional consequences of the use of this formula were different among Muslims from what they were among Zoroastrians. Zaehner states that "This near-identity of Church and State, which the Zoroastrians themselves admitted had been fatal to their religion once the Iranian monarchy collapsed, was nevertheless firmly embedded in their thought." [17] In Islamic history, by way of contrast, the decline of legitimized government as exemplified by the caliphate did not destroy the religion. If anything it might be argued that the decline of the Islamic political institution resulted in the strengthening of the religious institution through the identification of the latter with the entire community of believers. At the very least, Islam as a social institution was represented by the spiritual unity of all true believers. How or why Islam was able to develop such tremendous

staying power despite its almost complete lack of formal institu-
tionalization is a problem which scholarship has yet to answer.
One serious hypothesis at the ideological level might be the effectiveness of treating religion and politics as two separate entities
which may be related, even mutually sustaining, but which are not
intrinsically the same nor even absolutely interdependent. Obviously, Muslim theologians were not much interested in stressing
the illegitimacy of governments which did sustain the framework
of Islamic social life, but they were careful not to render that life
wholly dependent upon government—at least after al-Ghazali.

It is in terms of the diverse emphases of the mediaeval philosophers and theologians that we can understand the differences
between the two founders of Islamic modernism, Jamal al-Din
al-Afghani and his associate, Muhammad Abduh. Al-Afghani was
more imbued with the heritage of the philosophers and Abduh
more in the line of orthodox tradition. In Pètrement's terms, we
might say that al-Afghani's function was that of the dualist, raising
problems.[18] Abduh was the postdualist who set himself the task
of reconciliation. Al-Afghani inveighs against materialism in a
manner which renders Islamic religion all but material itself. He
renders it abundantly clear that he is concerned with matters of
this world and with the imperfect religion which characterizes the
imperfect society of created beings. His dualistic view is succinctly
recorded in his famous letter to Renan, "Les religions, de quelque
nom qu'on les désigne, se ressemblent toutes. Aucune entente ni
aucune réconciliation ne sont possibles entre ces religions et la
philosophie." [19] Abduh is concerned to free religion from material
circumstances. He does not render the material resurgence of
Muslims dependent upon the strength of religious asabiyyah as
does al-Afghani; he rather explains the decline of Islam as the
result of the mistaken involvement of religion with politics.
"Quant aux doctrines relatives aux khalifes et au khalifat, elles
variaient avec les dogmes comme si elles en faisaient partie inté-
grante." [20] As for Abduh's solution of the problem of the relationship of religion and reason, it was no less astonishing than it was
traditional in its conception: "La religion et la raison fraternisèrent
ainsi pour la premiere fois dans un Livre Sacré. . . ." [21]

These quotations are taken from the introduction to Abduh's

Risalah, which is described by Adams as unique among Muslim scholars "in showing an approach to the modern critical method." [22] It is this characterization of the introduction which led us to a closer examination of its method and an appreciation of the central doctrinal significance of some of the pronouncements made therein. Our limited purpose in the remainder of this chapter is to understand this unique contribution by itself, leaving it to others to consider what may be the implications of our analysis for the understanding of his work as a whole.

All of Abduh's introduction to his *Risallat al-Tawhid* has been translated into the French by B. Michel and Mustafa Abd al-Razik; and part of it has been translated into English by C. C. Adams. The chapter itself is brief, taking up but twenty pages in the Arabic; so it may be useful to present here a spare outline of its contents despite its availability to the interested reader.[23] The topics discussed in the introduction are as follows.

1. The subject matter of *tawhid,* unity of God, is defined.
2. This subject has gone by the name of *kalam,* or dialectical theology.
3. This subject was known before Islam but was not pursued by means of reason.
4. Then came the Qur'an, with its appeal to reason, and reason and revelation fraternized for the first time.
5. Religion may present something beyond understanding but never anything that is unintelligible (impossible according to the intelligence).
6. The Qur'an describes the attributes of God, at times in anthropomorphic terms, and also discusses the choices open to man, good and evil, and rewards and punishment.
7. Various theories developed as a consequence of these ambiguities.
8. During the time of Muhammad and the first two "rightly guided" Caliphs there were no important difficulties in understanding the meaning of the Qur'an.
9. The illegal killing of the third Caliph set the Muslims on the wrong track.
10. The seed of subsequent extremist sects is to be found in the

ideas of Abd Allah ibn Saba', a converted Jew, who believed that God manifested himself in 'Ali.

11. After this Muslims became divided over the question of the caliphate, each side supporting its position by falsification of *hadith* and of interpretation of the Qur'an.

12. Nevertheless, Islam continued to spread, and waves of non-Arabs were converted. . . . Attention turned from defense of the Islamic polity to the sources of dogma and laws . . . but the non-Arab converts kept some of their old beliefs and sought to link them with Islam. . . . Thus there developed divisions within Islam.

13. The first question dividing the Muslims was that of free will and predestination.

14. Then they disagreed over the relationship between the divine attributes and the divine essence and over the extent of the domain of reason in the understanding of the laws. . . . Some extended the domain of reason to cover secondary matters and matters of worship as well as first principles, . . . and doctrines of the caliphate varied with other doctrinal views as though they formed an integral part of Islamic dogma.

15. The followers of Wasil ibn 'Ata' thought it pious to support religious doctrines with whatever was proven by Greek "science," regardless of whether those things were derived from the principles of reason or from notions of the imagination.

16. The early Abbasids recognized the political importance of the Persians and gave them adminstrative positions, but these Persians did not believe in Islam.

17. While the science of *kalam* was still in its infancy, there arose the question of whether the Qur'an was created, an issue which led to the shedding of innocent blood.

18. Thus the central conflict was between those who would push reason to the limit and those who exaggerated emphasis upon the plain meaning of the law, . . . but both insisted upon the obligatory character of the religious laws concerning worship and social relations; . . . but the Dahrites, carrying with them their pre-Islamic beliefs, contrived to see some esoteric meaning behind every plain text.

19. The literalist *"salaf"* (theologians of the first Islamic century?) and their rationalist opponents both opposed the Dahrites, but continued their own violent dispute until the middle way solution of Abu 'l-Hasan al-Ash'ari was made victorious by al-Baqillani and al-Isfaraini.

20. Having established (their view of) the laws of existence as the basis of their doctrine, the Ash'arites insisted that their theory be accepted as an article of faith, believing that denial of the rational demonstration entrained denial of the object demonstrated, . . . but they were refuted by al-Ghazali and al-Razi, who argued that if one or more proofs were found erroneous, the object might then be proven by stronger demonstrations, so there was no need to be obstinate about demonstration.

21. The speculative philosophers were concerned with the expansion of their knowledge, and the Muslims permitted them to proceed in "acquiring the delight of their minds, in advancing the arts, and strengthening . . . the order of human society . . ." in accordance with the great importance which the Qur'an places upon reason, "in that it has the final decision regarding the matter of happiness, and in the distinction between truth and falsehood, and between what is harmful and what is beneficial. . . ." [24]

22. Difficulties arose for the philosophers because of their excessive regard for the Greek philosophers and because of the greed which dominated the people at that time. . . . The philosophers thrust themselves into the discussions of the theologians and, with their sciences, clashed with the prejudices of the masses, bringing on attacks from the theologians, first from al-Ghazali and then less moderate attacks, until they had no further influence among Muslims.

23. This is the reason why *kalam* and philosophy got mixed up, why the sciences got mixed up, and why science has stagnated in Islam.

24. Then came the trials of the contenders for political power, and and the speculative sciences declined further.

25. Then intellectual anarchy spread among Muslims under the

aegis of the ignorance of their rulers. . . . They drove reason out of its abode, . . . and they imitated some of the earlier peoples in declaring religion and science enemies.

26. This is the history of the science of *tawhid*; its roots are in the Qur'an. . . . Islam is a religion of unity and not divergence in its basic principles. . . . Anything to the contrary is the result of diabolical sowing of dissension and of the greed of rulers.

27. The purpose of this science is knowledge of God and of His prophets through demonstration and not traditional authority. . . . We have been commanded to use our reason, and we have been told the fate of peoples who failed to progress beyond their ancestors.

Abduh's purpose and his method are made clear in this introduction. While it is an introduction to a short treatise on Islamic theology, the central problem of the chapter is the relationship of Islam and modern science; that is, his subject is identical with the central problem at issue in al-Afghani's correspondence with Renan. To us it may be obvious that the reconciliation of modern science and religion differs from the problem of the reconciliation of mediaeval philosophy and religion; but there is some question as to whether Abduh understood this problem as we do. He uses a number of terms—*ilm*, *'aql*, *falsafa* or science, reason, and philosophy—without clearly distinguishing among them. While each use appears to fit into its own context, the consistency of theme throughout appears to justify our assumption that the dialectical use of each term is actually interchangeable with that of the others. If we can assume that Abduh's understanding of this problem is derived from Islamic philosophical sources, then we can confirm that he makes no modern style distinction between philosophy and science. The text itself strongly suggests that he accepts the mediaeval Aristotelian view that science is that sure knowledge which is the product of philosophy, while reason is the *modus operandi* of philosophy. After all, he argues that the stagnation of science in Islam is due to the mixing of *philosophy* and *kalam*. Hence, in attempting to reconcile Islam and modern science, Abduh follows the tradition of mediaeval philosophers and completely mistakes the metaphysical basis of modern science. Only such a view permitted Abduh's unequivocal acceptance of the axiom that there could be no essential opposition between religion and science. Science was the product of philosophy, i.e., that which could be absolutely demonstrated by speculative reason. Furthermore, as Abduh recalls in the following chapter, it was philosophy (and philosophy alone) which had demonstrated absolutely the existence of God.

In a manner of speaking, then, Abduh was flogging a dead horse. But to say this is hardly to do justice to the effect of his doctrine. One of the critical factors of which Abduh was aware, but which was not a part of the mediaeval notion of science, was that advancements in scientific knowledge might be made. Of this he was aware, if for no other reason, simply because of the disparity between Western scientific knowledge and that of Islam. It was al-Afghani who argued that scientific advances could be measured historically within any given religious culture.[25]

Given this awareness of the possibility of scientific advance, Abduh's purpose went beyond merely reconciling religion and science; but in keeping with the orthodox Islamic tradition in such questions which involve a dualistic mode of thought, his purpose was to permit the advance of science among Muslims. According to Abduh, the reason that science stagnated among Muslims was not the nature of Islam. So far he is in agreement with al-Afghani. But he goes on to argue that Islam positively encourages scientific research. The stagnation of science is due to the mixture of politics and religion, to the mixture of philosophy and theology, and to the conservative reaction of the orthodox ulama to these two challenges. The conclusions which emerge from this historical sketch are that neither politics nor speculation about existence touches matters of doctrine and that reason ought to replace prior authority in the interpretation of the Qur'an.

There is yet another step to be taken before we can complete this sketch of Abduh's thought. To pose the question in a completely naïve fashion, we may ask: How was it possible for Abduh to argue that philosophy does not affect matters of religious doctrine while at the same time arguing that reason must be the basis of interpreting the Qur'an?[26] There is no problem here if we separate philosophy and reason, in which case the relationship between religion and reason would become problematical. Holding, however, that for Abduh, reason and philosophy were two sides of the same thing, we seem to have caught him in a contradiction. This is only an apparent contradiction, though, for philosophy and theology both involve reasoning from first principles. The first principles of philosophy are the axioms concerning primary being; the first principles of theology are the verses of the Qur'an. The link between theology and philosophy is, therefore, no more nor less than the philosophic proof of the existence of God—the rest is either logic or explanation.

This is a reconciliation by means of the setting of a boundary, and the resultant dualism must be considered in the light of Abduh's assertion that Islam is a religion of unity. Despite Abduh's insistence that religion and reason are not inimical in Islam, it is quite clear that he does not equate them. Reason and religion fraternize, but they are not the same thing. His is a doctrine of the reconciliation of opposites, not a monist doctrine. In terms of the preceding analysis, Abduh's relationship to al-Afghani is that of reconciling the dualism—one is tempted to say the traditional Islamic philosophical dualism—of al-Afghani in the manner of mediaeval orthodoxy, that is, by juxtaposition.

While it is thus possible to understand Abduh in relation to al-Afghani, there are yet many questions that may be raised about this short but interesting chapter. Adams holds that the introduction is unique because it is critical, and he goes on to make much of the section on philosophy. Certainly the manner of Abduh's approach to his subject is more congenial to the modern mind because of its historical frame. It would be a mistake, however, to assume that Abduh's analysis is historicist in any of the senses of the term. The history of the science of *tawhid* is not the equivalent of the science of *tawhid* itself; it is rather the story of the deflection of Islamic theology from its true purpose.

Nor is it easy for us to grasp in what sense Adams used the term "critical." Our difficulty does not lie in the fact that Abduh approved of certain historical events and disapproved of others. The difficulty is in the manifestly ideological character of his historical interpretation. All of the specific events to which he refers are familiar from standard Islamic histories, but their methods were usually either annalistic or apologetic. Abduh's purpose, by contrast, is to deny the validity of the history which he recounts. This is not a critical history in the sense that some method of objective historical study is used. We shall, therefore, be sadly misled if we assume that Abduh's method need not be questioned; if we assume that it is a value-free application of critical reason to the science of theology as it developed and as it existed in his time. Rather, because of the traditional orientation of this greatest of the Islamic modernists, we are compelled to ask how it was that he employed this most modern of analytical methods.

In the absence of any testimony from Abduh himself, it is impossible to give a complete answer to the question we have raised. That Abduh had some acquaintance with European historical thought and theories of historical evolution is well known. This acquaintance is not enough to explain his adoption of an historical frame. Was an historical method particularly congenial to his views on theology? It would appear not, since he denied the validity of the history he recounted. Are we compelled, ultimately, to agree with Adams' suggestion of the original turn of the great shaikh's mind?

The latter possibility must be rejected also, because it can be shown that the bulk of the materials for this introductory chapter were drawn directly from the *Prolegomena* of Ibn Khaldun. It is well known that Abduh studied the works of Ibn Khaldun. He once gave a series of lectures on Ibn Khaldun's *Prolegomena*.[27] There may even have existed a manuscript of these lectures which has now, unfortunately, been lost to us. Sir Hamilton Gibb wrote that Abduh was deeply influenced by Ibn Khaldun, and most other scholars agree.[28] Yet I have nowhere seen any reference to direct borrowing, nor does Abduh himself acknowledge his debt to Ibn Khaldun in the introduction we are considering. We shall proceed with an attempt to show which parts of the introduction have been taken from the *Prolegomena*, but before doing so it is well to point out that in establishing Abduh's partial dependence upon Ibn Khaldun we will not have succeeded in explaining why it was that he chose thence to borrow in order to achieve his purpose. We can only show that his treatment was not altogether original and that it depended upon Islamic rather than European models of exposition. Obviously, the fact that Ibn Khaldun's work is congenial to the Western mind is not a matter of indifference.

Considering once again our outline of Abduh's introduction, we find his definition of the science of *tawhid* to be unexceptional, or rather standard. It is much the same as that employed by Ibn Khaldun in his chapter on *kalam* in Book VI of the *Prolegomena*. Ibn Khaldun goes on immediately with the philosophical proof of the existence of God, but Abduh reserves that for his first substantive chapter. Ibn Khaldun also indicates that the science of theology was practiced by other peoples. Ibn Khaldun does not assert that in Islam reason and religion fraternized for the first time. Instead, he diverts from his concern with theology itself into a long discourse on the limits of human perception and intelligence, the danger in seeking after the causes of all things, and the importance of converting merely verbal knowledge of the unity of God into an acquired state of belief. This is a theme to which Ibn Khaldun recurs in his discussion of Sufism. Ibn Khaldun further insists that the human intellect cannot comprehend God and His attributes. Ibn Khaldun, like Abduh, follows with a brief description of the message of the Qur'an, leading to the problem of the anthropomorphic description of the divine attributes. Like Abduh, he refers to these descriptions as ambiguous and states that they gave rise to theological disputation. Ibn Khaldun and Abduh agree that the first Muslims understood well the purport of the words of the Qur'an. The ambiguity is therefore not in the Qur'an but in man's understanding as the generations stretched out from the time of revelation. Abduh here departs from Ibn Khaldun in arguing that the turning point was the murder of the third Caliph and the extremism that surrounded the rise of Shi'ism. While insisting upon the baleful effect of political controversy upon the understanding of the Qur'an, Abduh also implies the responsibility of newly converted non-Arabs. The responsibility of the latter is even more clearly pronounced with regard to the rise of theological issues concerning predestination and the role of reason. Ibn Khaldun does not blame non-Arabs for the growth of theological disputations, but in his description of processes of ideological change and of cultural change in the intro-

duction to the *Prolegomena*, Ibn Khaldun offers Abduh the basis
for his own interpretation.[29] Abduh blames the Persian *katibs* for
continuing in their Zoroastrian beliefs and attempting to subvert
Islam. Ibn Khaldun, instead, describes the process whereby the
caliphate turned into ordinary kingship and suggests that political
authority came to conflict with religion.[30] Abduh argued that doctrines of the caliphate were not an integral part of Islamic dogma.
Ibn Khaldun, in his chapter on the Shi'ite theory of the Imamate,
declares that they falsely believed that the caliphate was "a pillar
and fundamental article of Islam." [31] Abduh's division of orthodox
theological disputants in the early period into those who would
push reason to the limit and those who held to the letter of the
law would appear to contrast the Mu'tazilah with the Zahirites.
The latter are opposed to the proponents of reasoning, or *ray'*, in
Ibn Khaldun's chapter on jurisprudence.[32] Abduh's treatment of
the Ash'arites and their insistence that their logical demonstration
be accepted as an article of faith is exactly paralleled in Ibn
Khaldun's chapter on speculative theology. On the relationship
between philosophy and theology, Abduh agrees with Ibn Khaldun
that the two were unfortunately mixed. Abduh, quite unhistori-
cally, asserts that the Muslims allowed the philosophers to pursue
their speculations quite freely until they got mixed up in theological controversies. We may note in passing that Abduh describes
one of the goals of the philosophers as "acquiring the delight of
their minds." Ibn Khaldun denies only that true happiness is
achieved by means of speculative reasoning. The soul finds joy
in perceptions unmediated by reasoning. "It greatly enjoys this
kind of perception, exactly as a child is pleased with its sensual
perceptions when it begins to grow up." [33] Abduh blames the
philosophers for thrusting themselves into theological matters. In
his chapter on speculative theology, Ibn Khaldun blames the theologians for getting involved with philosophy. But in his chapter
on the refutation of philosophy, Ibn Khaldun agrees with Abduh:
"They also think that the articles of faith are established as correct
through speculation and not through tradition. . . ." [34] It is in
connection with Ibn Khaldun's attack upon the theologians that
he mentions that the mixing of philosophy and theology was per-
petrated by non-Arab scholars.[35] Finally, Ibn Khaldun describes

the decline of learning in the Islamic West, whereas Abduh writes of the decline of learning throughout the Islamic world. Ibn Khaldun ascribes this decline to that of sedentary civilization, while Abduh ascribes the more general decline to secular struggles for political power.

It may be hoped that this brief sketch will suffice to establish the dominant influence of Ibn Khaldun in Abduh's introduction. What does this influence prove? Our first conclusion is a negative one. Abduh's introduction is not original, not unique, and not modern. Nevertheless, the introduction is not wholly derivative either. First of all, even in matters on which there is agreement, there are substantial differences of emphasis. Abduh's fraternization of reason and religion is a much stronger one than any formula used by Ibn Khaldun and is significantly similar to the more usual orthodox claim that politics and religion fraternize. Abduh emphasizes the role of the non-Arabs in the decline of Islam, a theme now familiar from contemporary Arab nationalist theory. Ibn Khaldun, by contrast, finds the decline of Islam (change from caliphate to kingship) the cause of the decline of the Arabs. Abduh blames the philosophers, only, for mixing philosophy and theology. Ibn Khaldun shifts his position but names only certain *theologians* who mixed the two. Abduh flatly states that the caliphate is not a matter of Islamic doctrine, while Ibn Khaldun says the same only in the context of a discussion of Shi'ite theory. Both authors agree that the early Muslims understood the Qur'an without ambiguity, but in explaining the later rise of controversy Abduh emphasizes politics and the role of non-Arabs.

Abduh did not change Ibn Khaldun's statement of the facts very much; but in using those facts to understand the state of Islam in his own day he drew very different conclusions. Abduh was willing to accept Ibn Khaldun's explanation of certain events, but he rejected his explanatory theory. It appears to me that the great attraction that Ibn Khaldun had for Abduh resided in the fact that their common difficulty was the reconciliation of contrarieties and incompatibilities in Islamic history and thought. Additionally, both were concerned with explaining what was held to be the decline of Islam. The work of Ibn Khaldun is, perhaps, the most ambitious and the most successful attempt at a grand reconciliation of all of the elements of a world civilization. Pètrement holds the method of historical synthesis to be one of the most important ways of negating dualism: "Les aristoteliciens sont d'ailleurs des historiens; Aristote est le premier historien de la philosophie. . . ." [36]

Ibn Khaldun and Abduh are agreed on at least one critical issue of method, and that is the method of *iqsam al-ulum*, or the division of the sciences. As Mahdi has shown, Ibn Khaldun must start with the *iqsam* in order to differentiate his own science of culture.[37] This science of culture then becomes the basis of Ibn Khaldun's explanation of the historical condition of Islam. But the *iqsam* is the key to the whole of Abduh's method of reconciliation by division into categories.

We can understand this difference better by approaching it from the point of view of the central problem of religion and politics. Here we must recall that the compatibility of religion and politics is one of the central themes of Islamic thought, at least until recent times. One of the main concerns of Muslim thinkers was to justify the coexistence of the Islamic community with a non-Islamic government. This was, until recently, a government of Muslims, but still a non-Islamic government. Political protection was considered essential to the survival of Islam. Al-Ghazali explained the deviation of Islamic government from the prescriptions of the *shari'a* as the consequence of necessity. To counterpose Islam and Muslim government would mean to counterpose religion and the nature of worldly existence. Ibn Khaldun rendered al-Ghazali's necessity as *sunnat Allah*, the habit of God.[38] His reconciliation of religion and existence or nature was accomplished by means of an historical method. This is what we learn from his description of the decline of the religious caliphate into kingship and his justification of Mu'awiya. It is in the nature of religious authority that it will be transformed into royal authority. The reconciliation is in the *sequence* of their appearance, for religion and nature are not contradictory.

Abduh rejected Ibn Khaldun's justification of history and his justification of events by history. For Abduh, history is not a natural sequence of necessary events. In a sense Abduh holds that all history is bad. History consists of the confusion of things that should be kept separate.[39] History consists of distortions and disputes. The principle of history is not ancillary to the *iqsam*, it is the antithesis of the *iqsam*. An ideal Islamic community would have no history. Abduh agrees that the Islamic revelation occurred at a certain time in history, that great numbers of non-Arabs were converted to Islam over a period of time, and that Muslims made glorious intellectual achievements at various times; still, for purposes of contrast with Ibn Khaldun, we may insist that consciousness of time is not the same as history.[40]

Abduh's modernity does not lie in his acceptance of an historical frame. His modernity within the Islamic context is not the result of his acceptance of a Western mode of analysis. It is rather the result of his rejection of the Islamic idea of history as being somehow religiously constitutive of right. It is in his rejection of history and the contemporary state of Muslims that Abduh becomes modern. In his rejection of the fraternity of religion and politics he opens the way for Ali Abd al-Raziq's ill-fated attempt to assert the separation of church and state in Islam. Abduh argued further that the contemporary state of Islam would be altered by the development of science in concert with Islam and not by political means. In this he was opposed to his teacher, al-Afghani, who, in the end, has been proven the more correct of the two. Abduh was unable to change the heritage of 1300 years of Islamic experience, for, to parody Margoliouth, with whom we began: although we are apt to think of the Arabs as a nation, it is probable that they think of themselves rather as a religion.

Abduh did not argue that religion and nature are opposed. From his point of view, science depends upon nature, and since Islam and science are compatible, religion and nature must be in harmony. What Abduh denied was that history necessarily revealed nature. Doubtlessly, the great shaikh, despite his deep affinity for the common people of Egypt and their simple virtues, would not have been a nationalist. Nevertheless, his contribution to Arab nationalism was second to none. He did not succeed in Islamizing the liberal tradition of the separation of church and state. Nor did he succeed in overcoming the secularist tendencies of those inclined toward modern science. In the main he helped to overcome the anti-Western and antiscientific prejudices of the traditionals. He weakened the political alliance between the ulama and the traditional authorities. And by weakening the constitutive character of history he opened the way to a romantic reconstruction of the history of the Arabs. It was not his clear and undeniable intention, but by separating history from nature he permitted later theorists to discuss the "nature" of the Arab people and of Arabism in terms which refuted the history of their decline. With regard to the relationship between religion and politics, his denial of the legitimacy of historical government in Islam did not establish the separation of the two. Instead, his theory led Muslim nationalists to seek a form of government which would be compatible with Islam. Since the Arabs were the vehicle by which the Islamic revelation was made, Arab nationalism could be rendered compatible with Islam even if not itself Islamic. In this manner could nationalism and religion "fraternize" in Islam.

NOTES

1. D. S. Margoliouth, *Mohammedanism* (London, 1911?), p. 75.
2. This is essentially the method employed by E. Tyan, *Institutions du Droit Public Musulman*, 2 vols. (Paris, 1954 and 1957).
3. Each of these works contains references to the relationship between religion and politics, the former from the religious point of view and the latter from the political point of view. Each uses roughly the same unsatisfactory formula for handling the problem.
4. See, for example, E. Rosenthal, *Political Thought in Mediaeval Islam* (Cambridge, 1958), p. 84; and M. Mahdi, *Ibn Khaldun's Philosophy of History* (London, 1957), *passim*.
5. Simone Pètrement, *Le Dualisme dans L'histoire de la Philosophie et des Religions* (Gallimard, 1946, 3rd edition), p. 69.
6. *Ibid.*, p. 60.
7. Y. Kaufmann, *The Religion of Israel* (London, 1961), p. 315.
8. *Ibid.*, p. 60.
9. *Ibid.*, p. 21.
10. Pètrement, *op. cit.*, p. 61.
11. *Ibid.*, p. 60, n. 1.
12. F. Watkins, *The Political Tradition of the West* (Cambridge, Mass., 1948), pp. 11, 12, 32.
13. R. C. Zaehner, *The Dawn and Twilight of Zoroastrianism* (New York, 1961), pp. 296–298.

14. Pètrement, *op. cit.*, p. 90.
15. H. A. Wolfson, *Philo*, vol. I (Cambridge, Mass., 1947), p. 337.
16. *Aristotle's Metaphysics*, tr. Richard Pope (New York, 1952), Book Iota, section 7, 1057a38, p. 214.
17. Zaehner, *op. cit.*, p. 298.
18. Pètrement, *op. cit.*, pp. 78–84.
19. Jamal ad-Din al-Afghani, *Réfutation des Matérialistes*, tr. A.-M. Goichon (Paris, 1942), p. 184.
20. Cheikh Mohammed Abdou, *Rissalat al-Tawhid*, tr. B. Michel and Moustapha Abdel Razik (Paris, 1925), p. 12.
21. *Ibid.*, p. 6.
22. C. C. Adams, *Islam and Modernism in Egypt* (London, 1933), p. 122.
23. I have used the seventeenth Arabic edition, edited and annotated by Muhammad Rashid Rida (Cairo, 1960).
24. Quotations are from Adams, *op. cit.*, p. 123.
25. Al-Afghani, *op. cit.*, p. 177.
26. This is the issue dealt with by N. Safran, *Egypt in Search of Political Community* (Cambridge, Mass., 1961), p. 69.
27. See Adams, *op. cit.*, pp. 45 and 273.
28. H. A. R. Gibb, *Modern Trends in Islam* (Chicago, 1947), p. 128.
29. Ibn Khaldun, *Muqaddimah*, 3rd ed. (Beirut, 1900), p. 28; see Mahdi, *op. cit.*, p. 152.
30. Ibn Khaldun, *op. cit.*, p. 202.
31. *Ibid.*, p. 196; also p. 465 in the chapter on *kalam*. The quotation is from F. Rosenthal's translation (New York, 1958), vol. I, p. 402.
32. *Ibid.*, Beirut edition, p. 446.
33. *Ibid.*, Rosenthal's translation, vol. III, p. 256.
34. *Ibid.*, p. 247.
35. *Ibid.*, Beirut edition, p. 466.
36. Pètrement, *op. cit.*, p. 83.
37. Mahdi, *op. cit.*, p. 73.
38. *Ibid.*, p. 257 n. 7 and p. 258; see also Safran, *op. cit.*, p. 68.
39. "Il est d'ailleurs plus facile d'expliquer le mal par un mélange que par un principe unique, et l'on a toujours aperçu que la force du dualisme était dans l'explication du mal." Pètrement, *op. cit.*, p. 13.
40. Safran, *op. cit.*, pp. 72–73, shows that Abduh entertained other views of history but adds that these views are incompatible with Abduh's theory of history after the revelation of the Qur'an. In other words, after revelation there is no history.

4

THE IDEOLOGICAL FOUNDATIONS
OF EGYPTIAN-ARAB NATIONALISM

I

"Every nationalist movement must have an ideology," states one
Egyptian writer, thus boldly stating the intellectual confusion by
which Arab nationalist writers have been able to avoid their responsibility for critically examining the values upon which political legitimacy and policy are said to rest.[1] We need not lose sight
of the fact that such a phrasing suggests the primacy of action and
sentiment and the but secondary quality of verbal explication and
elaboration in noting that the search for an ideology is one of
the central themes of contemporary Arab nationalist writing.[2]
Nationalism, and Arab nationalism as well, is itself ideology and
as such has to be explained outside of the framework of its own
component ideas. The tests of language, historical consciousness,
and all the rest are applications of the idea of nationalism and
depend on prior acceptance of the nation as the determinant of
the political community. For the examination of diverse applications of this sort, important though they may be, there is a rela-

75

tively easy method. When faced with questions such as whether or not a Lebanese Maronite or a Karaite Jew is an Arab, we know that the answer has but the remotest connection to any truly objective order of the universe. But nationalism itself as a general principle raises questions of another magnitude.

Our problem here is not an examination of the ideology of Arab nationalism in the sense of the value consequences of some historically objective fact such as the existence of an Arab nation. Our concern is rather with the more striking transformation of the ultimate value from which all others are but derived, from revelation to the postulate of nationality.

II

Regardless of whatever else is claimed for modern nationalism, the single objective ideological consequence of nationalism on which there can be near unanimous agreement is that it delimits the political community.[3] Arguments for the need to add ideology to nationalism merely accept nationalism as a basic premise and hope to derive therefrom certain consequences for political organization. This is the procedure of nationalist writers who must accept this "ought" on the basis of faith alone, for it has no rational basis and only the cloudiest of experiential referents.

The subjective, nonrational core of nationalism is clouded by alternative arguments which stress objective characteristics such as language, geographical proximity, and the like, but even these degenerate quickly into postulations of the existence of a common historical memory, a common destiny, and a common interest.[4] Nevertheless, the objective argument reveals some of the philosophical heritage of nationalism and some of the inherent difficulties of the concept as an ultimate value.

If the essence of nationalism is subjective and even personal, it follows that nationality, when not completely identical with citizenship and language, is a categorical quality which can become socially and politically relevant only on the basis of conventional agreement, much in the manner of our agreement that red is red. Hence the penetrating insight of Michel Aflaq's argument that nationalism is like one's name or physiognomy.[5] But if this is the case, then surely no social consequences can be derived from such a concept unless they are put into it to begin with.

Our two assertions, (a) that nationalism deals only and essentially with delimiting the political community and (b) that it is inherently a subjective sentiment from which nothing further may be logically derived, are both resisted, if not denied, by a great many nationalist writers. Furthermore, search though we may for really significant discussions of the first assertion as a critical problem in political theory before the rise of nationalism, we find next to nothing. How is it possible that so central a problem of modern politics was so neglected in earlier times? How can we explain the emergence of this question from an intellectual climate dominated by universalism?

While not entirely neglected, the problem of delimiting the political community received little serious philosophical attention because it did not demand any. In Islam as in Christianity, society came to be seen as separate from polity. Princes governed a part of the whole, and all princes were supposed to do the same thing anyway. It hardly mattered who was prince over how much territory. All Muslim rulers jointly executed the holy law throughout the abode of Islam, and the foremost among them were those who carried out the general responsibilities of the Jihad and the defense of Islam. In Christian Europe, the device of the Holy Roman Empire did much to paper over the issue. To some extent Ottoman suzerainty and investiture of Sunni rulers had a similar effect. Nevertheless, both Muslim and Christian writers were wont to discuss the responsibilities of the ruler in the sense of all rulers, somewhat in contradiction of the dedication of their works to "the ruler of the world," as caliphs, padishahs and shahinshahs might be addressed. Quite justifiably, as it appears to us, the rationalism of the enlightenment and of the French revolution was universalist. If it admitted the reality of separate states or political communities, it did not justify them.

In fact, it did not need to justify political boundaries, because it was primarily concerned with political relationships within existing boundaries. The only body of thought which concentrated on the order of relations between states, and hence with political boundaries, was international law. But the very concepts of that discipline clouded the issue even more by providing the ready device of transferring the base of sovereignty from ruler to subjects. The implication of this qualitative change from subject to citizen-sovereign has brought forth no response from international law, other than to sustain the anti-individualistic notion of the general will through the concept of a collective and still indivisible sovereign.

There were two ideas offered by political philosophy to fill the gap between universalist ideology and the existence of delimited states. Rousseau presented both ideas, the social contract and its all but contradictory complement, the general will. The idea of the general will does not necessitate a natural conception of political society as opposed to the convention of the social contract, but the moral quality of the general will if based only on the social contract becomes contingent and positivist. Either morality is impossible outside of civil society, or, if the general will can exist in the absence of the social contract, civil society itself as concretely constituted must depend on nature. Rousseau posed the dilemma and did not resolve the issue of the natural or conventional basis of the polity.[6]

III

The really surprising thing about the development of nationalist thought in the nineteenth century was the near abandonment of the rationalist argument for nationalism based on the conventional character of civil society. In its stead there emerged a decided preference, though not a universal one, for the natural conception of the polity as expressed in romantic nationalism. How did romantic nationalism derive from revolutionary rationalism? The inherent difficulty of this problem at the theoretical level is too easily glossed over by the historians. That such a shift occurred is admitted, but the task of understanding so complex a development requires more than the mere assertion of fact or a use of the terminology of inevitability, of dialectic, or of the changed spirit of the times.

In order to explain this change we have to explain some philo-sophical contradictions such as Herder's nationalism and his uni-versalist cosmopolitanism, Rousseau's rationalism and his roman-ticism,[7] Fichte's shift from welcoming the French revolution to opposing it, or even Burke's continued concern with both individ-uality and virtue.[8]

To get at the philosophical basis of these contradictions, and hence the pattern of ideological dynamics, we can trace the con-nection in ideas from Condillac's (or Locke's) science of ideas as the basis of a new interpretation of reason through Kant's and Fichte's subjective conception of reality, especially Kant's postu-late of the will as the basis of morality.[9] But it must be remem-bered that the relation between reason and the ultimate value was not the creation of the age of reason, but its heritage. Reason was already a conceptual receptacle into which a new content was put. Romanticism could arise from reason only when reason itself was made to stand on a subjective foundation. But the changed basis of reason is only a condition of such a derivation, and the existence of such an "idea slot" is but a permissive circumstance; for to derive romanticism from a critique of reason as a criterion for determining reality is an extremism.

On the other hand, we note the concern of thinkers to sustain a rational political order by the use of nonrational and nonuni-versal symbols; or to buttress romantic or idealist notions with positivist-rational argument. At another level goddesses of reason are set up, and historical rationalizations are used to sustain a non-rational legitimacy. In an era of mass political participation in which the relatively uneducated citizen has a large part to play, it does not seem so paradoxical that both rational and romantic symbols are appealed to simultaneously. The contradictions we found in philosophical works are not the consequence of muddled thinking so much as of a clear grasp of political reality. The diffi-culty lies in the inherent incongruence of logical thought and hu-man behavior; and one need not be a materialist to hold such a position. In any case, the capacity for logical thought does not exhaust the description of the human mind, nor does it compre-hend the only conceivable basis of discovering the ultimate good.

Be these things as they may, our conclusion is that there was terminological "space" for the development of new concepts of reason, that the treatment of reason by philosophers at the end of the eighteenth century was not wholly free of nonrational elements, and that the supposed contradictions in the thought of such philosophers are to be explained by reference to their own experience and their striving to put their notions of reality into words and is not to be explained away. At the very least we may say that those thinkers who contributed most to the origins of nationalism believed in the nonrational as a practical necessity for any polity.

Now practical necessity was not new to political philosophy at the time, either; it was rather part of the baggage of mediaeval thought. Practical necessity was the corollary of the views that held politics to be a practical art or a result of the fall of man or, later still, dependent upon reason of state rather than pure reason. It remained, however, for the rise of the nation-state as the ultimate value in itself for reason of state to become the particular form in which reason was associated with that nonrational symbol.

IV

In this sense the rational and the romantic are not wholly alternative or antagonistic, but at least in some measure complementary. The former is concerned with the conventional aspects of community and the latter with the nonrational elements of identity. From this point of view there is little wonder that the two forms are not separated by centuries or class differences, that they emerge continuously out of one another, and that they can be completely intertwined in a single piece of ideological writing.

The romantic form is essential to the solution of the problem of identity, for its content can only be categorical. Islam on the one hand and Arab Islam on the other are not simply the forms into which the real *weltanschauung* of romanticism is placed. It is not romanticism which is essential here as a view of reality; the real problem is posed by the question, "Who am I?" The answer is usually an examination of experience and sentiment, the justification for which can hardly be rational.

That the problem of identity is real is obvious to anyone who has had first-hand experience in the emerging countries. It is usually suggested that the following are general causes for the disturbance of previous identity solutions: (a) geographical mobility, involving separation from both locality and family; (b) education, which has weakened religious practices and sometimes religious belief itself, and which provided a new sense of history and a new perspective of the self as part of an abstract state community; (c) the new occupational structure, involving organizational membership, new formal rules, and new social-competitive norms; (d) the emergence of a new prestige-power hierarchy and the decline of the old statuses. Regardless of how we explain these, and doubtless other, changes, there is no gainsaying their effect in producing an identity crisis. As we have attempted to show elsewhere, nationalist ideologies in the Middle East have a false ring about them precisely because they are largely imitative and because identity or the psychological self is a culturally tabu subject in Islam.[10] But these circumstances should not lead us to believe that the Arab is either incorrigibly romantic or that his search for new identity through nationalism is a wholly fictitious notion.

As for community, is it essentially of a rational, conventional nature, or nothing more than the sum of individuals of common identity? The idea of nation is a romantic idea postulating the "natural" unity of a number of persons. In accordance with the romantic idea, the political and social arrangements of the nation are or ought to be an expression of reason in history.

There is an essential difference between this romantic idea of the community as an extension of individual identities and the idea of the ummah in Islam. On the one hand the ummah is the whole body of true believers, and on the other it has continuity in history quite apart from its component individuals. Of course there is a clear and sensible recognition of the generational basis of continuity in Islam, but it is not considered a very efficient way of providing for the spiritual continuity of the community, in marked contrast to nationalist theory, wherein the generational process is a central operating mechanism rather than a deficiency-producing but necessary material process.

The Islamic view of the community was strengthened rather

than weakened by the philosophical view that the nature of the state was dependent upon the ideas of the citizens. Nationalism has modified this notion of the *ummah*, but it has not really been effective in eliminating the Islamic faith as a characteristic of full membership in the Egyptian or Arab nation.[11] Furthermore, and despite the legalistic treatment of the office of the caliph in both classical and modern times, the utilitarian aspect of the specific political and social arrangements of the Islamic community was never wholly lost from view. It is, of course, characteristic of modern nationalist theory that attempts are made to relate these utilitarian and programmatic ideas to the "spirit of the nation." Nevertheless, the mode of thought by which these programmatic ideas are put forward is rationalistic and utilitarian—all the way from al-Afghani to Gamal Abd al-Nasser. This is the paradox of means-end rationalism being associated with a romantic conception of the nation, though the aforementioned rationalism might be applied to any political community regardless of how constituted. Moreover, the current emphasis upon economic development, technological advance, rational planning, political equality and participation, education, bureaucratization, and all the rest by radical-reform governments will hardly permit us to treat these goals as simple derivations of nationalism.

Let us see if we cannot elucidate somewhat the ideological connection between the romantic idea of identity and the conventional idea of the community. In nationalism, membership of the nation is absolute, categorical, and unchangeable. But any conventional solution of the problem of community which involves political values and a specific allocation of influence and rewards may, perhaps must, raise the question of whether generationally produced members of the nation are "true" members. Are reactionaries, the current enemies of Arab socialism, true Arabs? Are those who were subject to the land reform laws true Egyptians? Are those who help currency smugglers true nationalists?

In addition to this difficulty, a truly rational means-end approach to policy involves some trial and error, some shifting of emphasis and priorities. In the face of such pragmatic searching, the definition of the "true" member of the nation must also shift about. Rationalization, therefore, conflicts with certain elements of identity, and where no fixed formula has been worked out or where in an excess of rationalism there is an attempt to keep the society completely fluid and mobilizable, the result approaches the pure form of mass society.[12] This sort of result has nowhere been achieved among the new nations, nor is there so strongly and dangerously a rationalist sentiment among the political leaders of these countries.

The "mass" idea is clearly related to the problem of identity, for identity is essentially an individual problem. Masses do not become available until identity becomes a widespread problem. The mass movement is therefore an irrational approach to the problem of community, in the sense that the search for support in any chosen identity resolution through generalizing that concept of identity for others is substituted for the search for a rational and conventional basis of cooperation with others in a political community. The attempt to resolve the problem of community through nonrational ideology, or by treating it as a residue of identity, is irrational not only philosophically but also practically.

V

In the Arab East, nationalism was borrowed from the West as a means of entering into the modern world as that world was defined by the dominant West. It may or may not be true that such acceptance was a matter of life or death, but many thought it was. Nevertheless, the minds of Arab intellectuals, particularly those who knew something about traditional learning, were not a *tabula rasa*. They had ideas of their own, mostly derived from a system of thought which was in the main hostile to modern Western ideas, but which, when broken down into its component elements, seemed to comprehend a number of ideas of particular relevance to those of the West. At least they might provide a means of understanding (or misunderstanding) the terms in which Western thought was couched.

In addition to the divergent intellectual background into which national ideas came, the situational context of polity, economy, and society also differed appreciably from that which nourished nationalism in Europe. This is not the place to attempt an elaboration of these differences, and it would be misleading to suggest that there might be at our disposal adequate historical research for us to do so. What is clear is that, at the end of the nineteenth century, Europe was already, for the most part, comprised of self-conscious nation-states, and the Arab East was not; Western Europe was already industrialized, and the Arab East was not; Europeans thought in terms of a neat, three-class social structure, and Arabs thought in terms of millets first and a more complex occupational gradation second. The nations of which Europeans were speaking had already emerged as politically tangible things, while in the Arab East the nation was a remote abstraction at best, and even the notion of an Arab nation lacked all clear definition at the time.

The particular way in which Arab, and particularly Egyptian, nationalist thought developed may be understood against the background of these two elements—the Islamic influence on the understanding of Western ideas and the concrete problems of social structure, community, and national interest that arose once these Western ideas began to be incorporated into Arab thought. It may be argued that it is too mechanistic to attribute all ideological consequences to these forces and nothing to genuine intellectual inspiration, but in so arguing we do not deny the possibility of such insight; we merely deny that it occurred. That there has been considerable artistic achievement, and more scholarship, cannot be gainsaid, but our concern here is with ideology and its adaptation to material circumstances, and that has been almost wholly derived.

VI

Superficially, the social circumstances of the rise of Egyptian nationalism appear similar to those of Europe in the nineteenth century, but certain points of difference must be borne in mind. These points should prevent us from making too facile generalizations about the direction of both material and ideological development. Consider especially that Islamic civilization was a defeated civilization; that no part of Islamic thought provided for a condition in which whole countries would be under alien, i.e., non-Islamic rule; that Europeans had already gone through many of the changes affecting Egypt, so that modernized groups acquired their modern ways of thinking more rapidly and more self-consciously; that modernization was "imported" into certain social sectors only, so that there remains a sharp discontinuity in society between the old and the new; that Europeans already had ideas and a ready terminology to explain what was happening in the Middle East; that the period during which nationalist thought developed was one of foreign domination and its aftermath, a domination which was not unaccompanied by severe attacks on Islam at times; and that Egypt did not share the western European heritage of an independent ecclesiastical structure, free cities, the early rise of a *national* bourgeoisie, and the unified, bureaucratized, monarchical state of the enlightened, benevolent despot.

Therefore, when we compare Egypt and western Europe and find that it was similarly "clerks" and those who had left the "vicarage" (i.e., ex-ulama) who developed nationalist thought, we must bear in mind that these Egyptian clerks, who could so easily identify their European counterparts, did not until recently discover a similar clientele for their writing. Instead of an historically rooted bourgeoisie to consume their product, Egyptian intellectuals wrote for and cooperated politically with a town-dwelling agrarian middle and upper class, most of whom were absentee landlords and only a few of whom were business oriented.

At the same time, we note the disturbance of the traditional pattern of local ties and primary group loyalties. Exactly how much and where has not been documented, but we know that in nineteenth century Egypt an entirely new pattern of land tenure, cropping, irrigation, marketing, and taxation was developed. We also know that there was a change in the social composition of the largest landowners and a similar change in the means of acquiring large estates.[13] There was a gradual decline in the size of middle holdings, a decline in the political influence of one class of local notables, and a probable increase in influence on the part of another group which, in terms of individual families, became partially modernized. It is also held that agricultural changes brought in their wake a reduction of the traditional level of peasant cooperation in the villages, but the extent of this is less well known. Of greater importance is the increase of rural population, which has by far outrun the increases in crop area. Concomitantly with these changes, rapid urbanization has occurred, and more recently there is evidence of the growth of a literate public for whom modern technical and language skills (in the special use of Arabic, too) became of central importance.[14]

The development of a press, the cheaper printing of books, an increasing number of translations of foreign works, government-financed education abroad, and the increasing number of foreign visitors constitute parallels with the communications and information revolution which occurred in nineteenth century Europe.[15] In the Middle East it has still not reached the proportions of England in the 1870's, but it is sufficient to sustain a new class of literate and popular writers and give them at once a medium of expression and a small audience. But these are communications specialists. Professional philosophers in the Middle East remain strictly within the framework of the academic study of the classic Western or Islamic philosophers, leaving it to civil servants, military officers, secondary school teachers, and journalists to write ideological tracts.

The spread of education, though still limited by comparison with the West, had certain similar effects. It produced a larger audience for nationalist writings and produced a bureaucratic middle class desirous of political recognition and social change. But in Egypt there was little vocational education, nor was there until recently a serious effort to educate the masses.[16] Education meant a change in social structure, a change in cultural orientation, and above all an increase in the number of aspirants for "clerical" occupations. There is no real educational, cultural, or social difference between writers and readers. Amateurs and specialists write for one another. All education is geared to higher education, and nearly useless if not culminated thereby.

We can further contrast the class origins of the nationalist groups in Europe and in Egypt. In Europe, it was the urban bourgeoisie, the younger sons of the aristocracy, the guilds, and offshoots of the clergy who contributed most to the growth of nationalism. These groups were all urban groups and part of the rational and more or less workable order of mediaeval corporativism. In Egypt it is the urbanized segments of the agrarian middle class which have led the nationalist "struggle" to overcome the anarchy of the Islamic city.[17]

The hold of religion has also declined in Egypt, but for additional and complex reasons, among which we note: the weakness of the religious institution (the ulama) *vis à vis* the government; the administrative inroads into *waqf*-religious endowments for the support of religious education and ulama; the higher prestige which was accorded those who held jobs which required a Western type of education, as a consequence of the greater influence and higher salaries which most of these graduates received compared with the average graduate of a religious institution; the irrelevance of religion to the problems facing a country challenged by Western technology and power; the growth of a contrary philosophy of reason and naturalism;[18] and the alliance of the ulama with the throne.[19]

This last would have meant little had not the traditional legitimacy in Egypt, as in Europe, become undermined. But it must be remembered that the Egyptian monarchy was never fully legitimate in Islamic terms. It could only represent a compromise with necessity contingent upon adequate performance. The Muhammad Ali dynasty had been established within recent memory; it had itself attempted to bring about modernization, thus shaking its own social roots; through its efforts foreign advisers and administrators were introduced into Egypt; and when the time came, it failed to defend the country against foreign occupation. Later, when nationalism grew, Farouk failed dismally to give his leadership any nationalist character.[20]

There has been in Egypt, as in parts of Europe, a rediscovery of the peasant as the symbol of the nationalist spirit and nationalist solidarity, but the theme is much weaker, and does not account for the more important cultural and social difference between the impoverished peasant and the *"kulak."*

A further element of outstanding importance for the understanding of Egyptian nationalism, which was not shared in western Europe though of some importance in eastern Europe, was the special and enviable status of the minorities under colonialism. These people not only dominated the modern commercial field but also competed effectively for many of the administrative jobs which were the only goal of the educated Egyptian Muslims.[21] Hence, from the inside, Egyptian social structure was doubly distorted when viewed by the educated Muslim.

VII

The problem of the limits of the national community, often so little a matter of dispute on the objective plane in Europe, has no such simple solution for the Arabs and particularly for Egypt. In Europe, the national community was not so agitated a question, though the disposition of border areas led to many disputes and much violence. In the Arab East the limits of the national community is a question which involves the subjective identities of whole peoples. Persians and Turks after World War I have been clearly and willingly separated from their Arab fellow Muslims, though the question of the disposition of Mosul and Hatay or Alexandretta demonstrate that it was not a wholly clean break.

Despite this sundering of the Islamic community (Iran had to all intents and purposes been separated since A.D. 1500) it still remains impossible to separate Islam from the sentiment of national identity. Thus, one of the central questions of Arab nationalism remains the position of the Christian Arab minority. Paradoxical as it may seem, the Christian Arabs of the Levant were the initiators of the Arab nationalist movement, though primarily through literary and intellectual pursuits.[22] One of their major goals was to find a basis of closer cooperation with their Muslim neighbors. That which was shared in full measure was only the Arabic language. The early Christian overtures came to little, and later when the Muslims aroused themselves to nationalism, it was a nationalism so heavily laden with Islamic sentiment that it has made both the Christians of the Levant and the Copts of Egypt somewhat apprehensive of their status in an Arab nationalist state. Nevertheless, Christian Arabs are active in nationalist activities, but tend to prefer smaller political units rather than what is called "comprehensive" Arab nationalism, or unity from the Persian Gulf to the Atlantic. This is particularly the attitude of Lebanese Christians, and to a lesser extent of Syrian Christians after the separation of Syria and Egypt. Among the Muslims, Arab nationalism was not the immediate response to Western pressures. Instead we have an attempt at an Islamic political revival first and then an attempt to reform Islamic legal theory and philosophy to accommodate the requirements of a modern society, economy, and military establishment. Jamal al-Din al-Afghani is associated with the first, or Pan-Islamic, movement; and his disciple, Muhammad Abduh of Egypt, is most closely associated with the latter. The views of both, though especially the former, were reinterpreted, with some distortion and under a certain vague influence of the puritanical Wahhabism of Arabia, by Rashid Rida, who may be looked upon as the leading light of fundamentalist Islamic reaction. The goal of all three movements was to reinvigorate Muslims and create in them a self-conscious desire for dignity, modernity, solidarity, and the preservation of religious values. In the face of European nationalism, these leaders of Islamic modernism wished to have Islam play the role of nationalism among all Muslims.

Their efforts failed for many reasons: the demise of the Ottoman Caliphate; the ambition of various Arab rulers; the British occupation of Egypt; and, perhaps most important, the cleavage of outlook between the traditional elites, including the ulama, who were the main support of religion and the Western-educated moderns. Pan-Islam did not get off the ground, but its exponents, in their variety, did succeed in producing a number of new interpretations of Islam such as to render it compatible with a modern outlook and hence dignified the Islamic identity to the point where it is nowadays frequently written about by both Muslims and Christians as an integral part of Arab nationalism.

Egyptian ideas have undergone the greatest transformation during the last century, though the situation in other Arab countries was similar, if less ambiguous. As a "vassal" of the Ottoman Sultan-Caliph, the Pasha of Egypt aspired simply to greater independence and the raising of his status, with the ultimate aspiration of attaining kingship.[23] These ambitions, which were behind much of the nineteenth century modernization of Egypt, were transformed during the British occupation into a desire to achieve independence of the British through the action of the Ottoman Sultan. After the turn of the century, it seems that the Khedive entertained certain hopes of acquiring the dignitiy of an Arab caliph. The first Egyptian "nationalists" or patriots aimed at getting rid of foreign influence and limiting the powers of the Khedive. The first party of the same name was founded by Mustafa Kamil, and it was pro-Ottoman.[24] The partition of the Arab lands of the Fertile Crescent by British and French mandates discouraged any thought of cooperation with other Arab countries for most of the interwar period, and Egyptian nationalist leaders looked elsewhere for assistance. It was not until World War II, when it became clear that the Arab states would achieve independence and would be organized in some form of league or federation through the agency of Great Britain, that Egyptian leaders felt the need of entering into Arab politics. This they did to prevent any of the other Arab leaders, the Hashemites especially, from forming a united Arab state which might serve as a counterweight to Egypt and weaken Egyptian efforts to be free of British occupation. Egyptian leadership of the Arab League and the nearly unaccountable entry of Egypt into the Palestine war sealed the identification of Egypt as an Arab country at the political level, but certainly not at the psychological level.

During the interwar years, Egyptian writers and intellectuals sought about for a suitable symbol of Egyptianism. They fumbled at one point with a pharaonic revival which is now much condemned.[25] There followed Taha Hussain's now rejected assertion that Egypt formed a part of a much broader Mediterranean civilization.[26] In the mid-thirties, however, there was a much more powerful turn toward romantic Islamic symbols, through the medium of biographical writings on the Prophet and his successors.[27] Lately, these themes have been not so much abandoned as subordinated to Pan-Arab symbols. There is, however, a certain uneasiness about these as well, for despite Egypt's clear cultural leadership among the Arabs of both the East and the West, there appears to be too much political manipulation of Arab symbols and too little real empathy. On their own part, Sunni Arabs out-

side of Egypt have been too willing to use Egyptian power to settle their own domestic scores and too reluctant to work out the
basis of a real union. Part of the difficulty is, of course, that Egypt's
population is greater than that of the rest of the eastern Arab
states combined, and there is no leader of stature comparable to
President Nasser. Despite these difficulties, the nationalist die has
been cast, and Egypt has come, by a devious process, to be unequivocally an Arab country. Not even the traumatic separation
of Syria can change this, although there have been a few recent
evidences of a renewed use of pharaonic symbols and some com-
parisons of the progressive Arab West with the reactionary Arab
East.[28]

The Hashemite dynasts, of whom only King Hussain of Jordan
is now left, lay claim to the leadership of the Arab national movement. As is known, this claim is based upon the role of Sharif
Hussain of Mecca in the Arab revolt of 1916, which T. E. Law-
rence made famous.[29] After the brutal assassination of King
Faisal II of Iraq in 1958, the possibility of a Hashemite state unifying the whole of the Fertile Crescent and possibly the Hejaz,
in accordance with the early aspirations of the long-deceased
Sharif, is all but incredible. Nevertheless, there would appear to
be some sentiment for this type of more limited unity.

Islamic and Christian sectarianism has also played an important
role in limiting for some Arabs the territorial scope of their ideal
Arab state. The Parti Populaire Syrien, which failed in an attempted coup in Lebanon in early 1962, had a program of unifying the Fertile Crescent and Cyprus in an Arab nation-state. Many
of its members were Greek Orthodox in religion. Nearly 40 per
cent of the population of Syria are either non-Sunnis or nomads,
and this fact has certainly had an effect on Syria's lack of political
unity and no doubt lies behind the separation from Egypt in some
remote sense. But the most outstanding case of the effect of minorities and sectarianism is demonstrated in the incapacity of
Egypt and Iraq to agree on the procedure of Arab unification.
Less than half the population of Iraq is Sunni; the remainder are
Shi'ites. Somewhat less than a quarter of the population of Iraq
are Kurds, with their own national aspirations. Under Kassim
there were some tentative, but largely unsuccessful, attempts to

create an Iraqi nationalism, while attempting to stave off union with Egypt by using both sectarian and leftist sentiments against the Sunni minority. The present quasi-Ba'thi government represents a reassertion of Sunni domination.

The foregoing have been but the briefest suggestions of the magnitude of the concrete problems of welding a common national identity for only the Eastern Arab peoples. In the latter half of the twentieth century Arabism has been accepted in its broadest form, but it is clear that its psychological essence varies still from country to country on the basis of the particular experiences, the social structure, and the ethnic and religious composition of each. Ideological efforts in writings, speeches, propaganda, and songs have done much to bridge the gap; but the persistent demand for an ideology for Arab nationalism suggests that the path is still a long one. Nevertheless, so compelling is the idea of Arab nationalism itself and so insistent is its normative claim, that few may admit adherence to it in limited or conventional form. The fate of more recent discussions of Arab unity (April 1963 and after) sustain the point. Arab nationalism and Arab unity are now one aspiration. Federative unity is suspect.

VIII

It is apparent that Arab nationalism has been accepted, at least by the intellectuals of the Arab world, as an ideology, but it has not yet been applied in any meaningful way to everyday political life. Ideology may serve as a link between two kinds of meaning, a philosophical and a psychological. It can also help bring about change. The problem of Arab nationalism is not that it has no ideology, but that the link between abstract ideas and identity sentiments has not been fully forged. The weakness, however, is not so much between Islamic philosophy and nationalism as between nationalism and historically defined personal identity.

Islamic philosophy was brought into accord with nationalism by an ideological process which we shall shortly describe. In the accomplishment of this task, however, Muslims also became heirs to all of the ideational tensions of modern nationalism. It is not

an easy matter to join Arab identity and Islamic community ideologically. It is not at all self-evident that the romanticism involved
in the rejection of recent history and the rationalism whereby that
history is to be changed are ideologically compatible. Will, reason,
history, and nature are the philosophical terms that were used to
bridge the gap between Islamic philosophy and the nationalist
idea. The resultant weaknesses of Arab nationalism are the weaknesses of all nationalisms, caused by the intrinsic duality of identity and community, of subjective sentiment and the conventional
order of human society.

The most imposing problem of all is to explain how a people
imbued with a belief in a divinely ordained ultimate revealed in
holy writ could transfer their loyalty to a pantheistic notion such
as nationalism. As we have seen, this transfer was not complete,
nor has it extended to all Muslims; but the intellectual issue is
not diminished by these qualifications. All the evidence of social
and economic change will not tell us why this particular ideological change came about in Egypt, nor are such events truly explanatory of ideological change in Europe without reference to the
limiting channels of existing ideas. In the West, the gradual development of nationalist ideas depended upon the transformation
of a conception of natural law. The association between reason
and nature was an ancient heritage; and we recall that without the
new rationalism based on a new concept of nature we could not
have gotten the romanticism of the nineteenth century.

But Islam was also heir to Greek reason. It is true that "orthodox" Ash'arism succeeded in defeating the rationalist theology of
the Mu'tazilah at an early stage in Islamic history; but it is apparent that the Mu'tazilites were not fully in control of the Greek
philosophical tradition. The introduction of this tradition into
Islamic intellectual circles in its most influential form was the
work of al-Farabi.[30] The "philosophic" tradition in Islamic thought
which was thus introduced was highly suspect in the eyes of traditional, orthodox theologians, because it raised the controversial
issue of the relationship between reason and revelation—an issue
which penetrated into Western Christianity. The "philosophers,"
as were called the exponents of the received Greek tradition, were
not immediately nor widely influential. Nevertheless, for all their

fear of persecution, and for all the abstruseness of their expression, their works have been accepted into the Islamic corpus of learning, and their central postulate of the rationality of the universe and of revelation were adopted.

The philosophical position which aroused the ire of the Ash'a-rites was the assertion that the universe could be comprehended through reason, as well as through revelation. If pushed to its logical conclusion this view reduces the miracle of the Qur'an, which is itself the proof of its own authenticity and of the truth of Muhammad's prophecy, to the work of a philosopher. The opposed positions were reconciled by adding that human reason was nevertheless not as perfect as divine reason. Therefore revelation was necessary to provide for the true guidance of mankind. Despite the verbal acceptance of this compromise, the sincerity of the philosophers was held suspect; and even when formalized into a standard Islamized philosophic tradition, tension persisted between the legists and the specialists in divine philosophy. But the revised tradition was popularized and became widely available to intellectuals, especially in the work of al-Dawwani. Significantly, Dawwani's *Ethics*, a sort of compendium of true knowledge, combines, among other things, this watered-down philosophic tradition and the Iranian tradition of practical statecraft.[31]

There was a further complication, however, in the relation between reason and revelation. If the limitations upon reason were a matter of dispute, the difficulty of the Qur'an was a matter of general agreement. Of course, the obscurity of certain verses was attributed to the passage of time and the loss of live contact with the Prophet himself, and hence justified dependence upon *hadith* or traditions of the Prophet's words and actions. But these traditions are themselves subject to much suspicion of forgery. In addition to this basic difficulty, there are also passages in the Qur'an which are said to abrogate other passages or to permit of reconciliation only by the most complicated means. In other words, rather than revelation completing reason, the issue might have been put quite the other way around. But it is not the same thing to declare that reason may attain all the truth that is revealed in the Qur'an and that the difficulties of interpreting the obscurities of the Qur'an may be resolved through the application of reason.

Even the latter, more limited, position was further restricted by making such use of reason dependent upon only certain rational techniques, such as grammatical analysis, analogy, and the reconciliation of divergent texts. The really critical problem is in what is meant by reason.

Despite the fact that such matters were the concern of only a small group of traditional intellectuals, identical themes were rapidly taken up by Westernized writers, after being applied to the problem of the suitability of Islam to the modern age by Afghani and more especially by Abduh. Afghani's position on the matter is not at all clear, but two of his most important statements permit us to make some suggestions as to the effect of his teaching. His attack on the "naitchuri" movement among Indian Muslims demonstrates his opposition to a materialist solution of the problem of reason.[32] He insisted on the importance of will and spiritual strength in human affairs. This attitude is indicative, to some extent, of an inclination toward the traditional Islamic "philosophical" school. His reply to Renan's lecture on religion and science appears to contradict his writings aimed at Muslim audiences, for in that letter he asserts that all religions stand in the way of scientific progress, and that the problem of scientific progress is not resolved through a compatible religion but through devices of mitigating that influence.[33] One hardly knows what to make of a position of this sort, unless it can be shown that Afghani's notion of science was that of traditional philosophy, in the sense that knowledge is not essentially empirical but the product of speculative reason. Hence reason and religion are always in conflict, in the sense of the mediaeval controversy over whether revelation is necessary to complete reason. Eventually reason would prevail over revelation, but for the time being religion was necessary. Religion was to serve the function of political myth.

Abduh was also exposed to the teachings of the traditional "philosophical" school, but he was more deeply influenced by the conciliatory efforts of Ibn Khaldun. Abduh held that reason and revelation could not be in conflict. Islam, and only Islam among the religions, accords fully with reason. If reason, and its product, science, had declined among Muslims, the cause was not Islam, but the misrule of sultans and the fanatical conservatism of the ulama. Thus, Abduh attempted, without immediate success, to restore reason to a position of respect among the orthodox. His more immediate accomplishment was to convince a small group of Western-educated laymen of the harmony of reason (as they understood it) and religion in Islam.

As Safran has shown, it is probable that Abduh's concept of reason did not much differ from that of al-Afghani.[34] That is, he probably thought of reason as the mechanism of speculative philosophy. Nevertheless, he was not wholly consistent in his various references to reason, philosophy, and science or knowledge. One of the most interesting pecularities of Abduh's thought is his equating speculative reason with science and practical reason. It would seem that he reversed the philosophic tradition that tended to place the religious sciences among the practical sciences and speculative reason apart from them and presumably higher. In this manner, science and speculative philosophy are assimilated to politics, ethics, and the productive arts.[35] Philosophy may concern itself also with the laws of existence but not with the core of religion, i.e., the nature of God.

It is not at all clear that Abduh rested his notion of reason upon nature as revealed in history, a transformation necessary to the development of nationalist ideology. Nevertheless, his treatment of the problem of reason and its relation to his understanding of modern science permitted others to draw timely conclusions. He argued that Islam encouraged man to use his reason to discover the laws of existence. Though religion and not reason must be the basis of the ideal state, nearly everything else related to politics was in the sphere of reason. Material and scientific progress were associated with the application of reason to Islamic law (but not to theology). Reason and free will are materially conditioned, i.e., by the order of created existence, and they are sufficient for man's earthly needs. Intellectual order and harmony or the reverse determines the course of history.

By these means Abduh asserted the relationship between reason and nature which had been all but eliminated by Islamic occasionalism and by Islamic legal theory. In effect, Abduh approached a reconciliation of the views of al-Afghani and of the Indian "*naitchuri*" movement which al-Afghani had so bitterly attacked.

But, in mediaeval philosophic fashion, Abduh set reason in opposition to history—or at least Islamic history. The explanation of why reason had not manifested itself in history is due to the rigid acceptance of traditional authority. It is in his rejection of *taqlid*, or the acceptance of traditional authority, that Abduh comes closest to rendering reason and Islamic law as a consequence, dependent upon history. Had he carefully distinguished between speculative reason and practical reason, or had his followers had a better understanding of mediaeval philosophy, his solution of the problem of *taqlid* would not appear to be so revolutionary. After all, both politics and religious law (in Islam) had been considered in the realm of practical wisdom by Muslim philosophers.

On the problem of history, Safran has again shown that Abduh had a dualistic view.[36] Abduh saw human history up to the time of the Islamic revelation as steady progress and maturation. Thereafter, political cleavages caused the decline of Muslim society, and the decline is proportional to the passage of time from the appearance of the Prophet. Thus, Abduh accepts history as reason up to the time of revelation; thereafter, history represents unreason. It is further significant that Abduh attributes part of the reason for the Muslim decline to misunderstanding of the Qur'an, a condition caused, in some degree, by the rapid conversion of non-Arabs.[37]

IX

The most characteristic feature of reformist Islam, in all its varieties, is the rejection of *taqlid*, or the doctrine of the requirement to accept received authority. All reformers insist that the force of earlier consensus (*ijma*) be limited or subject to review in the light of new criteria. As the concomitant of this view they also hold that the use of independent judgment (*ijtihad*) to initiate new interpretations of the law is permitted for those who have the requisite qualifications of learning and piety.

The primary emphasis of Abduh's critique of *taqlid* and *ijma* was to reject the historical consensus of the Islamic community and to insist that only the consensus of reason was valid.[38] *Ijtihad was to be based on reason.* The controversy over the binding nature of *taqlid,* thus joined, was not a new one in Islam. For example, the Shi'a have always held that consensus meant consensus among the judgments of the Imams, and the "gate of *ijtihad*" remains open for the practice of qualified *mujtihads.* One of the four "roots" of the law for the Shi'a is *'aql,* or reason (intelligence), though there are diverse interpretations of its application. *Taqlid* for the Shi'a means only that certain ulama and laymen choose to accept the authority of a particular *mujtihad,* generally one with whom they may have some personal contact, i.e., who is living and resident in their locality. There were also, from time to time, Sunni ulama bent on reform who denied the extreme form of *taqlid* which had become the single most important constitutional feature of the religious institution of Islam. But these few, like Ibn Taiymiyya, are outstanding exceptions; while the differences with the Shi'a are of the most critical importance in understanding the theoretical centrality of *taqlid* and *ijma* to the Sunni position.

As Abduh mentions with some regret, opposing views of the caliphate became mixed up with various theological positions.[39] In his general avoidance of the question of Islamic government, he follows the spirit of al-Ghazali in the latter's doubts about the significance of the doctrine of the caliphate in the Shari'a or Islamic law.[40] Ali Abd al-Raziq pressed this attitude too far in arguing that it was incorrect to insist that Islamic law dealt with the state as well as with religious matters, thus demonstrating once again how Abduh's use of traditional ideas was distorted by his eager followers.[41] Regardless of this revised assessment, it is true that doctrines of legitimate government were intimately bound up with theological considerations. The Shi'a claimed that the Imams, who were the best qualified and impeccable besides, should have been the caliphs, and only they had the right of *ijtihad* during their respective lives. In their view, the Islamic community has been misguided in its majority and throughout the great bulk of its history. The Sunni argument was that those who had actually served as caliphs, especially before Ali, were sufficiently qualified and did not need to be impeccable. Their proof for this was the *ijma* or consensus of the community. Hence, according to the Sunni view, the Islamic community remained divinely guided, not by its caliphs so much as through the immanence of divine will in that community itself.

The fundamental religious attitude toward history in Islamic civilization is bound up with this position in the politico-theological controversy. There were, of course, many divergent schools of historiography, but we are here concerned with that which accords most closely with the Sunni theological orientation. From this point of view the purpose of history writing was essentially didactic, to show the consequences and explicate the nature of good and evil acts.[42] It was also a continuation of the religious work of describing in detail the life of the Prophet and of his Companions, in the sense of extending the narrative of God's intervention in human affairs: *gesta dei per "musulmanos."* But the subject matter of history is divided generally into political annals and biographical works, the former reporting the deeds of both good and bad rulers and the latter primarily the works of pious men, poets, learned scholars, and the like. Hence Islamic historiography recorded the decline of the community from the perfection attained under Muhammad and the first four, the "rightly guided," Caliphs on the one hand and the admirable upholding of the Islamic tradition by individual members of the community. The caliph, as the Sunni theologians insisted, need not be impeccable, nor was he. The Shi'a, by contrast, insisted that this was a dreary history of sin, and that if the Islamic community had been divinely guided through the Imams the perfection attained under Muhammad would have been maintained. In effect, the Shi'a challenged all Muslims to re-achieve that past perfection. The challenge of the West was not really much different.

To rephrase these generalizations, we may say that history represented a decline from a past point of highest ethical achievement. Hence, in one sense—and that, too, temporally restricted to early Islam—history was derivatively constitutive. In another sense, history represented the baneful effect of the interposition of an increasing number of generations between those who knew Islam at first hand from the Prophet and living Muslims who know it only by the handing down of tradition. This is the view behind the later doctrine that the true caliphate lasted only thirty years, or the view of some reformers that only the *ijma* of the generation of the Prophet is to be accepted as binding. Thus, only a certain period of history became constitutive of law in the later religious view.

Abduh did not oppose this view; in fact, his whole outlook on the decline of Islam is permeated by it; but in rejecting a *taqlid* which emerged out of particular historical controversies, he would argue that the nearest approximation of re-achieving the heights of early Islam might be attained by the application of reason to the law. Furthermore, as we have seen, he freely mixed experimental science, speculative philosophy, and practical reason in his notion of reason. The door was therefore open to a blending of his rejection of *taqlid* with that of the "*naitchuris*." The view which emerged most strongly in India was that *taqlid* must be rejected and the gate of *ijtihad* opened because *ijma* was valid only for particular times and particular places. When material circumstances changed, the interpretation and application of the law must change. This was Iqbal's "principle of movement" in Islam.[43] Nor was Abduh explicitly uncongenial to this point of view. "Indeed, the later generations have a knowledge of past circumstances, and a capacity to reflect upon them, and to profit by the effects of them in the world, which have survived until their times, that the fathers and forefathers who preceded them did not have." [44] The temporal and geographical limitation of *ijma* was particularly agreeable to the nationalist idea; but it also leads directly to a new view of history. History now becomes, in a certain sense, truly constitutive; but the dictates of historical circumstances must be interpreted by *ijtihad*, a striving to grasp its true meaning. *Taqlid* had prevented Muslims from adapting Islam and their own social and political arrangements to historical circumstances in the past.

It is significant that the new historical outlook permitted the early glories of Islam to be preserved in order to inspire the present. There was general agreement that the long middle stage of Islamic history was characterized by a decline—which was variously interpreted. The contemporary stage is one of awakening.

X

Obviously there was some ambiguity in the orthodox religious attitude toward history. On the one hand we have a determination to maintain the idea of the divine guidance of the Muslim community, and on the other the difficulty of the actual shortcomings of Islamic government. These shortcomings entered into the writings of the legists, generally without specific reference, however, so that they took the guise of recurring conditions. This treatment was due to the style of legal writing, which aimed at the theoretical resolution of every problem as a general case rather than providing for discretionary judgment on the part of the judge. Hence we find al-Baqillani discussing the problem of the simultaneous existence of two legitimate Caliphs, al-Mawardi discussing the "Amirate by seizure" and the problem of heretical praetorianism, and al-Ghazali discussing the problem of an unqualified Caliph.[45]

In order to cope with these situations and the doctrinal compromises in which they resulted, al-Ghazali employed the concept of necessity.[46] In the sense in which he used the term, necessity meant the general condition of social and political relations. There is a clear connection here between this doctrine and the philosophical one of understanding sensible historical reality. We must, however, distinguish between the notion of *sunnat Allah* and this necessity.[47] *Sunnat Allah*, or the "way of God," was used as an explanation of man's ability to make sense out of sensible reality; necessity explained the deviation of that reality from the Islamic ideal in such a manner as to render the validity of orthodox doctrine independent of sensible reality.

The connection between the two concepts results from the resolution of the problem of the origin of evil. If all human acts are created by God, then evil acts are also originated by God. Necessity and *sunnat Allah* cannot be fully separated, as a consequence. There were various devices for coping with this difficulty which do not here concern us, for none mitigated the basic principle. It is this connection which permitted Ibn Khaldun to use the idea of *sunnat Allah* to explain his theory of historical causation.

But we must bear in mind that there is an important distinction to be made between a perceived causal relationship between two objects (*sunnat Allah*) and the total societal configuration of such relationships (necessity) which al-Ghazali deemed to condition the morality of certain political acts. The justification of this transformation of necessity into political legitimacy was significantly referred to the good of the community.

We have already noted the influence of al-Ghazali on Abduh, and the doctrine of necessity is another instance. Here, however, we note a substantial departure on Abduh's part, perhaps under the influence of Ibn Khaldun, to the extent that al-Ghazali's use of the term is distorted. Abduh denied that Islam was spread by the sword and explained that Muslim conquests were prompted by self-defense, "thus the beginning (of conversion) was a consequence of the necessity of political society." [48] Here, it is apparent that necessity takes on a broader meaning, involving not a detraction from an ethical ideal but what is from the Muslim point of view a highly desirable consequence. Necessity is no longer something with which the human conscience must wrestle, but a general condition of morality. The implications of this view for the possibility of a relativist morality and the material conditioning of value are great indeed, even though Abduh hardly pushed it very far. It was left to his successors to twist the notion even further, as in a recent work on Arab nationalism, where the expulsion of all non-Muslims from Arabia is justified by reference to the security of the fledgling Islamic state. [49] In this manner Abduh's "necessity of political society," which referred to the natural order of human society, became transformed into materialistic prudence and self-interest. Necessity was now used to justify the acts of government instead of explaining its failings and serving as a warning to truly pious men to steer clear of political affairs. Al-Ghazali's necessity now became the equivalent of "reason of state," through the medium of a reformulation based on Western influences.

XI

Romanticism and vitalism are characteristic features of contemporary Arab nationalist thought. The foundation of these themes in nationalist literature is an insistence on the freedom of the human will. Without this link all of the interpretation of the various historical stages through which Muslims have passed would be meaningless, for all conclude with various reasons for the present decline. The true spirit of the Arab nation was revealed in history but must be discovered by an inner act of recognition, and the true place of the Arab nation among the peoples of the civilized world must be attained by an act of will.

The surprising thing about this romantic view, which parallels the ideology of many a European nationalism, is not that it contradicts the sort of rationalism which we have found in reformist Islam, but that it so flagrantly contradicts the Ash'arite-orthodox position on God's creation of human acts and man's mere acquisition of those acts. Presumably the Ash-arite doctrine of perpetual creation should have stood in the way of such a transfer, but there were other elements in Islam which, when stressed, opened a direct path to romantic vitalism. We have already pointed out where even the orthodox conception of history departed from the strict influence of Ash'arite occasionalism. We have also noted the distinction between the use of the terms *sunnat Allah* and necessity. And then we have the obscure Ash'arite device for reconciling occasionalism and responsibility, acquisition. Man acquired his acts by virtue of accepting them as his own, that is by willing them. This act of will, which is essential to all nonmaterialist rational philosophy, is also the foundation of modern nationalist romanticism. History determines the identity of the individual, and he "acquires" this identity by consciously willing it.

If Orthodox Islamic thought did not completely suppress the notion of will, the Islamic philosophical school preserved the idea of the rational will as received from classical philosophy. It was this idea rather than the Ash'arite view which Abduh passed on, and we take note of the amazing paradox whereby the modernization of Islamic thought is made more easily possible by drawing upon a secondary tradition. But Abduh's treatment of the will and its freedom, whether because of his desire to limit discussion prudently or because of his alleged "empiricism," accords very well with romantic nationalism.[50]

The Necessarily Existant, or God, necessarily has will, holds Abduh, and this will is a characteristic which informs the action of the Knowing One in any one of its possible manifestations. Thus all things created are in accordance with divine wisdom and will. The meaning of will is that all creatures have specific character- istics, time, and place, which characterize them in opposition to all other possible creatures. The question of decision or choice does not apply to God, who acts out of knowledge and will. But this question does affect created beings, in whom knowledge (reason?) is imperfect. Hence will is contingent upon knowledge. When there is complete knowledge only one decision can be forthcoming, and in God the will and the deed are one. The meaning of power in the sense of God's power over man is nothing but God's control over the act of creation, that is, creation in accordance with His knowledge and will. Choice or freedom of the will is nothing but the effect produced on "power" (ability to act) in accordance with the measure of knowledge and the determination of the will. That is, freedom of the will is contin- gent only upon human knowledge or reason. Man does not act without sense or will, nor is it beneficial to man to believe that he is compelled to act as he does, because such a view relieves him of responsibility. Rather the welfare of man and the order of creation are determined by the fact that they have been effected by the most perfect of beings, and the (degree of?) perfection of the created follows from the perfection of the Creator, in whom there is both complete knowledge and absolute will.[51]

From the foregoing paraphrase of Abduh's views on freedom of the will, knowledge, and choice we can see that classical occasion- alism is not permitted to affect human responsibility. There is a parallelism here between the position of Abduh and that of Aquinas, a parallelism going all the way back to the idea of the creation of man in the image of God. But there is no grace in Abduh's system; there is no transcending of the human condition. Material reality does not determine the will, it is the condition of the possibility of choice. Knowledge, will, and choice are at once free and contingent upon the order of creation. The contin- gency of will upon the natural order is the condition of its vari- ability, and variability is the definition of freedom. The limitation of knowledge or reason proceeds beyond this, so that either correct or incorrect decisions may be made even within the framework of the created order. There is still some distance between this view and the doctrine that the true spirit of the Arab people has revealed itself in history and that the recognition of such reality depends upon an act of will by a right-thinking vanguard of the nation; nevertheless, this is one of the ways in which the groundwork was laid.

There were other themes which contributed to the same end and are presently at the root of Arab nationalist romanticism and vitalism. These contributory themes will not long detain us, though it is well to bear in mind that there was more than a single ideological influence. One of the sources of such ideas is the concern with prophecy in Islamic theology, which produced the terms *ilham* and *wahy*, both referring to inspiration, the former emphasizing its human instinctive aspect and the latter the act of God in instilling an idea in a human being. Another sense of vitalism is in the mystic tradition of Islam, which tended to stress the importance of immediate religious experience above legal conformity. Nor should we overlook the implications of the *"naitchuri"* argument, which contributed to Iqbal's reconstruction of *ijma* as the "principle of movement" in Islam. Afghani's own antimaterialism is yet another source of vitalism, particularly important in view of his emphasis upon spiritual values as the source of political solidarity and social stability.

Not less important than these ideas, and in some instances contributing to their interpretation, was the revival of Ibn Khaldun's concept of *asabiyyah*, or social solidarity. Ibn Khaldun's theory was based in part on the observation of the effect of the decline of tribal solidarity when the tribe moved into urban surroundings. *Asabiyyah* meant this sort of prescriptive solidaristic norm, but was also used to refer to parochial fanaticism. Abduh substituted for this idea the theory that love held social units together and motivated their mutual assistance.[52]

The passage in which Abduh refers to love as the basis of the political community is interesting in itself, but it also has important implications for the subsequent development of Arab nationalist thought. Readers who are at all familiar with the ideas of Michel Aflaq of the Ba'ath Party of Syria will immediately recognize the contribution of the theme of love to his alternatively subjective and natural-historical conception of the basis of the Arab political community.[53] In Abduh's treatment, however, his main concern is to prove the necessity of prophecy. Prophecy, and particularly the prophecy of Muhammad, it is implied, is the functional substitute for love. Abduh does not deny that mutual affection can remain the basis of the polity; in fact he does not work out the precise relationship between prophecy and love. He is at pains rather to prove that the basis of the political community cannot be rational. Perhaps he believed that mutual affection could prevail only after a messenger had been sent by God.

Of the need which each member of a society has for his fellows there can be no doubt . . . as a consequence whereof there is the link extending from the family to the tribe then to the nation (ummah) and to all mankind. . . . The form which these needs take, particularly within nations worthy of the name, that is those characterized by relationships and ties which distinguish them from others, are the need to subsist, the need to enjoy the advantages of life, the need to acquire the things desired, and the need to fend off all sorts of adversities. . . . If human affairs proceeded according to the methods of the rest of creation, then these needs would be among the most important factors producing love among human beings. . . . It is of the nature of love that it maintains order within nations and inspires their subsistence, and it is of the nature of love that it is closely connected to human needs in accordance with the determination of the laws of existence. . . . There is no doubt that the persistence of a society under these conditions (the breakdown of love because it is not instinctive in mankind) is impossible, for it is necessary for humankind to preserve itself through love or some substitute. . . . At various times certain thinkers resorted to justice . . . thinking that justice might take the place of love . . . but who will lay down the rules of justice? Do they say that reason will do it? . . . But has it ever been heard of in the history of mankind and does it accord with human behavior that a whole society or its majority should submit to the opinion of a wise man simply because it is correct? . . . No. Such has never been heard of in the history of man and such is not in accord with his nature.[54]

The influence of Ibn Khaldun upon Abduh is apparent even from this omission-scarred quotation. Ibn Khaldun's *asabiyyah* was a natural solidarity, found among tribal peoples and subject to decline with the civilization of nomadic conquerors by their victims. Ibn Khaldun held, further, that Arab *asabiyyah* was greatly enhanced by the admixture of religious *asabiyyah* after the mission of the Prophet. Abduh, however, adds another term between natural asabiyyah and religious solidarity: subjective sentiment. It was in stressing this subjective sentiment and not in his rejection of the historical possibility of the rule of philosopher-kings that Abduh departed from Ibn Khaldun and the mediaeval philosophers. In rejecting the rational basis of the political community, Abduh is attempting to stress the subjective religious sentiment which remains so important a factor in the contemporary solidarity of Muslim Arabs.

XII

In the preceding we have been concerned to elaborate a few of the Islamic ideas which were capable of adaptation to meet the social and ideological crisis confronting Egyptians and all Muslims at the turn of the nineteenth century. We have not asserted that present day nationalism is the outgrowth of these ideas alone, nor of these ideas and a social context. The task of ideological analysis does not end with pointing out the parallelism of certain ideas. The explanation born of parallelism leads to the "Starkian" notion of social knowledge and to the language of the "spirit of the age." [55] Not only does such language lack explanatory meaning, it also fails to answer such significant questions as to why, as many Christian observers hoped and expected, Muslims did not merely accept Christian values and Christianity. Can one argue that it is the form of the ideas that is important and the content epiphenomenal, much in the reverse of the way in which the national question was dealt with by Stalin? That is, can we hold that it is the romantic or rational form that is significant, rather than the specific Islamic content of these ideas? Is *Weltanschauung* form or substance? If substance, how can we explain the persistence of both rational and romantic ideas among the same people, even in the writings of the same person, at the same time in history? Or is it preferable to argue with Stark that this contingent content is ideological, while the *weltanschauung* form of the age is knowledge in some sense? Which, then, is our age, the age of rationalism or the age of romanticism?

It is remarkable that the major works on ideology pay so little attention to nationalism. I think there is no good reason for this other than the kinds of theory with which the subject matter of the sociology of knowledge was associated and the universalistic biases of its exponents. One of the principle points of departure for such theory would appear to have been a lack of concern with ultimate values and a disproportionate interest in programmatic ideology.

As is well known, the study of ideology received its greatest impetus from Marx, but ultimately the central idea behind the sociology of knowledge goes back to Montesquieu and beyond. These two lines of thought, which have contributed so much to modern sociology and anthropology respectively, have also inspired two somewhat divergent kinds of analysis and theoretical approach to the study of ideology. The first attempts to explain ideology as a condition of the social position of the individual, primarily social class; while the second leans more heavily upon explanations based on a concept of stages of intellectual growth, maturation, or modernization. Mannheim, with his conservative-radical dichotomy and ideology-utopia distinction, follows from the first tendency. Dilthey and Weber, the former in his types of *weltanschauung* and the latter in his types of authority and types of rationality, follow from the second tendency. But ideologies (whether one insists that ideology distorts or not) differ in their evaluation of events even under the common intellectual umbrella of a single ontology. The difficulty is illustrated by these two tendencies in the sociology of knowledge. Marx considered ontology to be dependent upon ideology, but Dilthey, Weber, and Stark have all tried to establish the dependence of ideology on ontology. When we examine nationalism in the light of these considerations, especially the European nationalism to which these writers were exposed, we find that it does not appear to fit into either category. European nationalism has cut across class lines or has been the cry now of radicals and now of conservatives. It has affected a large group of nations of roughly equal intellectual maturity in Europe, but it has produced diverse ideological results; while it has affected peoples of quite disparate culture outside of Europe with amazingly similar results in our own day.

The tendency of the sociology of knowledge has therefore been to regard the nationalist idea itself, that is, the ultimate value to which the programmatic is attached, as mere epiphenomena. Even if not intentionally, surely the neglect of any serious treatment of the core idea itself has led to explanations of nationalism in such terms that one wonders why such a "meaningless" ultimate has become so uniquely appealed to when any other notion might serve equally well to mask the class interests of the rising bourgeoisie or a working class intent on preserving hard-won benefits. Nor, and this is crucial, would any serious person argue that nationalism represents a higher stage of intellectual maturity.

Thus the study of nationalism poses an enigma which is matched only by the nationalist's claim that his nationalism is *sui generis*, and cannot be understood by reference to any other idea calling itself nationalism. As a consequence of such theoretical neglect, nationalism has become a subject for the discipline of the unique par excellence, that is, for history. The best works on nationalism are by historians who trace the intellectual and political sequences by which modern nationalism has risen supreme and who have been able to point out how the shape of international politics has changed as a consequence. If statements are made about all nationalisms or even a group of nationalisms, no theoretical or ideological characterizations are given. Nationalism is either condemned for leading to political excesses domestically and internationally or praised for leading to the cultural enrichment of the world and as a way station on the road to universal harmony. It is explained in terms of its origins or its end, but almost never in terms of its essence. That essence is either affirmed as unique by nationalists or rejected as nonexistent by historians who well know of cases in which nationalism itself was nonexistent.

Perhaps there is no special essence; but even if not, existing explanations raise more problems than they can solve. It appears that the nationalist classes have changed over time, and rather than social change resulting in greater maturity of thought or rationalism it has resulted in nationalism's turning more and more to romanticism. These changes are amply brought out by the contrast between Kohn's characterization of the nationalist class and Benda's characterization of that same class in France.[56] We may contrast as well the rationalism of the French revolution with the romanticism of German nationalism.

It is instructive to compare Kohn's presentation with Benda's critique. Kohn holds that the national awakening in each case resulted in the integration of the dominant ideology or "philosophy" of the period into the more widely participant politics which were the consequence of admitting the bourgeoisie as citizens as well as subjects. Hence he finds within the same framework of nationalism distinct national ideologies, not national character but national values.[57] The emergence of nationalism is for him an ideological cutoff point, whereby social processes fix a particular value configuration. For Benda, however, nationalism is inextricably bound up with positivism and the conquest of French intellectuals by German romantic philosophy.[58] Whereas for Kohn French rationalism and nationalism go together, for Benda nationalism is unreason and represents the politicization of philosophy.[59] For Kohn it is almost the reverse: the philosophizing of politics.

It is significant that Kohn does not argue, as do some others, that the pattern of nationalist thought is everywhere the same. In fact, for him a national ideology is the same as a nationalist ideology: French nationalism was rationalist and German nationalism was romantic. But Benda might argue that French rationalism was not nationalist, as was French romanticism. Kohn does consider the romantic and self-regarding aspects of national ideologies, but these are looked upon as more truly ideological, i.e., as mere justifications of the core of national ideologies.

To contrast Kohn with Marx, it might be said that Kohn finds ideology determined by vertical divisions (i.e., not class or occupational divisions) within the bourgeoisie, while Marx finds the essential divisions to be horizontal within the socio-economic structure as a whole. It is clear, however, that Kohn does not argue that social position determines ideology, but only that it determines that there will be an ideology. It may be added that it is not at all clear that this ideology must be nationalistic, although historically it would appear that it must assume nationalistic features as a matter of self-defense. What was to be defended, of course, was the right to a national ideology.

Now the justification of the right to a national ideology may be called nationalism. Kohn was not primarily concerned with the connection between ideology and ontology, but the right to a national ideology surely calls into question the unity of mankind, the essential rationality of mankind, and the possibility of a wholly rational basis for the political community. Nationalism demands an historical ontology. Such an ontology was provided by Dilthey, Weber, Mannheim, and Stark, to leave out of account the historians themselves. All argued that ideology was based on ontology, which changed with historical conditions. What is the more remarkable is that all of these students of ideology believed that the spirit of the modern age is rationalist and, hence, in diametric opposition to nationalist thought. One might then expect, in Kohn's terms, that all national ideologies would be rationalist, that none would develop nationalistic elements, and that no ideational barriers of an ontological nature would be put up against the creation of a world state. Nevertheless, the very relativism with which they treated the rationalism of the modern age contributed to the strengthening of romantic nationalist ideas.

The crux of the problem is really the relationship between identity and community. In a purely analytical sense we may agree that identity is irrational and community necessarily rational. It might even be agreed that identity is "natural" in the historical sense, while community is conventional. Analysis aside, experience strongly urges upon us the conclusion that both needs must be satisfied for the maintenance of a stable polity. Viewed in this light both identity and community determine the political function of ideology; but this function is, itself, defined philosophically, i.e., by our ideas of the nature of the political community. The democratization of political life entrained the politicization of identity in place of its functional equivalent, divine right. The politicization of identity in Europe has thus far been more significant than the rise of industrialism in determining the nature of political cleavages. Vertical cleavages have been more important than horizontal.

Ideally, a national ideology (in Kohn's terms) ought to include symbols such as to requite both functional requisites of identity and community. The existence of a vertical cleavage is empirical evidence of the failure to satisfy identity needs, whatever their historical origin may be. This is one source of nationalist ideologies (in our terms). Political communities exist within a context of other political communities, and their separate existence may be challenged by their neighbors. This is a second source of nationalist ideologies. The justification of a challenge to the separate existence of another political community may be the antithesis of a nationalist ideology, that is, it may be an argument for the essentially rational basis of the community. Similarly, the justification for the refusal to recognize the existence of a vertical political cleavage may be that the conventional community determines identity. These incomplete generalizations are not very important for European history, but they are essential for an understanding of the rise of nationalism in the underdeveloped areas. The argument used by imperialism, justifying the subjection of colonial peoples, was an argument from the rational and conventional basis of the political community. It was argued, for example, that European administration was better than native administration. European imperialists were inconsistent, of course, for in Europe they argued that identity determined community while in Africa and Asia they argued that community ought to determine identity.

The rise of colonial nationalism may be attributed, in part, to the outcome of this simple debate. Still, if there was inconsistency on the imperialist side, there was incongruency on the colonial side. Nationalist modes of thinking developed without the prior appearance of national ideologies. There were occurrences of this kind in Europe, too, and Kohn takes pains to point out the differences.[60] But the important point is that the converging processes of social mobilization and the philosophizing of politics which have been described by Kohn and Deutsch [61] had not taken place when the vertical political cleavage between colonial and imperialist became too manifest to be resisted. The search for an Arab nationalist ideology expresses this deficiency. Instead of a western European type of combination of national ideology and nationalist-historical ontology, we find in the Middle East, as elsewhere among the new nations, a traditional, often religious, ideology sustained by a nationalist ontology which has been revised from the theological. Perhaps a national ideology is in the process of being created. We may even begin to suggest whence these incipient ideas are forthcoming. But for the time being the really significant element in the study of Arab nationalist ideology is the means by which the philosophical foundation was provided for nationalist modes of thought. The essential consequence of this ideological process has been the insistence upon the natural basis of the political community, and its dependence upon the subjective identity resolutions of individual citizens.

NOTES

1. Ibrahim Gum'ah, *Idiyulujiyyah al-Qawmiyyah al-'Arabiyyah* (Cairo, 1960), p. 25.
2. See N. Rejwan, "Arab Nationalism," in W. Z. Laqueur, *The Middle East in Transition* (New York, 1958).
3. E. Kedourie, *Nationalism*, revised edition (New York, 1960), p. 9.
4. E. g., Muhammad al-Ghazali, *Haqiqat al-Qawmiyyah al-'Arabiyyah* (Cairo, n.d.), p. 149.
5. See Chapter VI.
6. See the discussion of Rousseau in L. Strauss, *Natural Right and History* (Chicago, 1953), p. 252 f.
7. A. Cobban, *Rousseau and the Modern State* (London, 1934).
8. Strauss, *op. cit.*, p. 323.
9. Kedourie, *op. cit.*, p. 32 f.
10. This problem is dealt with in my "The Modernization of Egyptian Political Culture," a paper prepared for the SSRC Comparative Politics Summer Institute, 1962.
11. See L. Gardet, *La Cité Musulmane* (Paris, 1954).
12. W. Kornhauser, *The Politics of Mass Society* (Glencoe, 1959).
13. See G. Baer, *A History of Landownership in Modern Egypt, 1800–1950* (London, 1962).
14. D. Lerner, *The Passing of Traditional Society* (Glencoe, 1958), p. 251 f.
15. N. Safran, *Egypt in Search of Political Community* (Cambridge, 1961), p. 57 f.

16. Kamal al-Din Husain, *Al-Tarbiyyah wa'l-Ta'lim fi Khamsah Sanawat* (Cairo, 1957).
17. X. de Planhol, *Le Monde Islamique* (Paris, 1957), p. 5 f., on the anarchy of the Islamic city.
18. Safran, *op. cit.*, pp. 85 f. and 129 f.
19. M. Colombe, *L'Evolution de L'Egypte, 1924–1950* (Paris, 1951), p. 68 *et passim*.
20. *Ibid.*, pp. 270–271 *et passim*.
21. M. Berger, *Bureaucracy and Society in Modern Egypt* (Princeton, 1957), pp. 13–14, 22, 63.
22. G. Antonius, *The Arab Awakening* (London, 1938). The importance of these should not be exaggerated, however. See S. G. Haim, *Arab Nationalism* (Berkeley, 1962), p. 4.
23. H. A. B. Rivlin, *The Agricultural Policy of Muhhamad Ali in Egypt*, Cambridge, 1961, pp. 250–254.
24. J. M. Landau, *Parliaments and Parties in Egypt* (New York, 1954), p. 114.
25. Colombe, *op. cit.*, p. 167 f.
26. *Ibid.*, p. 124.
27. *Ibid.*, p. 147; see also W. C. Smith, *Modern Islam in India* (London, 1947), p. 64 f.
28. *The Charter* (Draft) May 21, 1962, Information Department, U.A.R., pp. 18, 19; M. H. Haikal, editorial, *al-Ahram*, September 14, 1962.
29. See letter of King Hussain to President Nasser, *al-Ahram*, March 31, 1961; also C. E. Dawn, "The Amir of Mecca al-Husayn ibn Ali and the Origin of the Arab Revolt," *Proceedings of the American Philosophical Society*, 104/1, Feb. 1960.
30. M. Mahdi, *Al-Farabi's Philosophy of Aristotle*, Arabic text (Beirut, 1961), Preface, p. ix.
31. E. I. J. Rosenthal, *Political Thought in Medieval Islam* (Cambridge, 1958), p. 210 f.
32. A.-M. Goichon, ed. and tr., Jamal al-Din al-Afghani, *Réfutation des Matérialistes* (Paris, 1942).
33. *Ibid.*, p. 174 f.
34. Safran, *op. cit.*, p. 69.
35. M. Abduh, *Rissalah al-Tawhid*, 17th ed. (Cairo, 1960), p. 20.
36. Safran, *op. cit.*, pp. 72–73; see also G. E. von Grunebaum, *Islam*, 2nd ed. (London, 1961), p. 189f.
37. Abduh, *op. cit.*, p. 14.
38. Safran, *op. cit.*, p. 65.
39. Abduh, *op. cit.*, p. 16.
40. *Idem.*
41. Ali Abd al-Raziq, *al-Islam wa-Usul al-Hukm* (Cairo, 1925); see Colombe, *op. cit.*, p. 127.
42. H. A. R. Gibb, *Studies on the Civilization of Islam* (Boston, 1962), "Tarikh," p. 121.

43. M. Iqbal, *The Reconstruction of Religious Thought in Islam* (London, 1934); Gibb's treatment of Iqbal in his *Modern Trends in Islam* (Chicago, 1947), is most relevant here.

44. C. C. Adams, *Islam and Modernism in Egypt* (London, 1933), p. 132.

45. Gibb, *Studies*, p. 151f.

46. L. Binder, "al-Ghazali's Theory of Islamic Government," *Muslim World*, July 1955.

47. M. Mahdi, *Ibn Khaldun's Philosophy of History* (London, 1957), p. 257, n. 7, and p. 258. Safran also treats this problem, but somewhat less satisfactorily: *op. cit.*, p. 68.

48. Abduh, *op. cit.*, p. 191.

49. Ibrahim al-Basati, *Wahdat al-'Arab* (Cairo, 1960), p. 36. The term used is the supreme interest of the state.

50. Safran, *op. cit.*, p. 64; J. M. Ahmed, *The Intellectual Origins of Egyptian Nationalism* (London, 1960), p. 43.

51. Abduh, *op. cit.*, pp. 40–41.

52. *Ibid.*, p. 98f.

53. Haim, *op. cit.*, p. 242.

54. Abduh, *loc. cit.*

55. W. Stark, *The Sociology of Knowledge* (London, 1958).

56. H. Kohn, *The Idea of Nationalism* (New York, 1961), pp. 3, 345, *et passim*. J. Benda, *The Betrayal of the Intellectuals* (Boston, 1955), p. 19.

57. Kohn, *op. cit.*, pp. 9, 273, 276, *et passim*.

58. Benda, *op. cit.*, p. 21 *et passim*.

59. Kohn, *op. cit.*, p. 259; Benda, *op. cit.*, p. 77 *et passim*.

60. Kohn, *op. cit.*, p. 457.

61. K. Deutsch, *Nationalism and Social Communication* (New York, 1953).

5

ISLAM, ARABISM,

AND THE POLITICAL COMMUNITY

IN THE MIDDLE EAST

The concept of the political community comprehends a range of
problems which are both interesting and significant and which
one may sidestep by means of a narrow definition only at the risk
of emptying the concept of much of its meaning to large numbers
of people. Our own view of the problem in its contemporary context takes the political community to be the terminal group to
which political allegiance is owed. But even this formal definition
gets us into so many philosophical difficulties and more empirical
difficulties that it seems better to define the problem in terms of
current political issues in the Middle East. There are two broad
issues which are of central importance: Islam versus nationalism
as the basis of the political community and one Arab state versus
several. Possibly of secondary importance, but of no small significance to the resolution of the central issue, are the questions of
legitimate political procedures and techniques, the integration of
small, traditionally organized groups (tribes, village communities,
minorities) into the larger social and political systems, and the

scope and purpose of government. If we further assume that the present arrangement of political communities as recognized in international diplomacy is unstable and subject to change, the preceding issues must be stated in dynamic terms, and our attention must be concentrated upon the ways in which the political community can change. This contemporary concern shifts our interest from the problem of the ideal state, but it cannot exclude the impact of such ideas upon the future of the political community in the Middle East. Our interest is in empirical theory which can throw light on what might be called gross system change, but insofar as ideological factors are operative, both the Islamic ideal and the nationalist ideal are relevant. Furthermore, there seems to be little doubt that contemporary empirical theory, if it is not openly value laden, has value implications which outrun in significance its predictive possibilities. Specific theories are not only analytical schemes; they are also, in some measure, programs.

Historically, theories of the political community have made the distinction between the natural and conventional order of society, but a rational conception of the state prevailed for most thinkers and in most communities with a written tradition up to modern times. The central aspect of the rational theory of the state varied from the postulation of a divine legal order which determined the relations among men holding the same religious beliefs, to an order in which beliefs and preferences were primary and laws dependent thereon, to one in which aspects of society were governed by divine law but other aspects were subject to natural law, necessity, or *sunnat Allah*, to one in which the rationally interpreted "nature of man" determined the form and purpose of the community. The natural conception evolved from the status of a rejected alternative, as *jahili*, that is, without revelation and necessarily less than ideal, to become a preferred objective of those who were disenchanted by the rationalization of society, who were dismayed by the technological differential between various states, who opposed tradition, and of those who opposed revolution.

The opposition of natural and conventional or rational became, for many, an opposition of ideal and material conceptions of the community. Or it might be better said that this later philosophical distinction was sorted out of the more diffuse conceptions of the earlier disagreement. Religionists generally combined ideal and rational views, liberals preferred rational and material views, revolutionary nationalists combined the natural and idealist views, and conservatives often held natural and rational views. In reality the categories are not so neat, and careful analysis might reveal ideas of all four types in a single work. The ideal and the rational stressed common belief and conscious or rational decision; the natural and material viewed existing societies as the only ones possible, given human nature, the conditions of the physical world, and the state of technology or the means of production. The meaning of both the rational and natural theories branched off into opposing types of theory and did not merely develop; and this branching permitted the development of the material conception of the community from the rational and the idealist from the natural. This is not the place to work out the causes of this branching and development, but the connection can be found in the influence of the neo-rationalist classical economists on Marx and in the influence of Rousseau on the nationalists. This dichotomy has informed contemporary theory in the form of the divergence of emphases of personality psychology and cultural anthropology on the one hand and of sociology on the other. As bodies of social science theory, all three are essentially materialist, but they emphasize the opposing elements of our dichotomy. Psychologists and anthropologists have been more concerned with what were called the natural and irrational bases of the community; sociologists have been more concerned with what went under the heading of the (neo-)rational and material bases. It may also be suggested that psychologists and anthropologists have been more concerned about the preservation of irrational values and about emotional problems, whereas sociologists have been motivated to preserve or realize rational values. Of course, these differences have been rendered more extreme and absolute than they are in the work of any individual for purposes of exposition. Our exaggeration is poetic and not scientific. Nevertheless, awareness of the contrast between these two types of theory will help us to isolate the broader issues on which the future of the political community in the Middle East depends.

I

". . . Polity [1] is the natural result of social solidarity.[2] It cannot occur as a matter of preference [3] but is solely the consequence of the necessity and order of existential reality. . . . Laws and religions and any other thing that men may be engaged upon require solidarity, since otherwise their object will not be attained." [4]

". . . The situation concerning the good [5] is that it is, in reality, achieved through preference [6] and will . . . and therefore any city is capable of achieving (true) happiness; and that city which seeks, in the association of its people, cooperation in those things which lead to (true) happiness is truly the ideal city. . . ." [7]

Ibn Khaldun's opposition to the hypothetical views of the *falasifa* is well enough known,[8] but the difference between his views on the essential nature of the political community and that of al-Farabi is not merely a curiosity of Islamic political thought. This difference is not unrelated to the continuing philosophical opposition between rational and irrational theories of the determinants of the political community. It is not surprising to find this suggestion of a later important philosophical controversy in the writings of two innovators, both of whom departed from the legalistic tradition of their predecessors, utilized an abstract theoretical framework, and employed a comparative method. Their predecessors were more interested in the prerequisites for maintaining the Islamic community and empire than in elaborating a general theory of society. The emphasis in classical Sunni thought was upon the maintenance of certain legalized relationships; and the legal operations thus defined were believed to form the bonds of community.[9] *Ibadat* both required and were the prerequisite of *mu'amalat*.[10] Belief in God and fulfillment of His appointed services required civil society; and divine law determined the nature of the ideal society. It is only in recent times that Muslim theorists have become concerned with political decline and, by implication, political change as secular phenomena rather than cyclical phenomena.[11] The transformation of the Islamic community and its division by political boundaries, even in mediaeval times, was accounted for by the legal doctrine of necessity, a presumably temporary and grudging concession to "reality." In more recent times, however, when the Islamic community has been deeply affected by alien influences, the need to adopt modern technology has been admitted by the minimalists, while the maximalists have advocated a complete cultural revolution and an entirely new concept of the political community based on nationality.

These introductory remarks are not meant to serve as a summary of Islamic ideas on the political community, but to suggest the wealth and variety of Islamic opinion on the subject. The concept of the *ummah* in Islam continues in an unbroken thread from the time of the Madina Charter, but as A. P. D'Entreves has said of natural law, can we be sure that it has been used in the same sense in all ages and by the exponents of all literary genres? [12] The initial question would appear to be whether the word *ummah* implied a designation of the legitimate limits of the terminal political community. In a manner more in keeping with the spirit of orthodox Islamic thought, we might ask whether the word *ummah* implied (in Kelsen's terminology) the personal sphere of validity of all law or of just law. The doctrine of necessity permitted and the grim facts of history compelled the Muslim legists to recognize the authority of local rulers, as Ibn Taiymiyya's *Siyasa Shari'a* indicates.[13] Nevertheless, it does not appear that orthodox Muslim law accepts any legitimate basis of the political community other than revelation. The views of the philosophers, despite their alien spirit and non-islamic terminology, do not depart from this position of the orthodox legists. Whether or not revealed law can be approximated by the rational effort of a pious philosopher, the ideal and hence the legitimate limits of the community are designated by that law. Ibn Khaldun, even in his acceptance of the classical theory of the caliphate, was the only important philosopher to specifically legitimize the rule of local warlords if they remained within the limits of the Shari'a. His doctrine of the natural cycle of dynasties did not stress disregard of the Shari'a as a cause of decline, as did both the *falasifa* and the authors of the "Mirrors for Princes," at least by implication. Loss of *asabiyyah* is not the same as disobedience to the law, although we may read as much as we like into that condition.

It is also significant to note that Ibn Khaldun is the only Muslim writer until modern times to have departed from the rationalist theory of the basis of the political community. In this regard, he may be said to have stood opposed to the major traditions of both Islam and Christianity. Neither law, nor contract, nor common rational belief are sufficient bases; laws and religion require *asabiyyah*. European writers through the mediaeval period had a similarly rational concept of the political community, which they had inherited from the stoic philosophers. "The formal aspect of Mediaeval Political Theory is to be found in that conception which is implied in the post-Aristotelian philosophy, in the Christian Fathers, and in the Digest and Institutes of Justinian, that the political and social order of society is conventional rather than natural, and represents the consequences of the fall of man from his primitive innocence." [14] But Carlyle hastens to add that this formal principle was not so important as was the emphasis upon justice through law as the only legitimate basis of political order. He further saw the basis of contemporary Western thought in the not unchallenged doctrine that the ruler is under the law. The crux of this doctrine turns on the nature of law. For Carlyle, law was in the first place the custom of the community: "the expression of the habit of life of the community." [15] In the second place and increasingly with the approach of modern times, law was authorized or at least consented to by the community. If Carlyle is right, then we have here the germ of an irrational theory of the political community—or of the community as the basis of the state. It is, however, problematical at best to attribute such a notion to mediaeval political philosophers, first for their emphasis on natural law and second for their frequent insistence that the relationship between prince and community was a contractual one. Natural law not only superseded any local custom in legitimacy, but it served as the basis of judging the validity of customary law. D'Entreves is at pains to point out St. Thomas' acceptance of the Aristotelian view: "homo naturaliter est animal politicum et sociale," [16] and his rejection of sin as the central factor in the rational justification of the state. [17] But the natural order of political society is a rational order: "Thus all humanly enacted laws are in accord with reason to the extent that they derive from the Natural law. And if a human law is at variance in any particular with the Natural law, it is no longer legal, but rather a corruption of law." [18] Nevertheless St. Thomas accepts, if he does not explicitly explain or justify, the particular and historical states of his time [19]—as did the Muslim theorists—and he asserted that man was subject to a triple order: the rule of reason, the rule of divine law, and "a third order, regulating the conduct of man to his fellows with whom he has to live." [20]

Aquinas' assertion that men would have organized politically even had they remained in a state of innocence became the mythical state of nature whence man's natural rights were derived. But the social contract which changed the locus of authority for the natural law still continued to render the state a rational order. It was left to Rousseau, Burke, Hegel, the romantics, the irrationalists, the historians, and the nationalists of the nineteenth century to reverse this perennial concept.[21] And it was from sources such as these that contemporary Muslim nationalists have drawn their ideas of the legitimate basis of the state—referring it to the "natural" political community.

II

What can we do with these ideas? Is there any way in which they can be related to contemporary problems? Will they determine future boundary lines in any way? Will they have any effect on the shape of the developing political systems of the Middle East? In asking these questions we are asking the more general question of the relationship of ideology to politics, but we shall attempt to answer this question within the somewhat loose boundaries of the question of the nature of the political community in the Middle East. We turn next, therefore, to an examination of some purportedly empirical theories of the political community, in order to see where these philosophical preferences may fit.

The juxtaposition of the rational and irrational conceptions of the basis of the state is a relatively modern contribution. In both Islam and Christianity the rational concept held universal sway, with the limited exceptions of the work of Ibn Khaldun and, much later, of Montesquieu. In more recent times there has arisen the idea that somewhere behind the politically and legally delimited society there exists a natural community which may or may not coincide with the former. The nineteenth century nationalists claimed that this natural community was the only legitimate basis of political society, but anthropologists and sociologists began to examine actual political societies under the intellectual influence of these conflicting theories. The anthropologists concentrated on the study of primitive communities which they assumed to comprise natural societies, man in the state of nature, or men in the state of innocence. Before the contemporary interest in the problem of the adaptation of these primitive societies to a changing environment, they were often treated as perfect communities. The *a priori* identification of primitive and ideal communities may have contained much that was erroneous, but it did contribute to the development of a theory of the prerequisites for the stable continuity of the political community. The twofold assumption of the related patterning of all cultural institutions and their functionality was constructed on Montesquieu's suggestions about the effect of climate and the distribution of resources upon the form of the community. But while theory developed toward the postulation of certain indispensible functions as the prerequisite of political community, empirical research uncovered situations in which the relative importance as well as the institutional form of the particular "function" varied tremendously. In some cases it appeared that the function might even disappear, as in the so-called stateless societies, although it might better be said that some of these functions, e.g., controlling the elements upon which grazing or agriculture depends, or settling disputes, are carried out in extremely decentralized fashion.[22] In any case it is clear that the empirical materials on which these views are based describe instances of successful adaptation by a variety of communities to a variety of environmental conditions. While such theory has extremely limited predictive value, it does suggest that successful adaptation to new and more rapidly changing environmental circumstances must bring in its wake new ideas and new values. If social, economic, and political institutions and their ideological justifications comprise a coordinate pattern of mutual reinforcement, changes in any one must bring about a degree of change in all the others. In the Middle East, we know that there have been important changes in the first three areas, but we are not convinced of the degree of adaptability of Islam to accommodate these changes. But must ideology follow "objective" social change, or can a firmly rooted ideology shape that change, i.e., can we look upon environmental changes and traditional ideology as a vector of forces acting upon social and political institutions and in the long run determining both the objective and ideological shape of the political community in the Middle East? Is ideology functionally autonomous or functionally dependent? If it is functionally autonomous to any large degree in a specific case (e.g., Sunni Islam) has it the efficacy to shape the political community or does it become a philosophical curiosity, an ideological fossil?

The same relativism and consequent comparative approach, based on the recognition of the functional diversity and diffuseness of concrete institutional structures, entered into sociological theory, most notably through the work of Ferdinand Tonnies. His postulation of two contrasting ideal types of human association has had a deep and lasting effect on social theory. The two types were called *gemeinschaft* and *gesellschaft,* usually and unfortunately translated as community and society, the first stressing familistic behavior and the second, contractual relationships. The *gemeinschaft* is a natural order of community; the *gesellschaft* is a rational order of society. The more contractual a society, the more will its artificial order conflict with its underlying natural tendencies. Nevertheless, these are essentially two types of association, as reflected in Weber's contrast of traditional, patrimonial society with rationalized, bureaucratic, and industrialized society. American sociological theory did not pursue the comparative leads supplied by this analysis in terms of ideal types, but rather tended toward preferring either the familistic or the contractual elements as the best explanation of the cohesiveness of society. The comparative emphasis was returned to this dichotomy by Talcott Parsons in his scheme of the pattern-variables,[23] but the problem was set in new terms somewhat closer to the outlook of the mediaeval philosophers. The pattern-variables were alternative modes of behavior the existence of which, in the end, depended upon the sharing of values and internalized norms among persons interacting with one another in an "action system" integrated by means of their mutually compatible expectations of one another's behavior. The question was no longer whether values or institutions were the more important, but whether or not they were compatible and mutually reinforcing in a concrete system. A further dimension was also added, in sharp contradistinction to mediaeval ideas: a consideration of the impact of the cultural-social institutional setting upon the integration of the individual personality and its consequent ability to adapt to new circumstances. This conception of the social system sought a common ground for the use of both theory and empirical findings from anthropology, sociology, and psychology. As compared with earlier theories, it appears eclectic, but the more reasonable for the complexity which it suggests is characteristic of all social phenomena. Nevertheless, in the relative centrality of values and personality it admits of a greater relevance for both philosophical and irrational psychological elements as against the instrumental logic of social, political, and economic institutions.

Shortly after having worked out this scheme, Parsons substituted for the pattern-variables a theoretical framework which was a modification of one used by R. F. Bales in his studies of small groups. The rather labored explanation of the compatibility of the two schemes need not detain us, for what seems more important is the shift in emphasis from a framework that provided the criteria for differentiating systems on the basis of shared values (i.e., ideology) to one which defined four processes essential to any system.[24] The shift was from a comparative framework to a theory of *the* system. In making this shift the essential prerequisite of shared values was rendered one component process of the social system. The four processes were goal seeking (policy making), adaptation (reality testing or learning), expression (satisfaction of psychological need dispositions by noninstrumental acts), and integration (acts producing a greater or lesser solidarity among the members of the system). While the locus of ideology may be found in the fourth process, i.e., integration, it is also clear that none of the other three can be freed from cultural values. Furthermore, the treatment of ideology and culture is further complicated by continuing to use the terminology of the action system, in which persons acting in social roles and having concrete statuses are the components of the system, whereas the form of the system has been altered to that of an analytical system in which certain processes (sc. the performance of certain functions) are mutually interdependent. One need not be wholly committed to this framework to see that such an approach tests an ideology among the four dimensions described; in instrumental goal achievement, cognitive adaptability, satisfaction of psychological needs, and ability to hold together the society despite the differential performance of these three functions. We have returned, it would seem, to a rational conception of society and of the political community.

III

Ibn Khaldun stressed *asabiyyah* as a prerequisite for a successful dynasty, but he certainly suggested that such solidarity could only persist within a particular social structure, i.e., tribal as opposed to urban. *Asabiyyah* characterizes a discrete system; and Ibn Khaldun's is a theory of the contact of two systems through conquest such that the boundaries between the two disappear, while the boundaries of the "conquered" system do not change appreciably, and its "integrative" capacity is sufficient to accommodate these new elements. Unfortunately, Ibn Khaldun's presentation stresses the military weakness rather than the cultural stability of urban society, but he does point up the contemporary problem of the inability of contractually ordered society to achieve a high performance on the expressive (psychological) scale. Is it possible, despite the justly stressed integrative ability of Islam, that urban Muslim society was not politically or socially integrated even before the impact of the West? I think that a good case can be made for this contention, not only from Ibn Khaldun's work and the observations of Ibn Rushd,[25] but from the character of urban revolutionary movements in Islam, from the consistent failure to Islamize the military and the bureaucracy despite the attempt at literary compromise, and from the persistence of Sufism. If this view is valid, we can hardly expect Islam as a disembodied ideology to accomplish now what it could not accomplish when faced with no serious rival.

These considerations run contrary to two recent attempts at more or less empirical interpretations of Islam. It should be borne in mind, however, that integration is a relative thing—that is, relative to goal achievement, adaptability, and expression for Parsons and Bales; relative to *asabiyyah* and its determinants for Ibn Khaldun; relative to the rational ordering of authority in the state for the *falasifa* (based, of course, on the prevalence of correct belief and philosophical wisdom); and relative to piety, scholarship, military power, administrative order, and physical and mental health for the orthodox jurists. This rather obvious interdependence of ideology as a factor in the integration of a social system, and hence in determining the limits and nature of the political system, appears to have been forgotten only by those who conceive of the problem in purely philosophical terms, who trouble themselves to study whether Islamic ideas render Muslims vulnerable to communism, democracy, socialism, or nationalism.

Two studies that emphasize the integrative capacity of Islam are *La Cité Musulmane* of L. Gardet and *Islam and the Integration of Society* by W. M. Watt. The philosophical orientation of the former is idealist, while that of the latter is materialist. Gardet's work is justly celebrated for his perceptive use of orthodox Muslim ontology as a basis for this analysis and for his recognition of the very powerful sense of community which exists among the Muslims which he observed. His comparison of what he determined to be the Islamic doctrine *ipsissima* with Christian doctrine is not entirely fair, because he was comparing what has become liberal Catholic doctrine, based on Aquinas' work of reconciliation, with his own able interpretation of Islam. In a sense, he stacks the cards against Islam by excluding from consideration those very adaptations of Islam to new political and social circumstances which would balance his choice of the perennial philosophy for the Christian side. It is only by separating the development of Islamic thought from its historical context that one can disregard the efforts to construct a legitimacy which, if it was not recognized by the legists, was nevertheless recorded by the historians—as T. W. Arnold has shown.[26] Only such a limited view would permit such a statement as "La Communauté Musulmane —et l'on ne serait pas sans trouver sur ce point une réelle équivalence en certains enseignements de Luther, voire une équivalence atténuée en telle attitude puritaine—la Communauté Musulmane, si attachée pourtant à sa notion de 'justice' positive, eut presque toujours comme un respect inné de la force qui triomphe et qui réussit." [27] It will not do to treat as a doctrinal and moral blindness what were manifestly "integrative" interpretations of Islamic doctrine when confronted with a new political and social structure. It is the greatness of St. Thomas and not his blindness that his doctrine rendered Roman Catholic Christianity more relevant to the conditions of his and our times than the doctrine of St. Augustine. In any case, Gardet's grasp of the problem of the future of the political community in Islam is not affected by his ideological bias. His view of the unity of the *ummah* is the most complete and sensitive I have ever seen, yet he shows how this unity is giving way to a growing "individualism" through the changes in family structure, tribal organization, the distribution of common property, industrialization, and the spread of liberalism. Orthodox attempts to cope with these problems by legal and philosophical devices without altering the letter of traditional Islamic law and by exploiting the close, almost organic, unity of Muslims (i.e., certain classes of Muslims) do not dispel these disintegrative tendencies and those arising out of linguistic and cultural differences. In the end, Gardet surrenders: "Tout va dépendre des réalisations sociales. . . . C'est ainsi selon une ambivalence sans cesse renaissante de cohésion foncière et de particularismes toujours nouveaux, que la communauté Musulmane continue de chercher, non point dans les principes mêmes—ils restent acquis—mais dans la réalisation terrestre, sa forme propre d'unité." [28] He notes that nationalist radical reform in Egypt is being carried out in an atmosphere congenial to the Islamic faith, so he can conclude that the Islamic community will continue to exist in some form; but he can do more than insist that the ordinary man in the street would prefer some kind of Islamic commonwealth "if it becomes possible." [29]

If we understand Gardet correctly, he believes that the Islam which he has described, especially the doctrines of equality and unity, inheres in the value system of the Muslim masses; but he fails to show us any manner in which this attitude can become politically effective. His faith in the eventual efficacy of these "dominantes non explicitées" is not supported by any historical example, while his illustration of the nondoctrinal aspects of Muslim unity suggests that the spirit he referred to was perhaps the culture of Sunni, Arab, urban, artisan, and clerical classes only, as developed in the purely male society of mosque, market, coffee house, and *tarikah*. If you change the condition of these classes or alter the institutions which regulate their association, will not the sense of unity fade before the sweep of individualism or the new rationalized order of the nation-state? Gardet, as might be expected, rejects this latter view and in the final analysis must impute the ideal Islam which he has described to the collective mind of the model of the organic community which he has constructed from Islamic law and selective observation.

Watt's study may be better comprehended against the background of this discussion. As a preliminary it may be admitted that Watt's work is methodologically confused, his evidence flimsy, and his application of ideas from Marx, Mannheim, and Weber unexceptional. The first difficulty is that he was not applying other people's theories to Islamic history so much as applying a few cases of Islamic history to social theory. The material he used was for the most part elaborated in his two volumes on Muhammad, but many critical factors have no more basis than speculation about what must have occurred—which are based, in turn, upon a materialistic interpretation of history. To turn around and use such speculation as the ground for developing social theory is hardly justifiable.

In his earlier work, Watt sought to find materialistic—specifically, economic—explanations of early Islamic history. In the present volume he is concerned to show that his use of economic "data" or suppositions does not make him a determinist. Belief systems or ideation, as he puts it, are not autonomous, but interdependent with economic and social situations, in the sense that they are called into being thereby and that they serve to integrate both individual and collective behavior. Nevertheless, this interdependence does not invalidate the possibility of the inherent truth of "ideation." To stress this point, Watt uses the term "ideation," as opposed to Mannheim's "ideology" and "utopia." Instead of standing on this manifestly Mannheimian position, however, Watt presumes to be able to use a test to determine whether false consciousness entered into Muhammad's Islam; his test is accomplished through an examination of the degree to which his ideas were "warped" by his social involvement [30]— despite his inability to suggest a method by which we can "know" the truth of any idea. In the end, however, his position is essentially Marxian, for he asserts that "material factors are fundamental"; [31] that there are types of social system more suited to certain economic circumstances than to others; that economic change produces social maladjustment; and that ideas channel social activity into adjusting social change to economic change. Economic change is evidently self-created; social institutions are neither material nor ideational; and the social effectiveness of any system of beliefs depends upon its correct "reading" of economic conditions, but to be effective these ideas themselves must appeal to men's emotions and not to their reason.

This position is not new, and it has been better stated, but its interest for us here is in the implicit argument that the system of beliefs known as Islam has successfully adapted itself to a series of economic changes during the last 1300 years. Hence its success was not due to its relevance to a specific set of economic conditions, but to its relevance to the human psyche, especially in the production of the "dynamic image of the charismatic community." [32] Now we find Watt's system breaking down, for neither the psyche nor the social structure is interpreted materialistically, and the failure of Islamic "ideation" to produce political unity is (astonishingly) attributed to the "proper autonomy of the sphere of politics." [33] Clearly, there are many crucial things left unexplained if we are to try to relate Watt's work to the problem of the future of the political community in the Middle East, for even if we stand on the author's own ground and accept the contemporary balance of power as a self-evident requirement of world "integration," this desideratum must be understood to comprehend integration at the level of control over the use of nuclear weapons and hence of the "ruling institutions" of the world. If politics are autonomous, then how shall the world benefit from the moral unity which Islam can provide?

If Watt provides us with no theoretical advance, his interpretation of the Islamic community may, nevertheless, be useful as a datum for consideration in another context. For him the Islamic community is founded upon revelation, which consists of those who accept Islam, irrespective of race or class: equal members of a charismatic community, the distinctive external characteristic of which is obedience to the Shari'a. While neither political unity,[34] intellectual unity (sc. cultural unity),[35] nor an adequate grasp of reality (see his interpretation of the psyche) [36] resulted, men of all races have been united in this moral community, and the major institutions of the family and inheritance became more or less uniform throughout Islam.[37] Government in Islamic countries, if it was to be legitimate, had to conform in some degree to the Shari'a; in the same manner, social institutions were affected to a limited degree. But if Islam did not shape the political community in the personal and territorial senses, it did define the purpose of government and organized society in the philosophical sense and within the broad limits set by historical and social circumstances. The latter conclusion is better illustrated by Gardet than by Watt, but I think that Watt is in agreement in his discussion of political integration.

The conclusions which we may draw from the analysis of these two studies sustain some of our earlier statements. Both Gardet and Watt are concerned to explain the deep psychological and social attachment of Muslims to Islam and the Muslim community. Both are also forced to admit that this attachment had little political efficacy, that is, it did not determine the limits of the political community. To put their views in our own terms, the concept of the *ummah* served as a referent for the identity resolutions of individual Muslims throughout Islamic history. But, as we have pointed out, identity was a religious and not a political category of concern until recent times. It is with the politicization of identity and the posing of the problem of the individual and the political community that Islam and politics have had to be reconciled within a new framework. Rational conviction is no longer held to be the basis of membership in a political community, but Islamic attachments could not be disposed of so easily. The solution, doubtlessly easier to reach because of the traditional treatment of Islam and politics, was to render Islam a part of the wider Arab national identity. In accordance with nationalist ontology, it was only historical Islam and not Islam as revealed religion that could be so reconciled.

The only way in which Islam alone could serve to resolve this problem of the individual and the political community is by the explicit extension of Islam to the issues of everyday politics. Furthermore, this extended Islam would have had to be accepted by most Muslims as the true Islam. Taking Zoroastrianism as our example, again, the possibly untoward consequences of the close joining of religion and politics in their institutional senses become clear. The Muslim fundamentalists do desire to extend Islam to comprehend routine political issues. The ulama, on the other hand, despite strong temptation, have resisted the intense urging of the fundamentalists and have retained traditional attitudes of ambivalence toward the political.

Material conditions, to which the rational conception of the political community must be referred, are also discussed by both Watt and Gardet. In examining Islamic history, Watt finds the impact of material conditions roughly the same in all periods, within arbitrarily defined political units. Gardet considers the affect of contemporary material conditions in sundering an Islamic unity which was not in any case a true political unity. Gardet believes Islam generally incapable of coping with changed material conditions; Watt believes that Islam is highly adaptable. Actually the difference between them is not so great, because Gardet is discussing Islam as a regulator of society, and Watt is discussing Islam as a psychologically integrative force. But this divergence of focus reemphasizes the very problem of identity and community that has concerned us.

The ulama denied that material conditions had any consequences for Islam. On the question of whether Islam had any consequences for the manner in which material conditions might be approached, their position was not at all clear. The modernists did believe that material conditions had consequences for Islam.

The fundamentalists, again, sought to reconcile both positions by a reinterpretation of Islamic government that probably would have rendered Islam subject to strict political control. The key to their reconciliation was doubtlessly that persons of their own fundamentalist persuasion take over the government. Nevertheless, the implication of their doctrine was that Islamic reform should be imposed politically. The political modernizers have not so well resisted the urging of the fundamentalists as have the ulama, but in the main they, too, have retained traditional political attitudes toward the relationship between Islam and politics.

IV

In his *The Political Community* [38] Sebastian De Grazia sets out to revive interest in the ancient Greek idea of the Great Community, bound together by "systems of beliefs, flexible bands weaving through and around each member," but his exposition denies both the spirit and letter of his model. His effort is directed at a restatement of the rational and idealist conceptions of the Catholic Church in a form acceptable to modern social science, but his product renders systems of belief dependent neither on reason nor on revelation. He attacks the separation of the concept of society as a collection of individuals from that of community, a unity of religious and political beliefs; and he blames the treatment of beliefs as superstructure or epiphenomena, as the "irrational elements of 'society.'" [39] But for the irrationalist bogey of the empiricists he substitutes the "irrational" psychology of the Freudians. It is not the content of beliefs that concerns him; it is rather their function: "Never mind their variety. There are many lands and diverse customs, but it is the same need in all men that brings them together." [40]

To analyze what brings men together De Grazia concentrates on the pathology of the community, on anomie, in the terminology of Emile Durkheim. The basic motivational force in man is the need for love, for close association with those who provide for his needs and protect him, and for evidence in the ways of evoking love, protection, and the requital of needs. Anomie is derived from and described in terms parallel to separation-anxiety in the child, and De Grazia accepts the dictum that the child is father of the man. Maturation is not dealt with after the manner of the rationalist social theories of the educationists; it is essentially a series of stages of affect-transference from parent to God to the State.

De Grazia distinguishes two major types of anomie, which he calls simple and acute. Simple anomie is produced by the conflict of ideologies coexisting in a single community—an indication of the underlying rationalist values of the author—while acute anomie is the result of the alienation of the ruler from the people, usually by revelation of the fact that the ruler cannot act as God or a parent surrogate and supply the needs of the individual. The consequences of simple anomie are found in modern romantic love, the silence on friendship, the growth of family "togetherness," the growth of associations and clubs, milder neuroses, and a preference for war and the companionship which it engenders. Acute anomie causes extreme psychopathic derangements, suicide, and revolutionary mass movements based on new ideologies. Let us consider the implication of these two conditions for the problem of the political community in the Middle East.

Simple anomie is the result of coexisting but conflicting belief systems. But not all systems of belief are mutually exclusive; it is the content of these beliefs that is the important consideration. Unfortunately, De Grazia fails to tell us how to distinguish compatible ideologies from incompatible ideologies. His concern is with proving empirically that simple anomie exists in the United States, and he goes on to attribute that fact to the conflict between an ideology of community and an ideology of society, to the conflict between Christianity, essentially in its Catholic form, and the competitive capitalist ethic which stands close to Protestantism. So we must modify our statement that ideological contradictions depend upon content. They appear to depend upon whether or not the ideologies in question accord with man's natural, i.e., psychological, disposition: Catholic Christianity does, but Protestant capitalism does not; and there is the implication that questions of truth are to be settled in this manner. De Grazia quotes Freud's *Civilization and Its Discontents* in his own support, but he does not accept its central thesis. For De Grazia there can be a community which eliminates the major causes of anxiety in the individual, but for Freud any form of civil society produces psychic tension—that is the human condition. But how much further is the human condition worsened by confronting the individual with two conflicting sets of directives? To what extent do the directives of Islam and of nationalism, Arab, Turkish, and Persian, conflict?

Modern critics of nationalism do not attack it on the grounds of its potential anomic affects within the political community which it defines, but for its tendency to break down larger unities and to foster war. This issue of the personal and territorial limits of the political community is what sets Islam and nationalism apart, but if De Grazia is right, one should expect the emergence of ever smaller, more closely united, and more culturally homogeneous units. We must bear in mind, however, that Muslim states are not now united under an Islamic empire, and that the political boundaries in the Middle East are such that no nation, or rather nationalist, is fully satisfied. The separation of Arab from non-Arab in what now appears to be a fairly permanent arrangement is in conflict with the classical concept of the Islamic Community, but attempts to establish security communities [41] comprised of Arab and non-Arab governments contravene the currently dominant ideology of Arab nationalism. Despite this contradiction, recent years have brought a greater awareness of common interests among Muslims and more frequent appeals for cooperation, which, if they have not overcome the Turkish-Arab and Persian-Arab antipathies, have been moderately well entertained between Arabs and those Muslim peoples who are not their immediate neighbors and among most non-Arab Muslims. It appears that the dominant ideological tendency is toward greater unity, as a consequence of both Islamic and nationalist ideals, even if few concrete results can be expected. One notes the great emphasis put upon the unity of Islam by both Gardet and Watt and contrasts this with the earlier interest in schisms and sects in the interpretations of Islam by Margoliouth and Gibb.[42] Still, Gardet makes an impressive point by suggesting that the nationalist movements among Muslims are essentially Islamic reactions to alien domination, and that given the choice the ordinary Muslim would opt for an Islamic state.[43] If he is correct, then the problem is not now that of the ability of Islam to withstand nationalism but that of the ability of nationalism to withstand the centripetal tendencies of Islam. If this view be accepted, then it must be further admitted that the cause of this "ideological conflict" is not the contradictions between Islam and Middle Eastern nationalism, but their very complementarity. In De Grazia's terms, we may say that the disruptive influences of western imperialism and Western culture (the competitive principle or universalist achievement values) created a degree of simple anomie, and there entered into the breach two types of ideology: fundamentalist Islam, which derived its inspiration from the period of the greatest Islamic unity, and nationalism, which postulated a new kind of unity. The confluence of these two ideologies may be viewed in a number of ways: from the point of view of doctrinal differences, they are wide apart; in regard to supplying the psychological needs of men in society, they are of kindred theoretical types; with respect to the organization of society and the goals of government, they do not appear to be in conflict; but as for the distribution of political power and the instrumental means of pursuing public goals, they are in sharp disagreement.

What is the importance of doctrinal differences? We shall attempt to avoid the methodological pitfall which beset Professor Watt and make it clear that in treating of Islamic and nationalist doctrine in the Middle East we are not proposing theoretical answers of universal validity but merely examining a particular situation in the light of existing theory. Different observers have drawn widely divergent conclusions about the political result of this doctrinal conflict. We have Gardet minimizing its importance, but Gibb has assessed Middle Eastern nationalism as the enemy of the Islamic cultural tradition.[44] The views of Sir Hamilton Gibb have had the greater influence and have colored the analyses of such widely divergent analysts as Professor Vatikiotis and Walter Laqueur.[45] Vatikiotis sees the conflict of Islam and nationalism as a dilemma facing the Egyptian political elite, but might have drawn another conclusion from the very evidence of the thematic ambivalence of official propaganda. Laqueur considers the struggle to be over, with nationalism the victor and Islam the vanquished. The significance of the work of Vatikiotis is precisely in the manner in which it sustains Gardet's impression, and its value is little affected by the caution with which Vatikiotis treats the motives of Egypt's leaders. In my own opinion, the confusion of Islamic and national principles is not opportunistic but a genuine reflection of the beliefs and social origins of that leadership. Indeed, the authority for the possibility of such an opinion is not only Gardet (and personal observation); further reference may be made to the extremely interesting analysis of Islam and Arab nationalism by S. G. Haim, who points out the doctrinal similarities and the special place of the Arabs in Islam,[46] Sir Hamilton Gibb's analysis of the latter theme,[47] and the suggestive study by Salo W. Baron of the historical interrelations between a variety of religions and a variety of nationalisms.[48] Further proof may also be supplied by the fact that the struggle for power in Iraq is essentially one between Sunni Arabs and Shi'ite and non-Arab groups. This confluence of Arab nationalism and Islam is not merely a political phenomenon in the materialist sense; it is the subject of rationalizing ideologies emanating from the pens of both religionists and nationalists. The writings of Hasan al-Banna recommend themselves as the probable source of Gardet's views, since they are so closely parallel. Al-Banna asserted that the Muslim Brethren did not reject any part of any ideology which was good; hence, if nationalism meant freedom from Western influence, it was good; if it meant love of country, it was good; if it meant regaining independence, it was good; if it meant strengthening the bonds of society, it was good; if it meant reconquering the country (by force?), it was good; but if it meant dividing the community, it was evil—and the community for Hasan al-Banna was a community of belief (aqidah).[49] It may be added that frequent statements of Egyptian government leaders have dealt with the brotherhood of all Muslims, and that no official statement limiting the ultimate scope of Islamic unity can be found. The Islamization of nationalism proceeds, however, and it is possible to look forward to the eventual accommodation of Islam and the nation-state. If Islamic ends, as they were limited in practice, could be pursued under all the varied circumstances of Islamic history, then why not under the nation-state? In a recent work Abd al-Rahim al-Fudah presents Islam as the natural religion, which recognizes the natural forms of human association, the family, the neighborhood, the city, and the nation.[50] Islam does not deny nationalism; Islam exalts it. Arab nationalism and Islam are closely related: Islam is the final and most perfect revelation, and Arab nationalism is the most perfect nationalism; and though the two are not identical, each has given of itself to the other—but the glory is not that of the Arabs, the glory is God's. Ahmad Hasan al-Baquri agrees with Fudah that Islam exalted Arab nationalism.[51] He agrees that the Arab nation can attain vigor and a renaissance only through religion. Islam made a nation of the Arabs by giving them the prerequisite of nationalism, i.e., common aspirations and thought, and the common goals of life, freedom, and dignity. We note that the *alim* used a "natural" definition of the nation, whereas the official uses the "rational" definition. Al-Baquri goes on to claim, with perhaps more truth than is generally acknowledged, that the beginnings of the reawakening of Arab nationalism were in the fundamentalist religious movements of the Wahhabis and the Sanusiyyah, under the influence of which there arose Gamal Abd al-Nasser. We note in passing the difference between al-Baquri's interpretation and the better known standard of George Antonius.[52] Even Muhammad al-Ghazali reflects a similar view.[53] He, too, proposes the theme of Arabism as the "vessel" in which Islam was contained; he goes on to develop the special qualities of the Arab nation that explain why it was so chosen, and he cites B. Lewis's quotation of Sir Hamilton Gibb's interpretation of the Islamic role of the Arab nation.[54] He then finds Egypt at the crossroads between nationalism and internationalism, both of which are bad: the first because it is a narrow *asabiyyah* and the second because the West will use internationalism to exploit the Arabs. But to have the benefits of both and neither of their evils, they should follow the obvious course of "Islamic brotherhood."[55] Yet al-Ghazali is opposed to nationalism in its usual sense. His counterpart on the nationalist side is Michel Aflaq, who declares that the Ba'th movement is in favor of religion, but true religion, not that apparent religion which prevails.[56] True religion and especially Islam is a revolutionary principle which can, in fact, only be understood by revolutionaries like the Ba'this. The implication of his opposition to the conservative ulama is clear.

This sampling will suffice to convey the tenor of contemporary discussion of the ideological conflict between Islam and Arab nationalism. The problem is there, but there is also evidence of the investment of much intellectual effort into the task of ideological reconciliation. For non-Arabs, the Turks explicitly and the Persians implicitly, Abd al-Rahim al-Fudah's views rationalize their nationalism within Islam. The problem is easier for Shi'ite Persians, for they are not yet full-fledged members of the *ummah*, despite efforts to have them regarded as simply a fifth school of law.[57] Nonreligious Persians are even more outspoken in subsuming their Shi'ism to their nationalism, as for example Mehdi Malikzadeh [58] and the Iranvij Society. The problem is more difficult for Christian Arabs, to whom, as is well known, Arab nationalism owes a very great debt. Where they comprise a small minority, i.e., outside of the Lebanon, they are interested primarily in maintaining or organizing special guarantees and a proportionate access to administrative and legislative positions. Ideologically, they do not oppose the idea of the Arab-Islamic state. Few even go so far in their public statements in criticism of traditional Islam as does Aflaq, but fewer still go as far in the other direction as the Copt Iyadi al-Abd al-Iyadi.[59] Once again Fudah's views are the most widely acceptable; particularly his emphasis upon the geographical basis of the nation and the equality of "neighbors," i.e., different kinds of people living in close proximity.

There appears to be little chance for an Islamic political unity which transcends the boundaries of language and sectarianism, so that the preceding ideological discussion cannot in any practical sense be read as one between Pan-Islam and Pan-Arabism. The real issues, despite the pre-1954 potential of the Muslim Brethren and despite Chaudhri Khaliquzzaman's highly overpublicized Islamistan, are those of the organization and goals of the state and of Arab unity.[60] The latter will be taken up below, and the former takes us back to De Grazia's *Political Community*.

If we see the political units of the Middle East as political systems in transition from the traditional type,[61] if we understand the nature of this transition in the psychological terms in which the theoretical findings of Lerner's communication study were stated,[62] and if we bear in mind both the degree of unity and the ideological compromises which existed in premodern Islam, it may be possible to come to a third theory, which is neither De Grazia's simple anomie nor his acute anomie. It is difficult to approximate De Grazia's direct sense of the malaise of American society with regard to Islamic society of the eighteenth and early nineteenth centuries. Still, we must try, and the general impression which I have is one of a decided lack of unity, both psychological and social. Moreover, I think this is characteristic of traditional and preindustrial societies. In comparison with modern industrialized societies with strong associational institutions, centralized organs of government, and developed systems of communication, traditional societies are probably all anomic. In Islamic countries, where the legitimacy of government was subject to question among certain classes, this condition was intensified. Of course, the term anomie may be misapplied in this sense, because it is existentially related to the disenchantment of the modern world and not of the traditional world.[63] The urgent calls for unity currently being uttered by both nationalists and religionists are not the result of the conflict between them, but the expression of their desire to mobilize the energies of a people still caught in the web of tradition. Freud's fundamental insight was doubtless the purport of the legal doctrine of necessity in Islam, but the twentieth century is the era of romantic utopian visions for non-Western civilizations. Visions of civilization without discontents are rampant.

As we have seen, De Grazia's acute anomie is caused by the inability of the ruler or the government to produce what is expected. This failure results in the alienation of the ruled from the ruler, regardless of whether the ruler stands for cooperation or competition, regardless of whether the problem of community versus society is called to the fore. In other words, in his discussion of acute anomie De Grazia passes on to entirely new theoretical ground; in fact, he leaves the psychological area of community and passes to the "societal" one of the performance of a government. It is true that he stresses the psychological dimension of the consequences of poor performance and the possibly irrational movements which may result, but is it not possible to say that given the failure of a government, people will seek an alternative; and that if they have "learned" (Parson's adaptive process) how to find an alternative, they will approach the problem more or less rationally? De Grazia gives us some examples of alternative seeking among primitive peoples, but disregards, for example, Bagehot's treatment of this problem in nineteenth century Britain.[64] When, however, does the solution demand a departure from existing ideology and existing institutions?

It is apparent that all Muslim governments failed to perform their appointed tasks during the nineteenth century, whether those tasks are understood as defined by De Grazia or by traditional Islam. Consequently, one is led to conclude that De Grazia's acute anomie is more relevant than his simple anomie to the contemporary Middle East, although it must be admitted that traditional Islamic beliefs and attitudes remain strong in the Middle East. It is not the conflict of ideologies that appears to be the most significant, for traditionalists can swallow nationalism rather more easily than fundamentalists. What seems to have occurred is that obvious political failure has triggered both a desire to change rulers and the latent Islamic disapproval of mediaeval Muslim political institutions. Indeed, the latter preceded the former, as al-Baquri suggested. But the early fundamentalism of the Wahhabis and the Sanusis was a protest against the preindustrial "anomie" which characterized Islamic society before the impact of the West was strongly felt. It is not "mass society" which calls this protest into being, it is a moral sense of injustice rooted in the content of Islamic ideology (and the compulsive morality of certain of the faithful). The answer of the early fundamentalists was still the traditional one of changing rulers. Afghani, on the other hand, did not advocate changing rulers so much as changing what the rulers were to do. It is this distinction of the concept of the scope of government which makes the crucial difference between the contemporary Middle East and De Grazia's example of Weimar Germany. In both cases the rulers failed, but in the Middle East a basically rational ideology proclaimed not so much that failure as the changed circumstances in which government found itself. The Germany of the 1930's may have reacted irrationally to the failures of the Weimar government, but it is difficult to attribute irrationality to Middle Eastern revolutionaries, except insofar as they grossly overestimate their resources. The real problem is not that of coping with irrational reactions to misplaced separation-anxiety, but the more rational one of functional adaptation to environmental changes. There is, of course, ideological conflict between those who seek change and those who would prefer to preserve received values; and to the extent that each group is partially successful during the lengthy, perhaps even endless, period called transition, we may say that anomie exists. But it is a special kind of anomie that applies to the developing areas, and its remedy is not only in the more efficient government performance, it is also in the continuity of the process of rational ideological change known as modernization. In the long run "modern" ideologies may be less satisfying psychologically (though we doubt the satisfaction produced by premodern Islamic society), but modernization is rational if Middle Eastern governments are to cope with an environment which has pressed in on them for about two centuries. What, however, are the implications of modernization for the political community in the Middle East?

V

Professor Karl Deutsch has been directly concerned with the problems of the growth and change of the political community, and in his search for empirical definitions which will isolate variables capable of measurement, he has worked out an interdisciplinary theory.[65] This theory is permeated by the world view of liberal rationalism into which the central propositions of contemporary American psychology, anthropology, and sociology are incorporated, but only as suggestions of the "black box" variety. Theoretical interest is concentrated upon social structural elements and a rationally conceived political process which can be measured, insofar as the interaction of individuals and groups is definable, in terms of geographical mobility, linguistic assimilation, and meaningful communication. Psychic forces, values, memories, symbols, and ideas are all left in the black box, constituting the machinery by which the aforementioned process is effective in changing either or both social structure and the human ecological and geographical field in which it exists, especially with regard to the composition of the political elite and the nature and scope of the monopoly of coercive and legitimate force.

Instead of approaching the central concepts of social science from the usual point of view of cultural unity, societal integration, political stability, economic dynamic equilibrium, and the healthy personality, Professor Deutsch starts by looking for discontinuities in social phenomena, the marking off of one unified, integrated, stable, equilibrated social unit from another; and he concentrates upon the application of the theory of communication at both its social (public opinion and propaganda) and mathematical (information theory) levels. The discontinuities of communication are the keys to his marking off. One can measure communication and its effectiveness empirically, and in the relation between such measurements and data on population growth, urbanization, literacy, and economic development, one can project the possible future discontinuities of society, culture, and polity. In this theory society, culture, and polity are the derivatives of social communication and social mobilization; as the author puts it, "the distribution of governments is therefore necessary in its essence, though it may well be arbitrary in its accidents." [66] The limits of the polity are determined by the successful "mobilization of consent and power"; [67] and both of these political phenomena are defined in terms of society: "a group of individuals made interdependent by the division of labor," and in terms of culture: "a set of stable habitual preferences and priorities in men's attention and behavior, as well as in their thoughts and feelings." [68] A community is a culture in which communication is facilitated. Political power is comprised of two things, "an inner structure of memories, habits, and values," [69] and the "execution of a will," i.e., the balance of power and consent.

This formulation appears to attribute all social phenomena to culture, or memories, habits, and values, but on closer examination culture and politics are both described in essentially sociological terms. For example, the "inner source of political power" depends upon existing *facilities* for social communication, but such facilities depend as much on the division of labor (institutionalized social roles) as on the ecology of communications. Culture, too, does not presume community, but community depends upon the frequency and mutuality of communication, which turns on a pattern of *interlocking roles*,[70] again a sociological definition. A further sociological emphasis arises when we attempt to understand relative preferences for an Islamic as against a nationalist ideology in a group which is at once a community, a culture, and a society, such as the Arabs claim to be. The answer, if it is not to be a naïve rationalization, depends upon differential levels of communication within classes, as determined by the division of labor.[71]

Since Deutsch is primarily concerned with the analysis of independence movements, he seeks to understand the ways in which ideological and political unity emerge in traditional and fragmented societies. His theory of social mobilization through social communication is essentially a theory of political development, i.e., a change in the nature and scope of political behavior. Two key elements are the circulation of elites and the "awakening" of the masses.[72] Once we have admitted that the process of political development is well under way, as it is in all Middle Eastern countries except those still subject to patriarchal government, the question of the organization and goals of the government depends on the resolution of the struggle among rival elites and "this inevitable question of power."

To restate the comments and conclusions derived from the "theoretical setting" of Professor Deutsch's communications approach, we argue that all of these questions which have a macropolitical relevance—ideological conflict, legitimacy, political institutions in the formal sense, public policy, economic organization —can be seen as the results of the interaction of groups and persons. Insofar as memories, habits, and values inform the behavior of individuals, ideological conflicts or the creation of consensus are concrete manifestations of a broad process of interaction. The working out of this process is infinitely complex, but it may be simplified by treating parallel cases as the broad units of analysis. These parallel cases are not arrived at by personifying ideologies, disembodying processes, or talking of societies "searching" for elites. Instead, we follow Lasswell in postulating that political influence is potentially indistinguishable from any sort of influence over any field of human endeavor.[73] If we are concerned with conflicting ideologies, it is not enough to compare their respective contents, nor is it enough to survey the current state of popular adherence to these, even in connection with gross economic and demographic developmental trends. We must look within the framework of each culture and society for those who are ideologically influential. Where, as in the Middle East, we find this group challenged by a rival ideological elite, we may attempt to cope with the problem of future developments by assessing the respective resources of power of each.

The question of the existence of a unified power elite is really an empirical one,[74] for as the history of Islam shows, despite the diffuseness of interests in traditional social structure and frequent role substitution, influence in various religious, economic, military, and political spheres was characterized by a well-defined division of labor. In the modern Middle East we may discover a tendency to reduce this degree of specialization, and may define the dominant aspect of Middle East politics as a conflict between traditional specialized elites and a modern rival elite.

In the Middle East, for a variety of reasons, it has been a military class which has everywhere emerged as the leading political class, able to apply both coercion and control over communications, subject to the limits of existing facilities and rates of social mobilization. These same limits on the ability of the military elite to manufacture the type of political community they desire were the conditions permitting them to rise to power in the first place. But to know the future of the political community in the Middle East we must first probe more deeply into the character of the military elite.

Most recent discussions of the political role of the military in the Middle East have concentrated upon demonstrating those aspects of social origin, education, and military culture which are common to all members of the military. Some have gone on to illustrate how the organizational structure of these armies and the dominance of a traditional military elite was conducive to revolt. Others have identified the same group with the modernized intelligentsia or "middle class" and have found the sole difference in the ability of the military to capture authority by force. This ability, again, is partly the consequence of their access to weapons and partly due to the relative disorganization of other groups, or, we might say, to the low level of social mobilization. Following this line of reasoning, from the description of the military "type," one would expect that a military coup would seal the fate of the old regime and of the future political community at one and the same time. Instead we find further coups, purges, lack of direction, ideological disunity, and excuses based on the argument for the need for gradualism.

It is not possible to bring about a complete social and economic revolution overnight, and in most cases ideological statements outline no clear-cut goal or a goal for which the requisite resources simply cannot be found. The difficulties in which these circumstances place the new military elites of the Middle East might suggest the possible resurgence of the old elites or provide for the emergence of new political forces. The fact is, however, that neither of these alternatives appears as more than an incipient tendency at the present time in Syria or in Iraq. Better explanations of the contemporary scene and of the means whereby these two incipient tendencies may become effective can be derived from a closer inspection of the "discontinuities" (in Deutsch's phrase) among the military class.

In the first place, as has been so effectively demonstrated in Syria, there are regional discontinuities. Secondly, it must be borne in mind that members of the military retain their religious, ethnic, tribal, and family affiliations. Often their family connections spread throughout a range of economic and professional interests including agriculture, religion, administration, commerce, and the like. There are, further, organizational and clique or friendship-group discontinuities within the military itself. Finally, whether as a consequence of these discontinuities or for other, unfathomable, psychological or intellectual reasons, there are ideological differences.

With this last point we have canvassed the third of three types of theory which have explanatory relevance to the contemporary problem of the political community in the Middle East. The first, the theory of social mobilization through social communication, has relevance to the division of the Middle East into linguistic, sectarian nationalities, especially insofar as Turkey, Iran, Egypt, and Israel are concerned.[75] The second, which we may call the conflict-of-elites theory, tries to explain why it is the military who lead the revolution; it bears upon the difference between those countries which have suffered military coups which have resulted in subordination of the traditional elites and those which have not. In this problem area the critical factor seems to have been control over the military by controlling its composition or by limiting its effectiveness. In a way this theory is skeptical of easy generalizations about the class origins of the military. In Jordan, in Lebanon, in Iran to some extent, and in the patriarchal or traditional systems, the army is heavily admixed with traditional elements. In Lebanon and in Iran under Qavam and Musaddiq, the army was kept weak. It should be borne in mind, as the events in Lebanon in 1958 and in Iran in 1952 demonstrate, that neutralization of the armed forces does not simply leave the traditional elites unchallenged, any more than a military coup eliminates all traditional influence. Nevertheless, traditional and/or parliamentary techniques predominate where the military have been thus neutralized. The neutralization of the military by granting high rewards for loyalty and through stringent security control, without controlling its social and ethnic composition or weakening it as a coercive instrument, appears to be but temporarily effective.

The third theory concerning the discontinuities among the military is derived from our previous discussions, but it has special relevance to the problem of the direction taken after the coup, if there is one. Thus we see the question of fundamentalism versus nationalism in Egypt worked out in the conflict between the Islamic romantics in the Revolutionary Command Council and Rashid al-Mehanna, and only afterwards in the open conflict with the Muslim Brotherhood and the subsequently successful wooing of the traditional ulama.[76] Similarly, the problem of the return of parliamentary government in Egypt was resolved in the Naguib-Nasser conflict, which resulted in a large-scale purge of the military and the bureaucracy and later in significant changes in the access and legitimacy granted to certain secondary interest groups, especially the downgrading of the lawyers and the upgrading of labor. Again, the question of right or left orientation was resolved by retiring the leftist members from the Revolutionary Command Council. Thus gradually did the ruling group gain in control, direction, and homogeneity. There are still some members of the inner ruling group who come from "good families" with substantial landed and commercial interests, but they do not have dominant voices and in any case have been able to transfer their interests to the growing administrative fiefs which have fallen to their lot.

This recitation of salient events in the recent history of Egypt is a success story. That of Turkey, did we know all the details, is doubtless similar. The situation of Iraq recapitulates the early history of the Egyptian coup, though in a far different setting. The second theory, that of the conflict of elites, suggests that the (undifferentiated) military seizes its opportunity and takes power. This assumption disregards the fact that the military are not always organized for a coup. In Turkey, the organization of the officers in the Committee of Union and Progress may be the key to its particularly stable development in the 1930's and 1940's. In Egypt, however, despite the attempt to read back the Free Officers into history,[77] their sole organization appears to have centered around the politicking in the Officers Club election of 1952. We do not know how many groups or cliques of officers, in which services, were thinking of and preparing for a coup in Egypt in 1952 or in Iraq in 1958. The group which pulled it off was widely hailed as fulfilling the wishes of the "military," but the honeymoon was short-lived. Due to the nature of clandestine preparation for a violent coup, a new leadership emerges from obscurity, or rather from among equally ambitious officers. As a matter of fact, leadership must be established after the coup by whatever means are available, including appeals to nonmilitary groups and even to groups outside of the country, so long as the principle of nationalism is not violated, as among the Arab countries. Obviously, the more religiously, linguistically, and ethnically divided is the country, the more discontinuities will be found among the military and the more significant will these discontinuities be. This rule will be mitigated by control over the composition of the military officer corps, as in Jordan, Lebanon, and Iran, but it has worked to a large extent in both Syria and Iraq. In Iraq the non-Arab and non-Sunni element maintained dominance until the successful Ba'thi coup of 1963. The series of Syrian coups and the attempts to win support from either Egypt or Iraq are clear indications of the discontinuities among the military of that country.

The prospects for Arab unity are to be seen in a similar light. The union of Syria and Egypt was largely due to an attempt to seek external support against a multivarious group of opponents. At the level of broad ideological and class orientation of the two military groups, the union was logical and desirable, if economically and geographically—even culturally and socially—difficult or impractical. It was thus an "idealistic" solution, which evolved out of a political impasse in Syria, grave danger arising out of growing Communist influence in the army, expectations of winning secure political positions as rewards, and a wholly unrealistic picture of the character of pragmatic Egyptian nationalism. Now the relevance of the theory of the discontinuities among the military appears decisive. Even the purged Syrian military could not bear their own subordination and the subordination of Syrian political traditions to the headlong program of President Nasser. Syrians had expected to determine their own future to some extent, through influencing the course of events in Egypt, as well as in Syria; instead, they found the Egyptians with a new and firm program developed after the Suez invasion. Union with Syria only complicated matters for Egypt; it did not cause any reconsideration of general policy lines. Syria's tribulations are by no means resolved, but the astonishing rapidity with which the revolution was accomplished points up another limitation on the prospects for Arab unity. That limitation is upon the use of force to achieve unity, for it is apparent that even the Egyptian army, despite Abd al Hakim Amer's recent boast, is not yet capable of operating far from its base and without supply lines over land. The current struggle in Yemen confirms rather than disproves this view. The Iraqi army would appear to be even less capable of applying force to the end of achieving Fertile Crescent unity.

These are the major lines on which the future of the political community in the Middle East will be resolved. There are many more questions of substance and theory, but they are largely subordinate and depend on the progress made toward economic development and social mobilization. Here, we will be satisfied to mention the few that come to mind and that appear worthy of future research. The familiar problems of the unifying capacity of charismatic leadership, the limits of the effectiveness of charisma and its connections with control over communications facilities, has added interest after the events in Syria. The rate of social mobilization under governments seeking to speed this process among tribesmen and villagers is another relevant problem. Are economic or educational programs the more effective? Does successful mobilization result in political pressures for increased traditionalism or for radicalism? What effect does mobilization have upon minorities, irredentism, and sleeping nationalities? What of the Kurds, the Arabs in Iran, and the Persians in Iraq? Above all, well-wishers of the peoples of this area may ask what are the prospects for conventionalizing the political processes comprehended in our three theoretical fields? Under what conditions can we hope for reasonable discussions in a peaceful atmosphere and on the basis of a recognition of these discontinuities as both real and legitimate, with a view to their tentative and possible resolution by agreed procedures? Under such conditions one could then discuss Middle Eastern politics in relation to the theories of functional integration and the process of federalism. Under such conditions one could conceive of peace and cooperation for mutual benefit prevailing in place of internecine and international strife. Then would the peoples of the Middle East have earned the dignity and respect which they seek and which they deserve with all mankind.

NOTES

1. *Mulk.*
2. *Asabiyyah.*
3. *Iradah.*
4. Ibn Khaldun, *Muqaddimah* (Beirut, n. d.), p. 202.

5. *Khair.*
6. *Iradah.*
7. Al-Farabi, *Ara,* ed. Dieterici (Leiden, 1895), p. 54.
8. E. I. J. Rosenthal, *Political Theory in Medieval Islam* (Cambridge, 1958), p. 94.
9. Al-Ghazali, *Al-Iqtisad fi'l-I'tiqad* (Cairo, n.d.), p. 105.
10. G. E. Von Grunebaum, *Islam,* 2nd ed. (London, 1961), p. 127.
11. *Ibid.,* p. 185ff.
12. A. P. D'Entreves, *Natural Law* (London, 1952).
13. Ibn Taiymiyya, *Siyasa Shari'a,* tr. H. Laoust (Beirut, 1948).
14. R. W. and A. J. Carlyle, *A History of Mediaeval Political Theory in the West,* Vol. VI (Edinburgh, 1950), p. 505.
15. *Ibid.,* p. 507.
16. D'Entreves, *Aquinas, Selected Political Writings* (Oxford, 1954). p. xii.
17. *Ibid.,* p. xvii.
18. D'Entreves, *Natural Law,* p. 43.
19. D'Entreves, *Aquinas,* p. xxv.
20. *Ibid.,* p. 109.
21. Carlyle, *op. cit.,* Vol. VI, p. 505.
22. H. Kelsen, *The General Theory of the State* (Cambridge, Mass., 1945).
23. T. Parsons, *The Social System* (Glencoe, 1951); also T. Parsons and E. Shils, *Toward a General Theory of Action* (Glencoe, 1950).
24. T. Parsons, R. F. Bales, and E. Shils, *Working Papers in the Theory of Action* (Glencoe, 1953), pp. 63ff.
25. Rosenthal, *op. cit.,* p. 194f.
26. T. W. Arnold, *The Caliphate* (London, 1923).
27. L. Gardet, *La Cité Musulmane* (Paris, 1954), p. 37.
28. *Ibid.,* p. 267.
29. *Ibid.,* p. 266.
30. W. M. Watt, *Islam and the Integration of Society* (London, 1961), p. 61f.
31. *Ibid.,* p. 284.
32. *Ibid.,* p. 142.
33. *Ibid.,* p. 175.
34. *Ibid.,* p. 175.
35. *Ibid.,* p. 251.
36. *Ibid.,* p. 282.
37. *Ibid.,* p. 207.
38. S. De Grazia, *The Political Community* (Chicago, 1948).
39. *Ibid.,* p. x.
40. *Ibid.*
41. K. Deutsch et al., *The Political Community and the North Atlantic Area* (Princeton, 1957).
42. D. S. Margoliouth, *Mohammedanism* (London, 1911), p. 154f; and H. A. R. Gibb, *Mohammedanism* (London, 1949), p. 107f.

43. Gardet, op. cit., p. 226.
44. H. A. R. Gibb, Modern Trends in Islam (Chicago, 1947), p. 120.
45. P. J. Vatikiotis, "Dilemmas of Political Leadership in the Arab Middle East: The Case of the U.A.R.," American Political Science Review, Vol. LV, no. 1 (March 1961), p. 103; W. Z. Laqueur, Communism and Nationalism in the Middle East (New York, 1956), pp. 5–13.
46. S. G. Haim, "Islam and the Theory of Arab Nationalism," in The Middle East in Transition, ed. by Laqueur (New York, 1958), p. 380f.
47. H. A. R. Gibb, Mohammedanism, p. 108.
48. S. W. Baron, Modern Nationalism and Religion (New York and Philadelphia, 1960).
49. Hasan al-Banna, Al-Rasa'il al-Thalath (Cairo, n.d.), pp. 14–18.
50. Abd al-Rahim al-Fudah, Al-Islam wal-Qawmiyyah al-Arabiyyah (Cairo, 1961), esp. p. 20f.
51. Ahmad Hasan al-Baquri, 'Urubah wa Din (Cairo, n.d.), p. 60f. I am told that al-Baquri is an ex-Ikhwani.
52. G. Antonius, The Arab Awakening (London, 1938).
53. M. al-Ghazali, Haqiqat ul-Qawmiyyah al-Arabiyyah (Cairo, n.d.), p. 9f.
54. Ibid., p. 198.
55. Ibid., p. 202.
56. M. Aflaq, Fi Sabil al-Ba'th (Beirut, 1959), p. 200f.
57. I. Goldziher, Hartzaot al Ha-Islam (Vorlesungen) (Hebrew) (Jerusalem, 1951), p. 211.
58. Mehdi Malikzadeh, Tarikh Inqilab-i-Mashrutiat-i-Iran (Tehran, n.d.), p. 31f.
59. 'Iyadi al-Abd al-'Iyadi, Al-Masihiyyah wal-Qawmiyyah al-'Arabiyyah, Cairo, n.d.
60. L. Binder, Religion and Politics in Pakistan (Berkeley and Los Angeles, 1961), p. 187.
61. L. Binder, "The Transition to Democracy in the Middle East," paper presented at the Annual Meeting of the American Political Science Association, 1960.
62. D. Lerner, The Passing of Traditional Society (Glencoe, 1958), esp. Chapters 2 and 3.
63. See L. Bramson, The Political Context of Sociology (Princeton, 1961).
64. W. Bagehot, The English Constitution (London, 1952), pp. 22 and 157f.
65. K. W. Deutsch, Nationalism and Social Communication (New York, 1953).
66. Ibid., p. 52.
67. Ibid., p. 53.
68. Ibid., p. 62.
69. Ibid., p. 49.
70. Ibid., p. 62, author's italics.
71. Ibid., pp. 16–17 and 75.

72. *Ibid.*, p. 78.
73. H. Lasswell and A. Kaplan, *Power and Society* (New Haven, 1950), Chapter 5.
74. R. Dahl, *Who Governs* (New Haven, 1961).
75. L. Binder, "Prolegomena to the Comparative Study of Middle East Governments," *APSR*, Dec. 1957.
76. Doubtlessly many former members of the Ikhwan are not satisfied with the demise of their organization, but the Egyptian government has made efforts to find positions within its fold for the most prominent of the "respectable" Ikhwan.
77. Anwar al-Sadat, *Revolt on the Nile* (London, 1957).

6

RADICAL-REFORM NATIONALISM

In an earlier chapter the major ideological tendencies in the Middle East were described,[1] and the following is a simplified typology derived from that description: (a) *traditional Islamic,* represented by the ulama; (b) *ijma-modernist,* represented best by older nationalist parliamentarians and wealthy urban classes; (c) *secular-nationalist,* best represented in higher civil servants, higher military officers, the more Westernized and the non-Muslim minorities; (d) *romantic-Islamic-nationalist,* best represented by semi-Westernized lower middle classes; (e) *fundamentalist-Islamic,* whose views are found among the traditional middle class as well as some of the partially Westernized lower middle class; (f) *communist,* a rather exceptional group drawing its adherents from the Westernized and the minorities, but by no means a widely popular tendency. It will readily be noticed that radical-reform nationalism is not included in this listing. It would most probably find its place in group (d), *romantic-Islamic-nationalist;* and it is all of these things and more. This chapter is intended to direct attention to this particular offshoot of Arab romanticism,[2] not because it is any more rational, nor even because its adherents are more numerous, but rather because it seems to be the ideology

154

which currently represents the thinking of dominant groups in Syria, Iraq, and Egypt.

Most discussions of current Arab thought are careful to include a statement to the effect that subdivision into pure categories is the device of the analyst and not of the exponent, who tends to be somewhat eclectic in his presentation. While such statements are generally correct insofar as they refer to any single work, the present writer believes that close examination and reference to active political groups will show that it is really only the romantics who are incorrigibly eclectic, and the least well organized in pursuit of their own interests. Because it is a composite of all the rest, Arab romanticism is nowhere explicitly differentiated in writing, unless one settles for certain expressions of the apologetic movement.[3] Despite this difficulty, it seems that "romanticism" best describes the attitude of most literate Arabs. The ability to read does not presuppose the ability to distinguish theoretical inconsistencies, particularly when such do not appear immediately in the form of a concrete political conflict. Moreover, in the absence of effectively and consistently oriented political organization, it is not surprising that the average literate Arab should nod approvingly at recitations of past Arab glory, lamentations on the decline of the Arabs, and diverse presentations of plausible diagnoses and remedies. Evidently, the average literate Arab believes that most of the diagnoses are correct and most of the remedies apt. Even if this attitude is not logical, it suggests the possible development of a moderate (in terms of domestic politics) consensus. The importance of this possibility is enhanced by the fact that education and literacy have increased at a faster pace than economic development and industrialization. In the long run, the development lag may weaken the consensus, but political events may already be overtaking it. Theoretical niceties aside, should anyone succeed in expressing adequately the romantic attitude and effectively organizing a movement based on such an ideology, he would win a wide following.

While the apologetic movement offers the closest approximation to the romantic approach, it no longer answers the intellectual needs of the literate Arab. In the new radical-reform movement, justifications of Islam have given way to emphasis upon the present low state of Muslims. The issue is no longer one of defending Islam against the direct and indirect attacks of Western imperialists; it is one of gaining international power and realizing the immediate and popular benefits of national self-determination. The old romanticism is not denied; rather, new things are added. The most important of these new additions are neutralism in the cold war, land reform and social welfare measures domestically, and an emphasis on political activism. Political activism is particularly opposed to the apologetic movement, since the latter tended to offer Muslims the complacent assurance of their superiority.[4] Activism is surely a factor which appeals to youth, and among Arab populations those under twenty predominate. Another aspect of radical-reform nationalism which appeals more to younger people than to older, more to intellectuals than to businessmen, and more to the proletariat than to the peasants, is an extreme emphasis on national solidarity, almost to the exclusion of any vestige of individualism. While this is a nationalist rather than a Marxist collectivism, it is often expressed by the term "socialism."

Although social and economic reform under the general name of "populism" was an integral part of the Iraqi Ahali movement ideology in the mid-thirties,[5] and although activism was a prominent part of the ideologies of both the Misr al-Fatat and the Ikhwan al-Muslimun movements,[6] neutralism could not put in an appearance until the opening of the cold war.[7] Some similarity of position may nevertheless be found in the Iraqi Hizb al-Ikha al-Watani and later the Istiqlal party (which supported the Rashid 'Ali al-Jaylani revolt of 1941) and among pro-axis Egyptians.[8] Thus the basic elements of radical-reform nationalist theory have been present in the Middle East for some time. They have probably been best expressed in writing by Michel Aflaq of the Syrian Hizb al Ba'th al 'Arabi al-Ishtiraki[9] and in action by the revolutionary government of Egypt. We shall here be mainly concerned with the literary expression of radical-reform nationalism as it is found in a number of Ba'th publications. But the recent unity negotiations among Syria, Iraq, and Egypt and the Egyptian demand for the dissolution of all political parties suggest the usefulness of comparison with the available writings of the leaders of the Egyptian revolution.

The Ba'th party was founded in 1940, and emerged into open activity in 1943, when Syria achieved formal independence.[10] As a small radical party it had little influence in the Assembly elected in 1943, in which the revived Kutlah al-Wataniyyah predominated. The Ba'th was suppressed along with all other parties by Husni al-Za'im in 1949. In the elections of 1949, after Za'im was removed by a second coup, the Sha'b won a plurality of seats and dominated the Assembly. Somewhat irresolutely, the Sha'b attempted to lay the groundwork for the union of Syria with Iraq. Shishakli's coup, the third in the series, blocked these attempts and drove the Sha'b into opposition to the regime. When Shishakli went on to promulgate a new constitution and to establish a mass national party of his own, both the Ba'th and the Arab Socialist Party of Akram Hawrani attempted but failed in a coup of their own. Michel Aflaq, Salah al-Din al-Bitar, and Akram Hawrani then fled the country and did not return until after the elections of 1953, in which Shishakli's Arab Liberation Rally won 72 of 82 seats. Despite his victory, Shishakli was apprehensive of the activities of the political leaders of nearly all parties except his own, and in January 1954 arrested a large number of them. On February 25, 1954 a fourth military countercoup reinstated the power of the political parties. Shortly thereafter the Ba'th and the Arab Socialist Party merged to form the Ba'th Socialist Party. In the elections held in October 1954 the Ba'th Socialists won 16 seats, the Sha'b won 28, the Hizb al-Watani (descendant of the old Kutlah) won 12, and of the 81 independent and liberal representatives, 30 formed themselves into the United Constitutional Front and 38 formed the Democratic bloc led by Khalid al-'Azm. Altogether, 142 seats were filled—one by Khalid Bakdash, the first avowed communist to succeed in any Middle Eastern election. The election of Shukri al-Quwatli as President tended to weaken the collaboration of the conservative groups. Nevertheless a government comprised of the groupings of independents and the Sha'b was formed in September 1955. The Ba'th, the Hizb al-Watani, and some independents went into opposition. In June 1956 the Ba'th entered a cabinet comprised of all parties, and Salah al-Bitar became the Foreign Minister of Syria.[11] Later the Sha'b, still favoring union with Iraq, was excluded from power, and many of its adherents in Aleppo were arrested, while various agreements preliminary to federation with Egypt were completed. Finally, in January 1958, Bitar, Quwatli, and Colonel Sarraj traveled to Egypt to insist on the immediate union of Syria and Egypt.

The Ba'th, therefore, never gained wide electoral popularity, and it was not above collaborating with certain conservative elements. Perhaps its strongest card was its ability to get along with some of the military. Apparently the Ba'th was genuinely popular among students and the middle and lower classes in both Hama and Hims, and to a lesser extent in Damascus. The prospect of new elections in a year or less could not have been very pleasant to the Ba'th, however. The independents, among whom landlords and tribal leaders predominated, would understandably win the lion's share of seats again; Khalid al-'Azm was preparing to contest the presidency; the reaction of Sha'b supporters would also be hostile; and, finally, the communists were gaining popularity on the strength of recent agreements with the Soviet Union and the Syro-Turkish border crisis. Despite the support of some elements of the military, the army was divided; and Colonel Sarraj, who was apparently in closest sympathy with the Ba'th, was in no position to effect a coup in their favor. It appears, then, that the most congenial solution for the Ba'th was union with Egypt in order to achieve their aims and to hold on to the power which they had at long last achieved. The Ba'th leaders overplayed their hand, and lost all control of developments in Syria to the Egyptians and to their military collaborator. Nevertheless it is significant to note that no explanation of the Syrian role in these events is acceptable without reference to the ideology and program of the Ba'th Socialist Party.

In the fall of 1961, after three and a half years of union, members of the Syrian army forced withdrawal of the Egyptians and jailed Abd al-Hamid al-Sarraj. Civilian government was restored, but the Ba'th, which had been gradually removed from power by Nasser, remained excluded. Though divided among themselves on the question of President Nasser's relation to the Arab national movement, the Ba'this were united in their opposition to the conservative government which followed the dissolution of the union. The Ba'this could not agree upon Nasser's exclusive right to leadership, but all Ba'thi groups agreed that he was on the right path. Most particularly, Michel Aflaq could not be brought to criticism of Nasser despite his own exclusion from influence in Syria. In March of 1963, a coalition of Ba'this and pro-Nasserist officers, encouraged by the Iraqi coup of the previous month and by Egyptian agents, overturned the instable conservative regime and installed a unionist government. In April, Syrian, Iraqi, and Egyptian representatives met in Cairo to lay the foundation for a new United Arab Republic. Despite the rapidly achieved agreement on general principles, implementation of the program broke down over Nasser's demand that all political parties be banned. The Ba'this were not willing to do this, and eventually they forced the pro-Nasserist elements out of the government.

Michel Aflaq is the chief Ba'th ideologist. He founded the party and edited its newspaper. He held political office only for a short period as Minister of Education. We know little more of him except that he studied in France before returning to his home city of Hama to teach secondary school and that he has traveled throughout the Middle East.[12]

To the Western critic, Aflaq's exposition of Arab nationalism presents a hodgepodge of vulgarized European philosophies. There is the usual reflection of Herder in the view that every nation has a peculiar mission to perform and through that mission each will contribute to international harmony. There is the Hegelian emphasis on history and national teleology, but instead of the dialectic, a cyclical concept of alternate glory and decline is substituted. There is a reflection, of course, of Rousseau's general will, but possibly even greater emphasis on his insistence on the relationship of personality and nationality. The Marxist theory of class struggle also appears, and considerable emphasis is placed upon the economic basis of politics, but determinism is rejected and materialism categorically denied. Aflaq's socialism is an aspect of his nationalism in much the same manner as Borochov's Zionism was part of his socialism.[13] And finally, as indicated, there is the vitalism of, say, Bergson.

But to criticize Aflaq in this manner is meaningless. The main point is that his expression of Arab nationalism is unique among

Arabs. If European ideas have influenced his thought, the cause is not to be sought in his European education, but in the relevance of these notions to the problems which Aflaq sought to solve. One of the most important of these problems, interestingly enough, was the maleficence of Western philosophy for young Arab students.

I THEORY

In a recent investigation of some contemporary Arab nationalist theories, Hakim Zaki Nusaibeh digresses from his main theme to discuss the question of the need for a nationalist ideology.[14] His answer is that such an ideology is necessary and should be so developed as to unify the great majority of divergent views among the Arabs. An efficient Arab nationalist ideology should include a description of the content of Arabism or the definition of an Arab, should assume that the Arabs have a common national interest, and should emphasize the positive aspects of nationalism against the contemporary revulsion therefrom. Much of Nusaibeh's work is a critique of a number of proffered theories emphasizing the nature of Arabism, and he concludes in general agreement with most of his predecessors that the Arabs are characterized by a common language, a common historical tradition, and a common interest, and adds that they should adhere to a common constitutional-democratic political ideology. Common religion, common race, and geographical contiguity are not included. The first two were specifically rejected except insofar as Islam may be incorporated into the common historical tradition, because of the problem of the Christian Arab minority and the admitted racial diversity of Arabic-speaking people. The third was omitted for reasons that may only be inferred: the problem of whether or not Egyptians are Arabs, or, more likely, the overwhelming emphasis on the subjective characteristics of nationality. Emphasis on subjective or "spiritual" characteristics is a common feature of ideological and religious movements which tend to consider conversion as separate from its environmental context, i.e., from social and economic factors. Subjective nationalism is similarly prevalent where insistence upon objective characteristics presents too many difficulties, and also where a liberal, nondeterministic outlook predominates.

Against this sort of theoretical background Aflaq's views stand out in vehement contrast. The first of his essays in a small book circulated in Iraq [15] begins with an attack on abstract thinking and theoretical definition.[16] Although written long before Nusaibeh published his analysis, Aflaq's essay seems to be directed against just such efforts: ". . . let not those who pursue foreign nationalist theories and philosophies think . . . that they can compound Arab nationalism of them . . . , their constructions are ridiculous regardless of how they dress them up." [17] Pure theory, he holds, dissolves things of their flesh and blood and divests them of their taste and color; it leads to inaccuracy and tends to represent opposites as similar, because it reduces real things to mere words.[18] A living thing defies analysis, is completely unique in its essence.[19] In an eloquent and revealing passage Aflaq asserts that Arab nationalism is not theoretical, but it gives rise to theories; that it is not the product of thought, but it rather nourishes thought; that it has not been contrived by art, but is the source and inspiration of art; nor is there any conflict between [Arab nationalism] and liberty, because it *is* liberty so long as it proceeds along its true path and realizes its full potentialities.[20]

In a direct attack on the thesis that a nationalist ideology is necessary, Aflaq insists that the Arabs have not become nationalists because they have embraced nationalist theory. Nationalism is neither theory, nor love, nor faith, nor will, although all these are necessary conditions of nationalism.[21] These attacks on "abstract" theory are meant to achieve much the same things that Nusaibeh and others desired. They are aimed against those who, educated in the West, tend to reject nationalism as a narrow and harmful ideology. Aflaq is also concerned lest emphasis on theory increase divisions among the Arabs. But he goes beyond this in insisting somewhat contradictorily that nationalism is love,[22] that it is an identity as intimate as one's name or physiognomy.[23]

At first sight all this looks as though Aflaq is striving to reject the objective or rational approach to nationalism, but it is evident that he is not merely insisting on subjective nationalism. Arab nationalism exists quite apart from anyone's positive acceptance thereof, whether for rational or sentimental reasons. Nationalism is like one's name or visage, bequeathed to him even before birth. Just as it is vain that a man wastes his life in regret that he was not born into some other family or that he did not have some other appearance, so is it wasteful if he tries to free himself of the bonds of his nation.[24] One's fate must be accepted, and one's destiny fulfilled to the greatest extent possible.

If subjectivism is rejected and nationalism imposed upon a group, surely that group must be defined in some objective manner. Despite his opposition to any effort to resolve Arab nationalism into its various components, we shall see that Aflaq does have a number of objective criteria of Arabism, the most important of which is related to the historical development of the Arab community. The important divergence of emphasis here must be understood in another sense. Contrary to the orientation of most theorists, Aflaq has no qualms about his own Arabism, or about the absolute worth of Arabism. Arab nationalism must not be measured by Western models. Above all, he has departed from the apologetic tradition. "We do not proclaim that we are better, but that we are different!" [25] Arab nationalism needs no justification, and hence needs no theory.

Nationalism is not theory, but it gives rise to theories. That is to say, Arab nationalism may not be subject to rational analysis, but there are logical consequences of the incontrovertible fact of Arabism. For Aflaq these consequences are determined by the contemporary degradation of Arab civilization and by the essential spirit of that civilization. The Arab decline must be overcome by an active movement based upon an ideology which represents the true spirit of Arabism. At one point, Aflaq is so carried away by his emphasis upon the importance of this ideology that he states that the nation is not a numerical group, but rather an ideology which is incarnate in that group as a whole or in part of it.[26] The minimization of numbers and the phrase "part of it" indicate again the relative unimportance of subjectivism, despite the apparently contrary implication of ideology. The nation has an ideology even if only a minority of its members adhere to or recognize that ideology. Conceivably that ideology might exist, and hence the nation, without anyone knowing or accepting it.[27] It is not difficult to derive from this theme a trenchant collectivism, and an authoritarianism which forces men to be free or compels them to realize their true destinies regardless of their conscious beliefs. Indeed, the problem is primarily that of making the Arabs aware of their true nature. But more of this later; suffice it for the present to record that Aflaq denies rational theorizing only insofar as it may affect the basic premises of his argument. The premise is to be accepted on faith; the rest follows logically.

The leaders of the Egyptian revolution were men of action and not theoreticians, yet one may note certain parallels with the tendencies of Aflaq in some of their writings. In the first place, the members of the Egyptian Revolutionary Command Council did not self-consciously question their nationalism. In his sole literary effort, President Abd al-Nasser would prefer to avoid using the word philosophy, for he is not sure where it might lead.[28] In stating this preference it seems obvious that he is wisely avoiding pretensions of the sort which are Aflaq's element. But Abd al-Nasser does not therefore deny that there is a philosophy of the revolution. He suggests that scholars must first investigate closely the history which led up to that revolution before its ideology may be expounded. Thus his position is not dissimilar from that of Aflaq. Nationalism itself is not brought into question, and certain logical consequences must be derived therefrom in accordance with a systematic historiography. Anwar al-Sadat concurs even more strongly with Aflaq's basic position: "I have always mistrusted theories and purely rational systems." [29] President Naguib's views are revealing when he explains that his differences with Abd al-Nasser were concerned with the "philosophy of the revolution." Since neither of them is a philosopher, Naguib would prefer to say the "psychology of the revolution." As Naguib puts it, the real controversy was over how far the revolutionary government should go in alienating various Egyptian classes and groups in attempting to achieve its goals.[30] From this, one may infer that Abd al-Nasser's views seem to accord with those of Aflaq again; that is, the philosophy of the revolution exists without being made explicit, and its conclusions ought to be imposed on the nation, even against its apparent will.

II ARABISM

Despite the fact that Aflaq vehemently castigates those who would define Arab nationalism and abstract its component elements, and even though he stresses ideas which have strong subjective connotations, his is an objective theory. Arabs are not free to be nationalists or not. Aflaq openly deplores the tendency of the Western educated to think of nationalism as only one possible ideology, whose superiority must be rationally proved. For Aflaq the basis of Arab nationalism is existential, not rational; hence, all Arabs ought to be nationalists. Furthermore, as we shall see, those Arabs who are aware of their own identity and of the consequences thereof must act as a vanguard of the nation. The role of the vanguard is to mobilize the nation behind the national idea, and to lead in the fulfilment of the national mission. Those whom the vanguard is to influence and those upon whom the national mission is incumbent are the Arabs. There is no room here for individual preference. Arab nationalism is not to be taken up or put aside like the latest fashion in clothing. Consequently, Aflaq's theory requires objective criteria for determining who is or who is not an Arab.

This logical consequence is never quite faced. The difficulty arises precisely because Aflaq is opposed to intellectual hairsplitting, because his target group have few doubts about their nationality, and because he desires to comprehend the largest possible group within his nation. This difficulty leads to a contradiction of sorts. In the constitution of the Ba'th party it is clearly laid down that an Arab is one whose language is Arabic, who lives in the Arab country, *and who believes in his connection with the Arab nation.*[31] Despite the subjective aspects of this definition and Aflaq's refusal to deal directly with the objective definition which his theory requires, it is possible to find some indirect evidence of his views on the "content" of Arabism.

At different places, Arabism is described as a living memory,[32] as love,[33] as similar to a family name or one's physiognomy,[34] as meaning optimism and the belief that every Arab has a capacity for good,[35] as having an ideology,[36] and as a means of realizing the mission of the Arab nation.[37] These are all poetic and powerful passages, and we may assume that their possibly contradictory emphasis is the by-product of the literary effect which Aflaq desired to achieve and his unconcern with thoroughgoing logic. But two additional references to the content of Arabism are more important. The first parallels the provision of the Ba'th constitution and similarly regards the problem of the marginal Arab. One of the interpretations of the manner in which nationalism is an expression of love states that Arab nationalism has a generous spirit and opens its ranks to whoever was associated with the Arabs in their history, to whoever lived in the atmosphere of their language and culture, and to whoever became an Arab in thought and feeling.[38] The second statement deals less with the marginal Arab, and emphasizes the unity of (racial) origin of the Arabs. The nucleus was then nourished and embellished by a common language, spirit, history, and culture. The decline of the Arabs begins when the common origin loses its importance.[39]

Both references recognize the fact the Arabs of today are not of pure racial stock, that Hamitic, Alpine, Armenoid, Negro, Aryan, and Mongolian infiltrations and admixtures have taken place. Both statements take it for granted that mediaeval Islamic culture was an Arab culture, even though not in its highest and purest form.[40] The first statement would bar none of the marginal Arabs, even if somewhat condescendingly; the second clearly regrets the corruption of Arab racial purity, even if not so strongly. Aside from the problem of common racial origin, both statements agree that Arabism includes a common history, a common language, a common culture, and a common spirit or common thought and feeling. A comparison of the two passages proves that there is implicit in Aflaq's theory an objective definition of the Arab nation which can be broken down into several components. Even more significant, however, is the fact that subjective nationalist feeling is important only in the case of the marginal Arabs, i.e., those who lived with the Arabs, not the Arabs themselves. The constitution of the Ba'th party goes on to say that those who do not identify themselves with the Arabs will be expelled from the Arab homeland.[41]

Until recently, Arab nationalist theorists have agitated themselves with the question of whether or not Egyptians were Arabs. The short-lived union of Egypt and Syria would seem to have settled the question once and for all, even if Egyptian membership in the Arab League did not. In his pamphlet on Arab resurrection, Aflaq does not specifically include Egyptians as Arabs, but the Ba'th constitution, in laying down the boundaries of the Arab homeland, does include all of North Africa to the Atlantic. In his philosophy of the revolution, Abd al-Nasser has an interesting view of the Arab relation of Egypt. The Arab sphere is but one of the three within which the Egyptian role is to be played. The Arab sphere is, however, the most important of the three, and some feeling of kinship is evident in his treatment. Despite the prior place he gives to the Arab sphere and his own metaphysical expression, it is significant that he emphasizes the rather practical point that the Arab area is united, particularly in that the same forces are united against it, i.e., the forces of imperialism.[42]

Naguib, like Abd al-Nasser, writes of the Arab connection of Egypt only as a matter of foreign policy. His only important reference to relations with the other Arab states is in his rather proud description of the program of the Liberation Rally. The eighth and the ninth of eleven points provide for friendly relations with all Arab states and a regional pact to increase the influence of the Arab League.[43]

The impression which is derived from these two books, that the leaders of the Egyptian revolution considered themselves Egyptians first and Arabs second, that they sought to solve first Egyptian problems and then Arab problems, rather than solve Egyptian problems by means of Arab nationalist activity, and that relations with other Arab states were primarily a matter of foreign policy for them, is corroborated by the absence of any important statement of the matter by al-Sadat, and by the texts of the few circulars cited by al-Barawy.[44] In these circulars, issued by the Free Officers, the other Arab states are mentioned in only two places, and Arab nationalism is never discussed. The two relevant statements oppose the MEDO proposal of the Western powers as an imperialist device, and the Arab Collective Security Pact because it was negotiated while Britain retained important preferential rights in Egypt, Jordan, and Iraq.[45]

III ISLAM

Islam remains a living ideology in the Middle East. Even though none of the Middle Eastern states conforms explicitly to the classical conception of an Islamic polity, neither does any, except Lebanon and Turkey, reject the legitimization of an established religion. The importance of religion in the governmental structure of Middle Eastern states tends to be thought of as a negative function of Western influence or the modernity of political outlook of the governing elite. But religion is not simply inversely proportional to Westernism, nor is nationalism directly proportional thereto. Egypt, which most certainly has a more highly developed nationalism than Syria, has had a much more severe religious problem. It is therefore possible that the active and efficient influence of religion varies directly with the influence of nationalism. The problem of a vigorous religious movement is in the opposition of some versions of Islamic fundamentalism to nationalism. In Pakistan, the Jama'at-i-Islami was outspoken in its opposition to nationalism. In Egypt, the Muslim Brethren emphasized anti-imperialism and condoned nationalism. Nevertheless, it is quite clear that the leadership of both groups was essentially reactionary and a potential rival of the Westernized elites which led both countries. The vigor of both groups and the wide popular respect in which they are held is evidence of the continued loyalty of Middle Easterners to Islam. Moreover, the Arabs, the Pakistanis, and even the Iranians have explicitly rejected the Turkish solution. Arab nationalists have agreed that their nationalism must accommodate Islam. The ulama seem prepared to help in finding some practical compromise. Heretofore nationalism, and particularly nationalist theory, was the private preserve of the better educated and the highly Westernized. The key to popularizing either nationalism or Islamic modernism of any kind is to include some of both in one's doctrine. But there remains the problem of which is the more important.

In Aflaq's treatment of this basic Middle Eastern ideological problem, nationalism is superior to Islam, Arab nationalism comprehends Islam, and it is possible to infer that Islam is one of those objective characteristics constituting the Arab nation. While Aflaq's views on Islam are definite, he does not consider the religious problem significant enough to require separate treatment. His references to Islam are all secondary to the mainstream of his thought, except insofar as Islam is an aspect of the historical heritage of Arabism.

At one point, Islam is recognized as an alternative ideology, at least for those who attempt to define Arab nationalism in terms of abstract theory.[46] But Aflaq rejects this view, insisting rather that Arabism comprehends Islam.[47] He does not assert that nationalism always comprehends religion; such would be the view of the abstract theorist: "But let us forget terminology and call things by their real names. Let us substitute Arabism for nationalism and Islam for religion; then the problem may be seen in a new light. Islam was created out of the heart of Arabism. It is impossible for them to conflict." [48] This is Aflaq's answer to the frequent questioning of students: "does it deny religion . . . ?" [49]

But the problem may not be disposed of so easily, for there are conflicting views of the nature of Islam. Which is the Islam which finds its place in Arab nationalism? Before answering that question, Aflaq is at pains to point out which is the Islam that does not accord with his Arabism. Neither the traditional nor the fundamentalist view of Islam is acceptable. Aflaq's nationalism emphasizes historical development, and the changed requirements of the times. The nation developed in history; at one stage its nature was determined by Islam, but this tendency led to certain difficulties. Islam must develop along with Arabism. Both stem from the heart and both proceed from the will of God. Each supports the other and embraces the other, "especially because religion resembles the genius of nationalism and flows along with its nature." [50] However, neither nationalism nor Islam (by implication) should be enclosed "in a framework of narrow definition as did the ulama al-Kalam in the old days. . . ." [51] And again,

Arabism denies the necessity of reviving the useless things of the past.[52] The past is studied not that it may be saved, but so that it may inform the actions of the present. Arabism is progressive; it reaffirms its heritage by rediscovering it, not by copying it.[53]

These statements indicate that Aflaq is opposed to both traditionalists and fundamentalists, but they do not clarify his position on *ijma* modernism. As a matter of fact Aflaq nowhere discusses the criteria for the development or reform of Islam. The emphasis of what he does say leads to the conclusion that Islam is to be reformed and developed in accordance with the development of Arab nationalism. That is, unlike its position for the *ijma* modernists, legal theory is of slight importance to his system. Islam, like nationalism, is a spirit and a memory.

In a discussion of the Arab mission and its relation to Arab history, Aflaq, with no prior indication, states that he has related the Arab mission, which is built on the "principles of humanity," to religion.[54] The abruptness with which he introduces the subject renders it somewhat obscure. However, it is probable that Aflaq means this mission to be, partly at least, the contribution of the Arab nation to the world. The vague term "principles of humanity" recurs frequently, and indicates recognition of some value greater than, or at least coordinate with, nationalism. Humanity can only be served through nationalism. The two may be in opposition in abstract theory, but Arab nationalism can bridge the gap to the principles of humanity, because it comprehends or is characterized by the universal religion of Islam. Thus it may be possible that Aflaq believes that Islam is merely the Arab version of certain higher universal ethical concepts, which he calls the principles of humanity.

We have already referred to Aflaq's view that a certain stage in Arab history may be called an Islamic period. Islam revolutionized the life of the Arabs, for it taught that values were no longer to be derived from the group. Values emerging from above the group and the individual alike counterbalanced the collectivism of the earlier period of ignorance and thereby brought harmony between the individual and the group. Islam gave the Arabs a sense of destiny, and turned them from being exclusively concerned with the present. The approval of the group no longer satisfied Arabs; they had to seek some higher goal. In the place of external anxiety, there was substituted a new inner anxiety.[55]

This is certainly a most favorable view of Islam. However, it is to be noted that this view is a very general one. No specific provision of Islamic law is stressed. The points emphasized are individualism and otherworldliness. Islamic political institutions and ideas are omitted. Later on, both individual freedom and "antimaterialism" are included in Aflaq's idea of the Arab spirit, but within the context of his discussion of Arab history, the Islamic period and especially its social contribution had certain untoward effects. "This is the period in which the Arabs moved from ignorance to Islam . . . distinctions among individuals were of little importance, and not long thereafter the Arabs were drowned in the bottomless sea of various foreign peoples." [56]

This is the beginning of the decline of the Arabs both nationally and morally. The importance of this interpretation cannot be too highly stressed. A key to differentiating among the multitude of Middle Eastern ideologies is almost invariably to be found in the theorist's explanation of the "decline." Of equal significance for an understanding of Aflaq's attitude toward Islam is his denial of its moral effectiveness. Not only did the Arabs lose their national feeling, but they returned to their antisocial habits of the period of ignorance. "Wherever national life does not prevail according to its true form, then narrow individualism and narrow-mindedness return." [57] Thus, by an indirect and complex path, Islam has become the cause of the decline of the Arabs. Islam has indeed contributed certain values to Arabism, but it is not in itself a foundation for individual morality.

Though Islam has been severely damned with very faint praise, we have seen that it has not been denied. Arab nationalism comprehends Islam and is not in conflict therewith. The dissemination of Islam is part of the Arab mission, but this Islam is no more than knowledge of the hereafter, the one God, and the notion of individual salvation. This Islam has no social ethic. The consequence of this theoretical approach is to render Islam subordinate to Arab nationalism, but it also tends to derogate the Arabism of non-Muslims.

Egyptian nationalists could not so easily dispose of the religious problem. Their views accord generally with those of Aflaq, but they are aware of other dangers besides those of rigid anachronistic authoritarianism. For years members of the Free Officers groups had maintained contact with the Muslim Brethren. Extensive cooperative efforts had been planned, and when all political parties were abolished the Brethren were permitted to continue. The final break came only after members of the Brethren had attempted to assassinate Abd al-Nasser. The dissolution of the Brethren in Syria in 1958 was a matter of course and was obstructed by nothing more substantial than a plaintive protest.[58] Even before the open clash with the Brethren, the Free Officers expressed their unwillingness to share power with them in the incident of Rashid al-Mehanna. Nevertheless, the Free Officers respected Islam, and were at once admiring and suspicious of the Brethren.

Anwar al-Sadat was for many years the contact man between the Officers and the Ikhwan.[59] His reports on meetings with Hasan al-Banna and intrigues with him and the Germans make interesting reading, but cannot obscure the fact that much mutual suspicion existed. Except for the ill-fated attempts to cooperate with the Germans, no combined efforts were ever carried out. Finally, Sadat's own version of his activities on the day of the revolution indicate that he was not completely in the confidence of the rest of the Revolutionary Command Council, or at least that he was not an important figure in the revolution.

Sadat sums up the attitude of the Officers toward the Brethren as follows: ". . . in its early days, the Muslim Brotherhood seemed a useful ally. . . . The Brotherhood opened its doors to good and bad indiscriminately. . . . [It] was to become an organization of unbounded fanaticism. . . ." [60] When Sadat asked Hasan al-Banna in 1942 to cooperate in a coup, the latter replied enigmatically and suggested that the two groups join. Sadat objected "that the ideology of the Brotherhood was essentially different from ours. . . ." [61]

Naguib is explicit in asserting that the Revolutionary Command Council sought to establish a secular republic. Col. Rashid Mehanna, as he put it, desired to go back to the theocratic state of Salah al-Din.[62] But it was not the intention of the RCC to do away with religion. When the old constitution was abolished on

December 10, 1952, the RCC announced its intention of providing in the forthcoming constitution for the establishment of Islam as the state religion, with full freedom of worship.[63] The constitution of 1956 reflects these views,[64] even though the provisional constitution merely provided for freedom of religion.[65] The principles of union upon which the new United Arab Republic of Egypt, Syria, and Iraq was to be founded include a similar article.

In Abd al-Nasser's discussion of three spheres surrounding Egypt, he refers last of all (after the Arab and the African spheres) to an Islamic sphere. His emphasis on Islam seems a matter of foreign policy, not of ideology. In his suggestion for an Islamic world parliament, he makes it clear that the resultant cooperation should not proceed beyond the limits of the loyalty of each to his own country. Despite the generally identical attitude of Naguib and Abd al-Nasser their writings present an interesting contrast with regard to the meaning of the Hajj. Naguib records that his second Hajj meant the renewal of his faith in the brotherhood of man.[66] Abd al-Nasser records the more jarring opinion that the only *raison d'etre* of the Hajj is to serve as an Islamic world parliament which "should become an institution of great political power. . . ."[67]

Despite the variety of emphasis and expression in the writings of these men, they all seem to be in general agreement. Aflaq and Abd al-Nasser put nationalism above Islam and would have Islam serve nationalism. Neither excludes or opposes Islam.

IV HISTORY

The ideological core of romantic nationalism is history. History comprehends institutionalized religion, history overcomes the problem of racial diversity, history defeats logic and defies "abstract theory," history affects the individual regardless of his conscious will, history emphasizes the collective character of the group, history foreshadows destiny, and history is a nonrational but nevertheless objective basis of nationalism. Arab nationalists are particularly prone to making sweeping statements on their own history, and together these comprise the Arab national myth.

Aflaq's theory takes advantage of all the facilities of the historical approach; he even offers an outline of a national myth himself.

Our discussion of Aflaq's notion of history falls into two parts, first his philosophy of history and second his sketch or interpretation of Arab history and the lesson derived therefrom. His philosophy of history is not presented as a coherent system, but some insights may be gathered from different essays. History is seen alternatively as being composed of cycles or of stages. The cyclical emphasis appears when Aflaq stresses the past glory of the Arabs and the importance of returning to it.[68] The same notion is reflected in the Ba'th constitution, which notes that the Arabs have suffered numerous historical reverses but have always recovered and risen to great heights thereafter.[69] The cycle is comprised of a series of rises and declines. The stages may be no more than phases of the cycle, but Aflaq insists that the present generation must judge the past as an historian would.[70] Its judgment must be interpretative, not imitative. The Communists reject the past in its entirety; those who admire the West reject only the Arab past; but the Arab resurrectionists "recognize the past without considering it perfect; they regard it as a stage to which return is impossible, but which is capable of influence, and which has a vital and intimate connection with the present. . . . We look to the past to benefit from it and not to benefit it." [71] Doubtless this stand accords with Aflaq's attitude toward traditional Islam which is typically related to a rigid return to the past.

The stages of history are closely related to the circumstances of the nation, that is, the nation as the subject of history. Aflaq seems to deny that there is any meaning in the idea of universal history. The mistake of the admirers of the West is that they take the historical development of the West as their own. Even though nations exist at the same time, their circumstances are different, and different actions are required of each.[72] It is the Arabs' misfortune to be living during a stage of decline rather than during the age of Walid (Umayyad) or al-Ma'mūn (Abbasid).[73] The present circumstances of the Arab nation contrast sharply with their own past and the present position of the European nations.[74] Recognition of these contrasts will cause the Arab awakening and their realization that the present stage is one of national struggle.[75]

History shows that the Arab mission was fulfilled only when national unity was maintained.[76] We shall return to the problem of the Arab mission, but here we may cite the manner in which Aflaq gets his view of history, mission, and Arab history together: ". . . the mission must be understood as a tendency and a propensity rather than a specific goal. To illustrate the discussion of the Arab mission in the past, we must draw a quick sketch of the major periods . . . of the life of the Arab people. . . ." [77]

The first of the periods discussed by Aflaq is the Jahiliyyah, the period of ignorance before Islam.[78] It was during this period that Arabs were united in a homogeneous group. Socially, the group dominated the individual. Culturally, the Jahili expressed himself in poetry and the language of the common people; the scholastic argumentation (*kalam*) of the middle ages was nonexistent. Ideologically, the Arabs of that period had no conception of the past or the future, only of the chain of the present. They had no notion of destiny and no understanding of the meaning of existence.

The coming of Islam revolutionized the social and intellectual life of the Arabs.[79] Values were now determined by a force above individual and group alike. The interests and values of individual and collectivity were harmonized. The Arab acquired a conception of destiny (hereafter?) and of the meaning of existence. Past and present were alike evil, places of trial over which the individual could pass only by "a bridge of effort and piety." The externalized concerns of the Arab changed to an inner anxiety over salvation. The approval of the tribe was no longer a source of security to the individual, who now sought to fulfill God's will.

As Islam spread among non-Arab peoples, and national differences were submerged, the Arabs lost their feeling of national unity and returned to their Jahili loyalties.[80] They engaged in tribal battles, and a narrow selfishness developed. Weakness followed this period, and the Arabs began to lose their national homogeneity.

This is certainly a confused passage. National unity supposedly emerged from the Jahiliyyah, yet here tribalism is stressed, rather than national homogeneity, as a characteristic of the pre-Islamic period. Evidently the meaning is rather that homogeneity developed during the Jahiliyyah, unity only during the early phase of Islam; later on some Arabs were submerged in the multinational Islamic society, while others, less advanced, reverted to tribalism. How tribalism is to be equated with individualistic selfishness (the bane of nationalism) is unclear.

As this development continued, values came to be determined by individuals and in accordance with personal power and rank. The equality of the Jahiliyyah passed away even as did the equality of Islam. Selfishness and competition prevailed under the rule that might is right.

After discussing the mediaeval situation of the Arabs, so similar to his view of its present stage, Aflaq goes back to sum up his interpretation.[81] This time he praises the vitality of the Jahiliyyah but deplores its excessive submission to tradition and its restriction of individualism. In early Islam, the true Arab ideal was realized for a short time; then came the decline. This short review is important because it illustrates the manner in which the romantic approach to Islam is worked into nationalist theory. The framework remains one of national history, and Islam is no more than a catalyst which brings out aspects of Arabism but does not change them.

The present period is one in which the Arab renaissance is beginning.[82] But this renaissance is endangered by the Jahili spirit, which may result in the tyranny of the group over the individual. Some higher authorization of values than that of group or individual is needed. "We believe that Arabism is above everything in the sense that it is above well-being and selfishness . . . but we believe that one thing is above Arabism, and that is truth. Arabism must be bound to a permanent principle. . . . Our slogan ought to be: Truth above Arabism so that the union of Arabism with truth may become a reality." [83]

It is difficult to know what to make of this passage. From the context and by obvious omission, Aflaq is not equating truth with Islam. Moreover, we have already seen that he rejects abstract theory and insists that the nation is the medium of the realization of all values. Is it conceivable that Arabism and truth can conflict? Perhaps the following passage will throw some light on the problem: "By Arabism they mean what is determined by the group. . . ." The antidemocratic implications of this statement will be taken up below.

Anwar al-Sadat's views on history, tradition, and Islam accord with those of Aflaq: ". . . respecting the customs of the people does not mean chaining them down to a dead past, it means respecting the essential and invisible continuities in a nation's life." [84] Al-Barawy accepts the idea of nationalism, but his is a Marxist approach to history. Naguib is much more concerned with explaining his own actions than with developing an interpretation of Arab history. However, President Abd al-Nasser does elaborate an historical sketch which is in conflict with that of Aflaq, in that it discusses Egyptian history rather than Arab history, and also because he holds a different view of the cause of the decline. In his sketch, Abd al-Nasser is concerned with explaining the lack of popular response to the revolution. After mentioning the strategic importance of Egypt, he briefly discusses the Pharaonic period, Greek cultural influences, the Roman conquest, the Islamic conquest, then the beginning of the dark ages for Egypt with the Crusades, after which Egypt was subjected to Mongolian and Caucasian (Mamluke) tyrants. Under these tyrants Egypt stagnated; the Mamlukes fought one another while the people stood aside unconcerned. Since that time the response of the Egyptian people has been the same dissociation from the ruling group. Under Muhammed 'Ali renewed contact was made with Europe, but this policy was overdone. The problem of the present is to unite the people behind a government which pursues the national interest, and to catch up with modern civilization. Like Aflaq, he says of the Egyptian nation: "Our destiny it is never to have fallen but that we rose again." [85]

It is possible to conclude that Aflaq and the Egyptian revolutionaries are in general agreement on their philosophies of history to the extent that these are made explicit. They are also in agreement that the present emerges from the past but that the past must not determine the ideology or the practice of the present. There is an important divergence over the conception of the nation which is the subject of a continuous history. Abd al-Nasser, moreover, is proud of the Pharaonic and Greek heritages of Egypt, although he blames the West for much. He does not ascribe the decline of Egypt to a mingling with non-Arabs, but to the domination of non-Egyptians. Furthermore, he ignores the pre-Islamic Arab period and both the Umayyad and Abbasid Caliphates. The Egyptians, after all, were some of the non-Arab peoples among whom Aflaq's Arabs lost their identity.

V MISSION

The national mission is of all the concepts of romantic nationalism least amenable to logical analysis. Despite the difficulty of this notion, it is almost perennially recurrent, and its frequency shows that it fulfills an important theoretical purpose. We have already seen that Aflaq insists upon the validity of the idea of nationalism regardless of the intrinsic value of the nation or its tradition. He also holds that nationalism is the constitutive principle of society, civilization, or humanity. In other words, value is created by, or by means of, the nation. The idea of a national mission, vague though it may be, seems to tie together a number of loose theoretical ends.

In the first place, the mission is another way of saying that the Arab national tradition is of universal validity, for there is nothing which is universal which is not also national. In the second place, the mission is a claim upon all other peoples to recognize Arab nationalism. In the third place, the mission denies that one may be complacent in one's Arabism; the mission is the basis of nationalist activism. Finally, the mission seems to be an ideological device by which the past imposes obligations upon the present and future. To put the matter simply, the idea of a national mission answers the question: "Yes, but so what?"

The eternal Arab mission holds a central place in Aflaq's thought, and in the constitution of the Ba'th party. In the Ba'th constitution the single Arab nation is described as having an eternal mission, ". . . manifested in the shaping of a perfected regeneration through the stages of bitter history, leading to the reform of human existence, spearheading human progress, and increasing harmony and cooperation among nations." [86] The consequences of this principle are two: (a) opposition to colonialism and support for all peoples struggling for freedom, and (b) the mutual responsibility of all humanity for human welfare and civilization.[87] The mission is related to the special character of the Arab peoples, which is distinguished in its special merit, revealed in its successive awakenings, and marked by the abundance of its vitality and inventiveness and by its tendency toward reform, and its resurgence is ever related to the growth of individual freedom and the (increased) scope of the harmony between (individual freedom) and national welfare.[88] The Arab mission bridges the gap between the individual and the nation, and the gap between the nation and all humanity. It therefore answers the criticisms that nationalism is collectivist, suppressing individual freedom, or that it is exclusive, claiming superiority over other nations. At least this is true of Arab nationalism, because of the content of Arab history. Insofar as the mission is rooted in history, or at least in the Ba'th conception of history, the nationalist movement is almost guaranteed of success, for the Arab nation, whenever it was united, has always achieved its mission in the past during its successive reawakenings.[89] Unfortunately, Aflaq fails to describe the time and circumstances of all those past reawakenings.

The foregoing discussion suggests that the concept of the national mission is a theoretical device which serves to solve a number of problems which derive from the absence of logic in romantic nationalism, from the vulnerability of nationalist theory to liberal criticism, and from the unsatisfied character of Arab nationalism. But the word "mission" itself seems to indicate that some specific program is to be deduced from Arab history. There is, however, no such program, and this is the real difficulty with the mission concept. The mission is in fact tautological, because it cannot be achieved until Arab nationalism is "satisfied," but once nationalist aspirations are realized, the mission is realized. Consequently, the mission is nothing more than the satisfaction of the first principle of the Ba'th constitution: "The Arabs are a single nation having a natural right to exist within a single state and (having a right) to realize its capabilities." [90]

That the Arab mission is, in fact, the realization of this principle is substantiated by Aflaq's treatment of this issue. Aflaq is at pains to point out that the mission is not a concrete or a specific thing to be realized at a particular time.[91] The mission is a propensity or a tendency [92] or simply faith.[93] It is self-evident, and a necessary complement of nationhood.[94] The mission is capable of immediate realization in the Arab struggle for independence, for through unaided struggle the Arabs "will learn anew the meaning of truth, righteousness, purity, work, sacrifice, clear thinking, . . . and free creativity . . ." [95] After "illustrating" the nature of the Arab mission by reference to the brief historical sketch which we have already described, Aflaq goes on to discuss the Arab mission today: ". . . that the Arabs rise to bring about the resurrection of their nation; that is the best they can contribute to humanity. . . . The eternal Arab mission is in understanding this present time . . . and requiting its needs. . . . Then they will not merely have built their nation and created a national character, but they will contribute to all humanity the result of that experience. . . ." [96]

The leading Egyptian revolutionaries are silent on the question of the Arab national mission. Only President Abd al-Nasser spoke of a role in search of a hero. That role was essentially international, and the hero was not the Arab nation but Egypt.

VI REVOLUTION

The Ba'th calls itself a revolutionary party, but the term revolution is given special meaning in Aflaq's theory. Except for relatively short periods the Ba'th cooperated in working the various constitutions which Syria has had since its independence. Even the union of Syria and Egypt, which involved a change of revolutionary magnitude, was accomplished by constitutional means. Obviously, Aflaq's is a romantic, non-legalistic conception of revolution. The Ba'th constitution, however, states that revolution and struggle are necessary for the achievement of an Arab renaissance and for building socialism. Gradual development and partial amelioration will be self-defeating. "Therefore the party decides upon: (1) a struggle against foreign colonialism . . . (2) a struggle to assemble a union of all the Arabs . . . (3) a revolution against existing evils comprehending all intellectual economic, social, and political forms of life." [97]

The goals of anticolonialism and Arab unity are revolutionary and justify the use of the term. The problem of economic and political revolution will be taken up later within the framework of a discussion of Ba'th socialism and democracy. Aflaq, himself, tends to stress the intellectual and social aspects of the revolution.

First Aflaq is concerned with why revolution is necessary. Once again reference is made to the decline of the Arabs, a recurrent theme in this work.[98] Because of the low state of the Arabs, gradual development and evolutionary change is not enough. The advanced nations are healthy and may therefore progress by normal means, but the Arabs are diseased, and ordinary methods will only redound to the further detriment of their health.[99] The advanced nations may progress by changing some laws or removing and replacing governmental personnel, but such palliatives would tend to worsen the condition of the Arabs.

Political changes and, by implication, economic changes do not comprehend the full or even the fundamental idea of revolution.[100] Aflaq places the ideal above the material. He rejected abstract theory because it denies that things may change in form and yet remain the same.[101] He rejects superficial change because it does not affect the spirit.[102] He asserts that spirit not only "controls matter and instrumentalities, but creates them as well." [103] The resurrection movement must be capable of controlling "circumstances," and this will be achieved primarily through its conception of the past.[104]

"When we speak of revolution, we mean an intellectual and a moral change." [105] Since the environment reflects social values rather than creating them,[106] the revolutionary struggle is with one's self.[107] This struggle is not merely a means, but an end in itself.[108] Only in an *atmosphere* of struggle will unity be achieved.[109] The aim of the revolution is to change the social values of the Arabs. "Our aim is therefore a long-term one: a revolution to be brought about in people's way of thinking." [110]

The social change which Aflaq seeks is less directly reflected than the intellectual change he is after. The intellectual revolution which he equates with a changed value system is to be manifested by the nationalists through struggle and sacrifice. The part which struggle plays in this theory has already been described: it is an end in itself. In order to carry on the struggle one must be ready to sacrifice the easy life and seeking individual interests. Sacrifice for one's nation leads to a more fruitful life and more exalted spirit than sacrifice for one's self alone.[111] The Arab youth may not live the comfortable life of the youth of the advanced nations.[112] Theirs must be a life of struggle.[113] They must shun pleasures and enjoyments if they are to be the instruments of a true and complete revolution.[114] Not all of those who oppose the Ba'th movement are evil; most simply seek to live a natural life under unnatural conditions.[115] But to seek such a life under existing conditions is to deprive the majority of the people of their opportunity of living a "natural" life (i.e., in accordance with the true Arab spirit) and is therefore illegitimate.

Muhammad Naguib's vision of the Egyptian revolution is straightforward. There were serious abuses of political and economic power in Egypt, and the army took action against the King who was the keystone of the whole system. Naguib's chapter on the revolution is a recitation of the action taken by the Revolutionary Council during its first months in office.[116] Naguib does, however, indicate the importance of inculcating pride, self-discipline, and a spirit of sacrifice in the younger generation.[117]

Abd al-Nasser's view of the revolution is somewhat vague, and yet aspires to greater sophistication. In the first place he writes of the "philosophy of the revolution," thereby indicating that it has some sort of intellectual dimension. He also presents his interesting theory of a twofold revolution, a political and a social revolution, whose coincidence constitutes Egypt's special problem.[118] Colonel Anwar al-Sadat reflects the same view when he says that Egypt had two bastilles: feudalism and British imperialism.[119] Al-Sadat goes on to say, ". . . once one fortress was breached, the other was sure to crumble." Abd al-Nasser does not agree with the latter view, for he felt that the political revolution tended to unite the people of Egypt, but that the social revolution divided them,[120] a lesson he learned by bitter experience. He relates how he had sought the advice of elder statesmen and of university professors, and how all saw remedies in their own advancement or the penalization of their enemies. He confesses he thought all that was needed was a vanguard to lead the way, but he found the people standing aside, allowing the revolution to pass over their heads, while the opportunist politicians sought to climb on the bandwagon.[121] His view conflicts somewhat with that of Professor al-Barawy, who is at pains to show that the revolution was a popular one and not a military coup d'état.[122] In an interesting chapter on the economic background of the revolution, al-Barawy describes the growth of a nationalistic petit bourgeoisie and locally educated intelligentsia.[123] But, of course, the Revolutionary Command Council did not appeal directly to this class nor to the less articulate workers and peasants for help. It first turned to Ali Mahir and was disappointed when he procrastinated on land reform.

Despite this divergence of view, Abd al-Nasser denies (and seemingly contradicts Naguib) that the revolution stemmed merely from rage over the defective arms with which the army had to fight in Palestine or from the refusal to permit Faruk to manipulate the election of the officer's club. The Egyptian revolution, he held, was rooted in the history of Egypt.[124] The task of Egypt was to catch up with the advanced nations, but the major obstacle was egotism.[125] Thus the main object of the revolution was how to unite the people of Egypt.[126] It would therefore seem that experience has taught him the truth of Aflaq's view, that superficial political and economic changes are not enough. Unfortunately, Aflaq gives us no formula for realizing the goals of his revolution. From his emphasis on a revolution in values, one gathers that he considers education and propaganda the most important method, but education must accompany the elimination of class exploitation.[127]

VII SOCIALISM

Socialism and nationalism, despite possible theoretical conflicts, have often been found together. The German National-Socialist Party stands out as a recent and impressive example of the potential political appeal of the two, but even the more orthodox socialists like the SPD in Germany and SFIO in France evidence strong nationalistic tendencies, and the British Labour Party, when in power, pursued a similar policy. Nevertheless, none of these except the National-Socialist Party raised nationalism to an ideological level equal to that of their socialism. The Syrian Ba'th is primarily a nationalist party, but it insists on the indispensability of socialism to the realization of its goals. The combination of nationalism and socialism in a single ideological system is not necessarily a contradiction in terms, especially when we are not concerned with Marxist socialism. Since Marxism rejects nationalism, Aflaq rejects Communism outright. What Aflaq calls "theoretical socialism" is rejected for the same reason.[128] What, then, is Aflaq's socialism?

Our tract offers little besides these negative statements, so we must turn once again to the Ba'th constitution and to another tract written by one of Aflaq's followers. Article 4 of the Ba'th constitution explains the necessity of socialism for the realization by the Arab people of their potentialities.[129] Socialism will cause the Arab genius to unfold in the most perfect manner, "and it will guarantee to the nation continuous growth in its spiritual and material development and strong fraternization among its individuals." In addition to this article, with its strong suggestion of ethical socialism, the constitution has a number of specific provisions for economic reforms. These include the redistribution of immovable property among all the citizens and the prohibition of the exploitation of the labor of all large-scale enterprises, the transport system, public utilities, and important extractive industries. Agricultural ownership is to be limited by the capacity of the individual to work the land without exploiting the labor of others. The ownership of small-scale industries will be regulated so as to permit the owner no more than the average national standard of living. Workers will have some say in management, and their wages will be determined by the state. The ownership but not the renting out of real property in buildings will be permitted, and the government is to guarantee to all a minimum of such property. Nevertheless, private property and the right of inheritance are guaranteed. The government will take over all banking services and supply credit without interest. The government will regulate foreign and domestic commerce and will draw up a comprehensive economic plan for the purpose of increasing national production.[130]

This summary of the Ba'th proposals for the future economic policies of an Arab national government poses two questions. (a) Is this "true" socialism or just "welfare-ism"; and (b) how is such a program theoretically required by Ba'th nationalism? There is, of course, no agreement on the nature of true socialism, but it is obvious that this series of proposals does not coincide with Marxist doctrine nor the policies of west European socialist parties. We may note briefly that these reforms will hardly touch the urban lower middle class and the peasantry, except to guarantee each a house in which to live. Owners of large tracts of land, large-scale entrepreneurs, and foreign enterprises are the only ones to be seriously affected. Workers will be organized in trade unions but will be controlled by the government. If al-Barawy is correct about the nature of the revolutionary class—and we believe he is—then Ba'th socialism does not lead to a dictatorship of the proletariat nor to a nationalization of production. Ba'th socialism means the dictatorship of the lower middle class and the levelling down of all those who stand above them in the social and economic scale. This interpretation is corroborated by the reasoning which finds "socialism" necessary to the realization of Arab aspirations.

Dr. al-Razaz is not nearly so persuasive a writer as Aflaq, but he has much the same approach to his material. His discussion of Ba'th socialism shows all the marks of Aflaq's influence. Socialism, he holds, is not solely concerned with economics; it involves a way of life and a way of understanding economic, political, educational, social, health, moral, literary, scientific, and historical matters.[131] Capitalism, feudalism, and tribalism are all comprehensive systems. Though Al-Razaz rejects determinism, he states that science has within the last century proven that economics directs and connects the other aspects of life and that economic considerations may either unite or divide individuals. Socialism is the economic system which unites and produces cooperation in all fields of life. In any case, life may not be compartmentalized into economic, political, and social spheres. Thus, whoever takes a position on political matters must take a complementary position on economic affairs.[132] Socialism, freedom, and unity are all aspects of the same thing. Unity cannot be achieved by means of colonialism or feudalism, and those who desire unity at any price (the Sha'b party of Syria?) are mistaken. The crises of democracy in Egypt, Iraq, Lebanon, and Syria come from the mistaken belief in constitutions and laws, but the success of democracy really depends on the abolition of feudalism. Moreover, it is impossible to say that first either freedom or unity must be achieved and afterwards socialism.[133] Socialism has a beginning, but no end; it is not laws, but a way of life; hence it changes with the times. The first step toward socialism is not organization, but understanding. Socialism helps us to understand the laws of history and teaches us how to struggle more efficiently; it eliminates trial and error.[134] Socialism does not give us exact goals; it is merely a means to an end. Some people say that the salvation of the Arabs is with the Russians, with diplomacy, military dictatorship, oligarchy, or intelligarchy, but they are all wrong. Socialism tells us that we must depend only on the people, and our understanding of socialism is important, because knowledge is the first step toward correct action. This belief in and action for socialism is something which strengthens our efforts now. That is why we must be socialists now. Moreover, socialism will be realized only to the extent that freedom and unity are realized, no more and no less.[135]

In view of the fact that determinism is specifically rejected by both Al-Razaz and Aflaq,[136] this interpretation of socialism is rather surprising. But we must note that even though socialism explains the laws of history, it is an integral part, but only a part, of the whole of life. Moreover, if socialism is understood as being the equivalent of respect for human dignity, and if it involves no specific program but rather grows and changes through history, then the whole notion can be reduced to the "welfare state" idea. In any case, socialism is here treated almost exactly as nationalism is treated by Aflaq, and may be considered no more than the recognition of the importance of economics to politics in a general way. There is, however, another dimension to the problem: the belief that certain entrenched economic interests are opposed to the realization of Arab nationalist aspirations. It is the latter point which is the real tie-in between the nationalism and the socialism of the Ba'th. An understanding of socialism will lead one to recognize the reactionary role of these interests. Socialism will be realized to the extent that freedom and unity are realized because, for the Ba'th, socialism, freedom, and unity are all the same thing.

Al-Razaz gives us the "socialist" interpretation of the Arab nationalist problem: feudalism and colonialism are natural allies; colonialism uses the feudal class as an instrument of control.[137] The colonialists attempt to exploit the feudalists as well as the people, so the feudalists lead nationalist movements until such time as the colonialists realize that it is better to cooperate with the feudalists against the people.[138] The example of Egypt proves that only after the feudalists were suppressed could real freedom be achieved, and only then did Egypt realize its own Arabism. Shishakli said he was a socialist, but he appointed large landowners to implement land reform, and capitalists to the ministries of Economy and Finance. Therefore, Syria was not freed of colonialism.[139]

This theory of the national problem is not implausible, nor is there any doubt that much unabashed economic exploitation exists in the Middle East. The real point is, however, that despite the achievement of independence, the lower middle class and the professionals so well represented by the Ba'th are dissatisfied with the domestic and foreign policies of their governments. Or, more accurately, they are dissatisfied with the policies of the neighboring Arab governments and the former policies of the Syrian, Iraqi, and Egyptian governments. Thus the issue is primarily a domestic one. But the effort of the West to maintain stability in the Middle East lends plausibility to the theory that colonialism and feudalism are allied against nationalism and social reform. The meaning of the revolutionary character of the Ba'th becomes much clearer now, despite the emphasis on the intellectual and ethical aspects of socialism. Ba'th socialism itself, if it is anything more than an ideological explanation of why imperialism must still be fought, and why land reform must be instituted, is aimed at expanding the economic and political opportunities of the lower middle class and enhancing their social status. Nationalism rather than socialism is the legitimizing institution which is their justification. In this regard, it is worth recalling that Al-Razaz is content to accept the Egyptian revolutionary reforms as having eliminated feudalism, and to equate that result with socialism.

Land reform is an important part of the Ba'th program, even though Syria has large stretches of unexploited or partially exploited land. Aflaq's own constituency of Hama has an acute agrarian problem, but what extensive agricultural development has taken place in Syria has been the result of private efforts in the Gezira. The "merchant-tractorists" who have ventured into the Gezira are mostly northerners who tended to favor union with Iraq. The extension of "land reform" to these areas of extensive, mechanized farming will most certainly deprive the "merchant-tractorists" of an important source of income. Conditions within Syria do not warrant such an extension. Syrian industry is small, and most of what there is of it was controlled by northerners and a single large holding company. These financier-industrialists were displeased by the union with Egypt and by the Ba'th's countercoup of 1963. The Syrian lower middle classes received the union with favor, but civil servants, teachers, journalists, and professionals of other kinds, including middle level military officers, found the competition with Egyptians to be severe.

The Egyptian version of Arab socialism will be discussed in the next chapter.

VIII DEMOCRACY

It is, perhaps, superfluous to point out that there are important differences among democracy, nationalism, constitutionalism, and socialism. There is no reason why all four of these elements cannot coexist in a single political system, even as the Ba'th argue that all four will characterize the future Arab state. There is, furthermore, something to the argument that all four will be but facets of one and the same social reality. While distinction among these four in a real state can be analytical only, they may be more reasonably separated from one another in discussing a theory and a constitution.

Democracy is a system of government in which the people are

the supreme authority for all official acts. While the people are taken as a whole, pure democratic theory postulates that ideally the will of all is the same as the will of each, given universal freedom, rationality and goodness. Theoretically individualism and social responsibility are reconciled in pure democratic theory. Nationalism insists upon the sameness of a certain group of persons and their difference from all others, which distinctive character entitles them to a separate statehood. Nationalism also reconciles individualism and social responsibility by insisting that nationality determines interest, preference of political institutions, and modes of cultural expression. Nationalism does not, however, insist upon some manifest expression of the popular will, as does democracy. Constitutionalism may be alternatively the principle of government under law or the limitation of governmental power. In relation to democracy, constitutionalism limits not only government but the operation of democracy itself. Insofar as the constitutional rules may provide for only periodic expressions of popular will, they also limit democracy, but in the interest of making it workable. Socialism involves not only public control of all economic activity, but also public ownership of the means of production, i.e., land and capital. Socialism postulates the identity of individual and collective interests once private property and private economic decision-making are eliminated. When the political is viewed as an aspect of the economic, socialism may become a necessary adjunct of democracy or nationalism.

If this brief explanation of these four exceedingly controversial concepts is accepted, it appears that the crucial assumption is that the will of each individual is the same as that of the collectivity. Insofar as the nation is comprised only of those who subjectively feel themselves to be its members, no theoretical problem arises. Since Aflaq's is essentially an objective theory, the issue is more problematical. The divergence of view between a nationalist leadership which asserts its belief in democracy, nationalism, constitutionalism, and socialism and an upper-middle-class elite which insists on the empirical discovery of the will of the majority is great indeed. The former have tended to set up plebiscitary dictatorships, claiming to act in the name of the nation, if not also of the people. The latter distinction is valid, since the nation may include past as well as future generations. Such dictatorships are legitimized by constitutions which may or may not recognize the fact that only a single will will be expressed. The socialism of such regimes empowers the dictatorship to control the economy. The justification of these regimes is that they act in the interest of the people even if they do not obey the people. Aflaq's views reflect at once a desire for democratic-constitutional devices and the realization that the will of the people will not accord with the will of the nationalist leadership.

According to Dr. al-Razaz, true freedom cannot come to the Arabs until foreign colonialism and "feudalism" are both abolished. When, however, the Ba'th movement is successful, it will enact a constitution which will guarantee a comprehensive series of civil rights and which will make government responsible and responsive to the will of the people. In the meantime, not only are constitutional means useless, but their continued pursuit has brought on the crisis of democracy in the Middle East.[140]

The Ba'th constitution lays down its program. It provides for freedom of speech, association, and creed.[141] The constitution declares that the Ba'th is a populist party which believes that dominion belongs to the people.[142] Full citizenship rights will be guaranteed to women. The system of government will be representative and constitutional. The executive will be responsible to the legislature which is to be directly elected by the people.[143] All Arab citizens will be guaranteed equality before the law and the freedom to vote as they please in honest elections.[144] There will, however, be certain limits upon these freedoms, as determined by the "higher interest of the Arab nation." Intellectuals and ulama are to be protected by the state [145] but "every manifestation of intellectual life . . . will be stamped with the Arab national impress." There will be no private educational institutions. The freedom of private association, of forming parties, and of the use of the media of mass communications will be limited, not by law, but by Arab nationalist ideology.[146]

Let us remember that this is an ideal constitution, to come into effect when the Arab nation is united and awakened. "When the nation was in an advanced state . . . the responsibility of the individual was smaller. Even if he was capable of serving the state he was not required to do so. There was no conflict between serving the state and benefiting from it; rather, both harmonized most of the time." [147]

Until that earlier level of advancement is regained, there is no such harmony between the individual and the general welfare. During the period of decline most individuals seek their own welfare, while only a few seek to serve the whole nation.[148] These few are the vanguard of the Arab national movement, which will save the nation from itself. The vanguard will struggle to awaken the nation, and they will be aided by the "hidden will which agitates the breast of the whole nation." [149] This elitist strain is further strengthened by Aflaq's insistence that "the nation is not a numerical group, but rather an ideology which is incarnate in that group as a whole or in part of it. Nations do not perish because of the decrease in the number of their individuals. . . . The ideology exists as a seed in certain individual members of the nation; therefore, it is right for people of this kind to speak in the name of the group. The leader during a period of weakness and ideological contraction is not the one who pleases the majority, but the one who resists . . . ; not he who substitutes numbers for ideology, but he who directs the 'number' toward the ideology." [150]

Another revealing passage may justify "forcing men to be free": ". . . in this struggle we shall preserve love for all. If we are hard on others let them know that we press them in order to restore them to themselves . . . and when others are hard on us we shall know that it is their own true selves which they ignore. Their concealed will which is not yet made apparent is with us though they themselves are against us." [151] Clearly the will of the nation is to be determined by a small group of enlightened nationalist leaders. This approach is not basically modified by Aflaq's insistence that truth is above nationalism.[152] He seems to realize that the nationalist renaissance may develop into a tyranny of the group over the individual, but he denies that Arabism is that which is determined by the group.[153] Who, then, is to determine the truth which will in turn define Arabism?

An interesting insight into Ba'th democracy may be gained from the way in which the problem of Egypt is dealt with. As Dr. al-Razaz puts it, Egypt seems to contradict his doctrine, because

Egypt has eliminated both colonialism and feudalism but does not enjoy internal political freedom.[154] Al-Razaz answers his own question by asserting that freedom will return to Egypt, because it is in the nature of things, the result of a kind of physical law.[155] Aflaq is less concerned with the laws of history and politics. He stresses the transitional nature of the present period in Syria and Egypt: "In those countries where the popular movement has grown to the extent of participating in the government, as in Syria and now in Egypt, we believe that we can allow some enlargement of the power of the executive and restriction of personal liberty to allow faster progress towards our objectives." [156] Apparently, it is Aflaq's belief that individual freedom must be expanded until the radical nationalists begin to acquire power; then it must be restricted in proportion to their increase in power, until such time as the educational efforts of the government have awakened all Arabs to the identity of their interests, when individual freedom may safely be expanded again. The success of such an experiment in social engineering ultimately depends on the validity of Aflaq's contentions about the "real" will of the Arab nation.

It is evident that the Ba'th found no ideological barrier preventing it from cooperating with the admittedly undemocratic government of Egypt. In this regard it is less important to examine the written views of the leading Egyptian revolutionaries than to refer to the actual institutions which they have established. The Egyptian constitution has its full complement of political and social rights limited by law or by their gradual extension as adequate means are found. The executive, legislative, and judicial branches of government are separated, and popular elections are provided for. But only a single party which includes almost the entire nation is permitted to campaign, and many candidates have run unopposed. Moreover, the President himself was elected by a plebiscite which offered no real alternative. Evidently it is the purpose of the Egyptian government to awaken and mobilize the people to an awareness of their interests.

It appears that the ideological tendencies and general political outlook of the Ba'th and the Egyptian leaders are essentially the same. Clearly the people are not to be consulted but directed. Eventually a system of democracy, nationalism, constitutionalism, and socialism (or "antifeudalism") will be justified by the absolute coincidence between the wills of the individual and the group. Until that time radical nationalist governments will disregard individual wills in order to serve what they *know* to be the wider nationalist interest. They know this because they are the vanguard of the nationalist movement.

NOTES

1. See Chapter 2.
2. For the use of the term *romanticism*, see H. A. R. Gibb, *Modern Trends in Islam* (Chicago, 1947), pp. 108f.
3. See W. C. Smith, *Islam in Modern History* (Princeton, 1957), p. 85f.
4. W. C. Smith, *Modern Islam in India* (London, 1946), p. 83.
5. Majid Khadduri, *Independent Iraq* (London, 1951), p. 71f. The National Democratic Party of Kamil Chadirchi is the indirect descendent of the Ahali.
6. Smith, *Islam in Modern History*, pp. 89f, 156f.
7. Michel Aflaq, *Fi al-siyasa al-Arabiyya* (Damascus, 1948), *passim.*
8. Anwar al-Sadat, *Revolt on the Nile* (London, 1957), p. 34f. Both the Istiqlal and the National Democratic Party were members of the Popular Front with the Iraqi Communists in support of Abd al-Karim Kassim. Apparently the Istiqlal now supports the present Ba'thi government of Iraq.
9. The Arab Resurrection Socialist Party.
10. N. Ziadeh, *Syria and Lebanon* (London, 1957), p. 202. An interesting summary of Ba'th history, somewhat at variance with what follows, will be found in W. Z. Laqueur, "Syria: Nationalism and Communism," *The Middle East in Transition*, ed. W. Z. L. (New York, 1958), pp. 326–329.
11. Gebran Majdalany, "The Arab Socialist Movement," reprinted from *Cahiers Internationaux* in Laqueur, *op. cit.*, holds that "the Ba'th has led the campaign for federation between Syria and Egypt; and the party's acceptance of two ministerial posts in the present Syrian Cabinet has no other explanation but the Ba'th's desire to promote this plan." P. 341. (The article was completed in the Spring of 1957, some eight months before the union.)
12. A short sketch of Aflaq will be found in the *Middle East Forum*, Vol. 33, no. 2 (February 1958), p. 9. The suggestion that he was once a member of the Parti Populaire Syrien is of interest. Laqueur, *op. cit.*, p. 327, reports that Aflaq was a member of the Communist Party of Syria up to 1943.

13. Ber Borochov, *Nationalism and the Class Struggle* (New York, 1937). p. 142.
14. Hakim Zaki Nusaibeh, *The Ideas of Arab Nationalism* (Cornell, 1956), p. 57f.
15. Michel Aflaq, *Fi Sabil al-Ba'th al-Arabi* (Baghdad, 1953), p. 5.
16. *Ibid.*, pp. 9–11; see Rejwan, "Arab Nationalism," in Laqueur, *op. cit.*, pp. 146–147 and 161 on the controversy over an Arab ideology. Nusaibeh's book is not so much out of date as Rejwan suggests, but is itself a contribution to this debate.
17. Aflaq, *Fi Sabil*, p. 11.
18. *Ibid.*, p. 9.
19. *Idem.*
20. *Ibid.*, pp. 10–11. Note the divergent emphasis from that of Sati al-Husri, *Safahat min al-madi al-qarib* (Beirut, 1948), pp. 57–58, cited in S. G. Haim, "Islam and the Theory of Arab Nationalism," Laqueur, *op. cit.*, p. 283.
21. Aflaq, *Fi Sabil*, p. 12.
22. *Ibid.*, p. 13; see below for the way in which "love" permits him to force men to be free.
23. *Ibid.*, p. 15; compare citation from *With Arab Nationalism* (Cairo, 1957), in Rejwan, *op. cit.*, p. 156.
24. Aflaq, *Fi Sabil*, p. 15.
25. *Ibid.*, p. 11.
26. *Ibid.*, p. 59.
27. *Ibid.*, p. 58.
28. Gamal Abd al-Nasser, *Egypt's Liberation* (Washington, 1955), p. 17.
29. Al-Sadat, *op. cit.*, p. 53.
30. Mohammed Naguib, *Egypt's Destiny* (London, 1955), pp. 215–216.
31. *Dastur Hizb al-Ba'th al-Arabi al-Ishtiraki*, p. 10; compare citation from Sati al-Husri in Haim, *op. cit.*, pp. 300–301.
32. Aflaq, *Fi Sabil*, p. 12.
33. *Ibid.*, p. 13.
34. *Ibid.*, p. 15.
35. *Ibid.*, p. 30.
36. *Ibid.*, p. 59.
37. *Ibid.*, p. 66.
38. *Ibid.*, p. 14.
39. *Ibid.*, pp. 43–44.
40. Bertold Spuler, "Iran, The Persistent Heritage," in G. E. Von Grunebaum, *Unity and Variety in Muslim Civilization* (Chicago, 1955), p. 171, holds quite a different view: "Anyone who is even superficially acquainted with Islam knows that . . . this culture, at least in the Middle East as far as Egypt, was largely a continuation of the Iranian."
41. *Dastur*, p. 10.
42. Nasser, *op. cit.*, p. 98.

43. Naguib, *op. cit.*, pp. 184–5.
44. Rashid al-Barawy, *The Military Coup in Egypt* (Cairo, 1952), p. 199f.
45. *Ibid.*, pp. 209–210; but see the citation from Nasser's preface to a work on North Africa in Jean Vigneau, "The Ideology of the Egyptian Revolution," in Laqueur, *op. cit.*, p. 137.
46. Aflaq, *Fi Sabil*, p. 9.
47. *Ibid.*, p. 10.
48. *Idem.*
49. *Ibid.*, p. 13.
50. *Ibid.*, p. 15.
51. *Ibid.*, p. 9.
52. *Ibid.*, p. 33.
53. *Idem.*
54. *Ibid.*, pp. 45–46. Rejwan, *op. cit.*, p. 156, illustrates the influence of this view on the Kuwaiti student publishers of *With Arab Nationalism.*
55. Aflaq, *Fi Sabil*, p. 47.
56. *Ibid.*, p. 48; for an expression of a similar view see Sa'adun Hammadi, "The Question of Arab Nationalism: Its Problems, Solution and Method," *al-Adaab*, Beirut, cited in Rejwan, *op. cit.*, p. 148. Hammadi's views, as presented by Rejwan, parallel those of Aflaq so closely as to leave little doubt about his inspiration.
57. Aflaq, *Fi Sabil*, p. 48.
58. *Al-Difa'a*, Jerusalem, March 3, 1958, p. 1.
59. Al-Sadat, *op. cit.*, p. 30.
60. *Ibid.*, p. 28.
61. *Ibid.*, p. 44.
62. Naguib, *op. cit.*, p. 150; as here used the statement is deprecatory, but all the more interesting for the parallels later drawn between Nasser and Salah al-Din after the union of Egypt and Syria, and particularly during his surprise trip to Syria, where he visited that hero's tomb. See *Rose al-Yusuf* for March 1958.
63. Naguib, *op. cit.*, p. 177.
64. *Constitution of Egypt*, articles 3 and 43, pp. 3 and 9, official translation.
65. Naguib, *op. cit.*, p. 186.
66. *Ibid.*, p. 197.
67. Nasser, *op. cit.*, p. 112.
68. Aflaq, *Fi Sabil*, p. 29.
69. *Dastur*, p. 4.
70. Aflaq, *Fi Sabil*, p. 56.
71. *Ibid.*, p. 45.
72. *Ibid.*, p. 21; compare Hammadi, cited in Rejwan, *op. cit.*, p. 149.
73. Aflaq, *Fi Sabil*, p. 17.
74. *Ibid.*, p. 19.
75. *Ibid.*, p. 22.
76. *Ibid.*, p. 43.
77. *Ibid.*, p. 46.

78. *Idem.*
79. *Ibid.*, p. 47.
80. *Ibid.*, p. 48; Hammadi differs somewhat: Rejwan, *op. cit.*, p. 148.
81. Aflaq, *Fi Sabil*, p. 49.
82. *Ibid.*, p. 50.
83. *Idem.* Hammadi, perhaps, makes this point more explicit: "The final aim of Arab nationalism is Right (al-haqq)," Rejwan, *op. cit.*, p. 151. In this book al-haqq has been translated as Truth.
84. Al-Sadat, *op. cit.*, p. 53.
85. Nasser, *op. cit.*, pp. 61–68.
86. *Dastur*, p. 5.
87. *Idem.*
88. *Ibid.*, p. 4.
89. Aflaq, *Fi Sabil*, p. 43.
90. *Dastur*, p. 3.
91. Aflaq, *Fi Sabil*, p. 32; in *With Arab Nationalism*, nationality is referred to as a being, while religion is described as a mission. Rejwan, *op. cit.*, p. 156.
92. Aflaq, *Fi Sabil*, p. 46.
93. *Ibid.*, p. 42.
94. *Idem.*
95. *Ibid.*, p. 33.
96. *Ibid.*, p. 51; Abdul Latif Sharara distinguished European nationalism from "humanist nationalism" in *al-Adaab*, October 1955, cited in Rejwan, *op. cit.*, p. 160.
97. *Dastur*, p. 8.
98. Aflaq, *Fi Sabil*, pp. 7, 11, 16, 28, and 29.
99. *Ibid.*, pp. 20–21; see Ali Baddur on the nature of the disease, Rejwan, *op. cit.*, p. 162.
100. Aflaq, *Fi Sabil*, p. 27.
101. *Ibid.*, p. 9.
102. *Ibid.*, p. 28.
103. *Ibid.*, p. 31.
104. *Ibid.*, p. 35.
105. *Ibid.*, p. 24.
106. *Ibid.*, p. 38.
107. *Ibid.*, p. 26.
108. *Ibid.*, p. 27.
109. *Ibid.*, p. 28 (italics supplied).
110. "Forum Interviews Michel Aflaq," *Middle East Forum*, Vol. 33, no. 2 (February 1958), p. 9. In the same issue, Professor G. H. Gardner comes to the conclusion that "the will for social change has not yet taken deep root in the Middle East, if our respondents are at all representative." His respondents were heavily weighted toward urban, university-educated Egyptians! "What Men Live By," *Ibid.*, pp. 11–14.
111. Aflaq, *Fi Sabil*, p. 13.

112. *Ibid.,* p. 20.
113. *Ibid.,* pp. 22.
114. *Ibid.,* p. 32.
115. *Ibid.,* p. 39.
116. Naguib, *op. cit.,* pp. 145–180.
117. *Ibid.,* p. 74.
118. Nasser, *op. cit.,* pp. 40–41.
119. Al-Sadat, *op. cit.,* p. 17.
120. Nasser, *op. cit.,* pp. 40–41.
121. *Ibid.,* pp. 32–33.
122. Al-Barawy, *op. cit.,* p. 43f.
123. *Ibid.,* pp. 75–80.
124. Nasser, *op. cit.,* p. 17 *et passim.*
125. *Ibid.,* p. 36.
126. *Ibid.,* p. 71.
127. *Forum,* p. 10.
128. Aflaq, *Fi Sabil,* pp. 44 and 60. *Forum,* p. 10.
129. *Dastur,* p. 7.
130. *Ibid.,* pp. 14–17.
131. Dr. Munif al-Razaz, *Li Madha al-Ishtirakiyyah, Al'an?* a lecture, n.d.,
     n.p., printed at Jerusalem, p. 46. But see Majdalany's definition, *op. cit.,*
     p. 337.
132. Al-Razaz, *op. cit.,* pp. 6–9.
133. *Ibid.,* pp. 16–20. Akram Hourani expresses the same view that socialism,
     freedom, and unity are single aspects of the same thing, in "Face to face
     with Akram Hourani," *Middle East Forum,* Vol. 32, No. 3 (March
     1957), p. 33.
134. *Ibid.,* pp. 21–22.
135. *Ibid.,* pp. 23–24.
136. *Ibid.,* p. 7, where al-Razaz holds that economics is not the sole determi-
     nant, Aflaq, *Fi Sabil,* pp. 35, 36: ". . . political circumstances, which
     are the result of economic circumstances . . ." pp. 40, 44: ". . . we
     control our way and make our destiny. . . ." See also A. Hourani,
     Middle East Forum, loc. cit.
137. Al-Razaz, *op. cit.,* p. 10.
138. *Ibid.,* p. 11.
139. *Ibid.,* p. 12–14. Cf. also G. Baer, in Laqueur, *op. cit.,* p. 95, and
     Egyptian views cited in Rejwan, *op. cit.,* p. 158.
140. Al-Razaz, *op. cit.,* p. 79.
141. *Dastur,* p. 4.
142. *Ibid.,* p. 7.
143. *Ibid.,* pp. 10–11.
144. *Ibid.,* p. 12.
145. *Ibid.,* p. 20.
146. *Ibid.,* p. 22.

147. Aflaq, *Fi Sabil*, p. 52.
148. *Ibid.*, pp. 6, 30.
149. *Ibid.*, p. 31.
150. *Ibid.*, p. 59.
151. *Ibid.*, p. 29.
152. *Ibid.*, p. 50 (discussed above).
153. *Idem* and *Forum*, p. 10.
154. Al-Razaz, *op. cit.*, p. 14.
155. *Ibid.*, p. 15. But Ali Baddur, in Rejwan, *op. cit.*, pp. 162–163, argues for "planned dictatorship" in an attack on Ba'th Party slogans.
156. *Forum*, p. 33.

7

NASSERISM: THE PROTEST

MOVEMENT IN THE MIDDLE EAST

I "NASSERISM" AND PAN-ARABISM

The pan-Arab movement is a protest against three related political situations. The most obvious target of pan-Arab protest is the division of Arabic-speaking peoples into a number of independent states. Secondarily, it is a protest against the existing economic and social systems of all the Arab countries and against the political power structure of some. The third protest is against the bipolarization of international power.

The form of Arab nationalism that is characterized by these three protests is sometimes referred to as "Nasserism," with the implications that the policies of the United Arab Republic have substantial support beyond the borders of that country and that they are an accurate reflection of pan-Arab ideology. But in equating "Nasserism" or pan-Arabism with the policies of the UAR we may be confusing a diffuse symbol with but one of its concrete manifestations.

The problem rests upon the multiple meanings and usages of

the term "Nasserism," and the confusion which results from the failure to probe more deeply behind it. Nevertheless, it may be argued that the truly important thing is the diffuse ideological and social movement of generalized protest known as "Nasserism," rather than the specific policies of the Nasser-led UAR. The concrete policy, however, is the test of what is essential in the ideology. It is the policy rather than the internal logic or philosophical foundation which gives us the meaning of the theory.[1]

The first thing to bear in mind is the fact that "Nasserism" is not used by the Arabs themselves to describe their aspirations. This is a term of Western construction. Arab writers generally ignore the term, but when they do not, they find it objectionable. According to Dr. Abd al-Qadir Hatim, the West talks of "Nasserism" as though Nasser were intent on establishing an empire, because they are imperialists and believe that everyone else is too.[2] Al-Rimawi asserts that the whole purpose of the imperialists, Zionists, and certain Arab ruling circles may be summed up in the single slogan "the destruction of Nasserism."

But this Nasserism does not refer to a single individual, and does not refer to a specific government such as that of the UAR. It refers clearly and precisely to the national revolutionary force —in its ideological position, its principles, its goals, in whatsoever it has realized by way of victories in the spheres of nationalism, liberation, unity, and in the economic and social spheres of life. That slogan is a war cry repeated by the forces of opposition and their stooges in the Arab homeland, a war to destroy the national revolutionary force and the new Arab national movement.[3]

But barely concealed beneath Rimawi's breathless prose is the assertion that "Nasserism," as used by the opponents of Arab nationalism, attempts to isolate President Nasser and the government of the UAR from the Arab people, while what they really oppose are the aspirations and the interests of the people. These aspirations are to be carried to fruition by the government of the UAR.

The birth of the UAR has come to declare, for the first time in modern Arab history, and for hundreds of years, the establishment of a united Arab state in which (a) there is no hostile or basic contradiction, in terms of will or interest, between the people and the government, and (b) there is no hostile or fundamental contradiction, in terms of will or interest, between that government and the Arab nation.[4]

The author's apologetic for the policies of the UAR and of President Nasser is directed against the unregenerate Ba'this who have mischievously refused to recognize that the formation of the UAR initiated a new stage in the Arab struggle.[5] According to Hatim, the third stage of Arab nationalism appeared when President Nasser added a philosophy or creed (madhab) to the socio-historical existence of the Arab nation and to the consciousness which gave birth to solidary action in Palestine and Port Said.[6] Nasser did not move directly from the first stage to the third stage because the landmarks of the ideology of the Arab nation were not clear. They are not written on paper as is the Communist Manifesto, but they are written in the hearts of the Arab people.[7]

The argument of these two authors is clear. They hold that the consciousness and aspirations of the whole Arab people, as represented in certain social facts and as evolved in a particular historical process, are concretely manifested in the policies of the United Arab Republic. Hatim does little more than assert this justification, but Rimawi outlines the goals of the Arab national revolutionary movement and attempts to prove that the UAR is objectively capable of realizing these goals—despite his attack on its wisdom and practicality. Hence, those opposing Nasser do not oppose the legitimacy of his leadership, they oppose the Arab national movement.

These opponents number more than a few; they included Bourguiba, the Syrian Nationalists, the Lebanese Confessionalists, the Hashemites, the "Communist-infiltrated" government of Iraq, and the traditional Arab rulers. With so many opponents claiming to speak for the interests of the Arab people, or for parts of them, it is probably not incorrect to assume that there is a good deal of interaction between policy formation in the UAR and expectations about popular reaction throughout the Arab world. The policy of the UAR, therefore, may be seen as an adaptation of the practical choices of the Egyptian political-military elite to the exigencies of the opinion of the (politically) participant Arab classes.

Even this careful definition of "Nasserism" is none too specific, but it has the merit of suggesting that the policy indicated by that term is dynamic and responsive. It is probably highly personal, because of the overwhelming dominance of President Nasser—politically within the UAR and symbolically elsewhere. If nothing succeeds like success, then it follows that to some extent the Arab national movement has adapted itself to the policies of the UAR. In other words, the two elements of our equation—the policies of the UAR and those things "written in the hearts of the Arab people"—are not equal, but they influence one another in the direction of equality.

In seeking to lead the Arab national movement and to benefit by its support, Nasser may not do as he likes, but he is at the same time under no compulsion to do any specific thing at a specific time. There is no ideological rigidity here, even if Arab nationalism appears less flexible at times than Communism. Up to a limit, a shrewd calculation of gains and losses, rather than a perverse, affective rebellion, is the more appropriate expectation in dealing with the leadership of the UAR.

II POLICY AND IDEOLOGY

The essentially nonideological character of UAR policy has been proposed, but there is some controversy over this matter. In most writing on Arab politics by Arab writers there is frequent reference to the principles of the revolution and the ideals of the Arab people. In President Nasser's speeches there is also a good deal of emphasis on the same theme. Of course, a set of principles is not an ideology, but even such principles as may be found do not set narrow limits to the range of policy choices before the government of the UAR. Furthermore, it is a generally well-known feature of contemporary Arab nationalist thought that the national movement lacks an ideology.[8] This does not mean that there are no Arab ideologies, or that the philosophical foundations and logical derivatives of statements on Arab politics may not be fruitfully investigated. It does mean that there is no widely accepted theory which satisfies the majority of the Arab intelligentsia. From the search for an ideology, it is possible to understand that to be without one is a source of shame to many. An official ideology, however, can be a serious embarrassment to a government as well as a welcome support to legitimacy.

The difficulty here is typical of that discovered in studying many areas of Egyptian politics, for the very reason that policy grows and does not spring full blown from the head of Zeus. We have already seen that Hatim propounds the view that only in the last stage, after 1956, did President Nasser provide the Arab movement (né the Egyptian revolution) with an ideology, the source of which was in the hearts of the people. Another minister, Dr. Tharwat Ukasha, presents a similar view and suggests, more specifically, that the idea behind the National Union will be found in the statements and speeches of President Nasser, but that this idea was always present in the hopes of the people and was represented by the Revolutionary Council, which laid the plans leading to the admirable state of affairs now existing in Egypt.[9] In his recent introduction to a newer edition of Nasser's *Philosophy of the Revolution*, Kamal al-Din Husain writes that Part Two of the book answers the two questions: What was the aim of the revolution and what is the way of achieving that aim? [10] The answer to the first question is simple: the revolution sought what every Arab seeks for his homeland. The second question was more difficult, but its answer is primarily to remove the obstacles from the path and give leadership to the lost caravan.

If these semiofficial statements follow the same line of according President Nasser ideological leadership, while asserting that he is doing no more than expressing the will of the Arab people, his own statements and many unofficial statements uphold the view that the ideology of the revolutionary movement is still not fixed. The most graphic of these is Nasser's report of the results of his seeking the advice of those "with opinions and expertise."

> *Every idea we heard had no aim other than to destroy some other one! Had we followed all that we heard, we would have killed them all and destroyed all the ideas.*[11]

Much later, Nasser was to admit openly that the leaders of the revolution had no idea of what to do when they suddenly found themselves in power. They made mistakes, especially in appointing that first civilian cabinet, for they did not appreciate the difference in mentality between themselves and the politicians and administrators whom they appointed.[12] But, more pointedly, Nasser has stated that there is no fixed plan for the National Union; progress is to be made by trial and error.[13] At a recent cabinet meeting the President was importuned to consider revising the system of administration in government-controlled companies to bring it more into line with the ideology of "Arab socialism." His answer was to point out the difficulty and the length of time necessary to study such a project, and he added that the accepted basis of administration in both East and West is efficiency.

These views of Nasser are borne out in most conversations with informed Egyptians. In answer to inquiries about the ideology of the UAR government, an admittedly unfair question,[14] two sorts of answers are forthcoming. Either people say that there is none, or they refer the inquirer to President Nasser's published speeches. If one inquires more specifically about certain policies of the UAR, then the answer is almost invariably that the policy is not rigid, it does not stem from any fixed idea, it will be tested pragmatically and discarded if found wanting.

Of course, opposition nationalist groups may have their favorite ideologians. If you ask Ba'this about the ideology of the Arab national movement, they will no doubt refer to Michel Aflaq and several others. Some of these ideologically inclined pan-Arabists have come over to Nasser's side behind Rimawi; and it is of great interest to note the way in which that ex-Ba'thi has turned the tables on his former comrades in justifying the pragmatism of Nasser against the romanticism of Aflaq. Without mentioning Nasser or Aflaq, he asserts that the Arabs must work to construct a theory on the basis of the experiences and successes of the Arab and Afro-Asian peoples. They must ask, he goes on, whether the slogans, policies, and positions of the government of the UAR are a correct expression of the revolutionary aims and of the interest of Arab nationalism. Then they must ask whether there is any fundamental hostile contradiction between the Arab people and that government. (We have already noted that Rimawi answers the latter in the negative.) Rimawi continues:

Those who pretend that a theory already exists are simpletons, and their productions are superficial and confused. The ideology of Arab nationalism is in the process of coming into being, and that process must be encouraged. Every Arab group or party has a part to play in this effort, but the part played by those who experience the realities of the Arab nation will differ from that of the ivory-tower theorist. The latter borrows from old philosophies or from the experience of other countries or strains to point out secondary contradictions and in the end finds himself consciously or unconsciously a tool of either the Communists or the imperialists.[15]

The primary premise has become the identity of the policy of the UAR and the interest of the Arab nation. Once this has been established, building the theory of Arab nationalism becomes a process combining exegesis, justification, and generalization.

Despite the lack of ideological limitation, the policy of the UAR can be shown to be more or less fixed at the present time and to have gone through a sort of rational (in the historic sense) growth. This growth, no doubt, is due to a gradually increasing awareness of the attitudes of the broader Arab public, as well as to the effect of international pressures and the blind logic of history, which never permits an act to be completely erased from the consciousness of man.

III PAN-ARABISM

The pan-Arab ideal of the Ba'th Party of Syria has become the goal of the UAR, even if not an unequivocal one. The Ba'th called for (and still does) comprehensive Arab unity; that is, for the creation of a single Arab state stretching from the Atlantic to the Persian Gulf. The exact means of achieving this unity and its institutional complement, whether a unitary state or not, is left conveniently open. Nevertheless, as Abdullah Rimawi insists, the formation of the UAR has pointed the way to a possible answer. That answer is the complete merger of Arab states whether neighboring or not.

But the implication of this simple, no-buts-about-it answer is now clear, for all to see. Given the size, wealth, military power, and demographic composition of the Arab states (with the exclusion of the Maghrib, perhaps), the implication is the domination of Egypt. The fact that even with this implication the idea is very attractive to many Sunni Arab intellectuals is a testimony to the charismatic qualities of President Nasser, as well as to certain other factors. These other factors may be summed up briefly as follows: None of the Eastern Arab states is either homogeneous or large enough to provide, at one and the same time, sufficient bases for Arab nations and sufficient scope for the aspirations of the educated classes.[16] To be a Syrian, Jordanian, or Iraqi has none of the appeal and little of the ideological reality of being an Arab. As for the possibility of an Arab state comprising the Fertile Crescent—Nuri Sa'id's plan or that of the Syrian nationalists—the statement attributed to Sa'd Zaghlul about the consequences of adding zero and zero seem to apply.

There are significant differences between the society and culture of the Nile Valley and those of the Fertile Crescent, but the intellectual classes and their medium of cultural exchange are similar. Furthermore, if Nasser's repeated emphasis upon power, glory, honor, dignity, independence, self-reliance, and, in the special sense of the local idiom, personality has any meaning, it is because Nasser himself appears to have achieved these, and one can identify with the "champion of Arabism" who was born in a village in upper Egypt. It must take a good deal of forebearance for any Arab to deny himself the vicarious glory of feeling himself to have shared in Nasser's "victories."

For those who seek some more concrete sense of the reasons for the success of "Nasserism" in this pan-Arabist sense, Professor Karl Deutsch's analysis of the formation of national communities in Europe is applicable here, perhaps even more than in the areas he studied.[17] In line with that analysis, Egypt is the core area, not because of its geographic location, nor because of its surplus wealth, but because of its size, population, stability, relative security, and intellectual leadership of the Arab world. Egypt does not offer many economic attractions to other Arab areas, and its surplus educated elite is potentially competitive with those from other Arab countries; nevertheless, there is some expectation that Egypt may be able to manage effective economic development.

Despite these tendencies, we should beware of overexaggerating the seriousness with which comprehensive Arab unity is advocated outside of Egypt. In many cases, the fate of Syria appears to have given solemn pause to those who have something to lose, although others assume the pro-Nasserist stance as the most acceptable of the Left or radical positions in opposing their own traditional or conservative governments.[18] In still other cases the pro-Nasserist position is to some extent a communal position for Sunni Arabs, who are in the minority and who, thereby, may wield the international prestige of the President of the UAR in their domestic battles. The balance of attractions and repulsions cannot be estimated yet, for, even if Syrians, and especially Ba'this, found themselves with little policy-making power, Egypt knew that it was being judged in the "Northern Region," and efforts were bent to developing the resources of Syria, even to the extent of transferring funds (directly and with moderate fanfare) to the regional budget from Cairo.[19]

Of course, no one explicitly advocates the subordination of all the Arab states to Nasser's leadership, but no other practical course is suggested. Rimawi is outspoken that the UAR has the capability of realizing all the Arab aims, but he does not draw the logical conclusion. The UAR leaders themselves were circumspect about expressing their aspirations even before the Syrian break with the UAR; first, because they were, doubtless, not yet ready to cope with another "region," though they were willing to if necessary; and second, because there was no need to be explicit. Hatim vigorously denied that Nasser had imperialist aspirations, and Nasser was careful to point out that the UAR came into being as a result of Syrian initiative. But the facts of the situation were all in favor of the UAR anyway. Its population numbered over 26 million, compared to a maximum total of 15 million for the Fertile Crescent. All that needed to be done was advocate unity, not in any legal sense, but the unity of brothers and the solidarity of the family.[20] When Kassim offered a proposal for federal unity shortly after the Iraqi revolution, Nasser pointed out that there was no hurry: first let Kassim consolidate his revolution, then one could consider ways and means of achieving unity.[21]

To illustrate the current policy of the UAR on the pan-Arab issue, there is no better or more interesting set of documents than the exchange of letters between King Hussain of Jordan and President Nasser. Relations between Jordan and the UAR have gone from moderately good, during the Nabulsi period of 1956 and early 1957, to bad, after Nabulsi's dismissal and the landing of British troops during the Lebanese and Iraqi crises of 1958, to slightly better from the appointment of Majali as Prime Minister until after the Bhamdun conference, when al-Majali was assassinated. Both sides accused one another of this murder and of worse; and the incident reversed an agreement between the two countries. Then, just as suddenly, relations improved after King Hussain sent a personal letter to President Nasser. The letters do not cover the differences between the two rulers, but they constitute a cautious agreement to disagree.

Hussain's letters expressed his desire to seek a better future for the Arab nation, "leaving the judgment of the righteousness of intentions and deeds to God, to history and the people. . . . The Arab nation will never be the property of Husain ibn Talal or of Gamal Abd al-Nasser." Both of them are simply responsible servants of the Arab nation. The dangers and problems facing the Arabs are great; hence, it behooves the Arab leaders to cooperate rather than dispute.

But Hussain's main plea was contained in his statement of his belief that the most elementary principles of cooperation and of steadfastness in the face of danger were "the equality of all the sons of our nation in good or bad times, their full equality in their rights and duties, and *nonintervention of some in the affairs of others*." [22]

It need hardly be pointed out that the principle of nonintervention has lost much of its meaning throughout the world today, but nowhere is the definition of an internal affair so anomalous as among the Arab countries. Some Arabs have insisted on the rule of nonintervention in both domestic and foreign affairs, but in Arab politics any statement about Arab nationalism necessarily affects the internal affairs of several sovereign states.[23]

President Nasser's response was in the same noncommittal tone, though it was interpreted as a friendly, if frank answer. That letter is an admirable summary of the UAR position. A précis of its relevant sections follows:

The disputes among the Arab states are not superficial; they reflect factual contradictions in the present Arab situation. But Arab solidarity is essential in the face of grave dangers and powerful enemies. True solidarity is needed, not a façade; nor should it be a solidarity which limits the Arab effort or restricts the Arab vanguards. . . . We praised you when you dismissed Glubb Pasha, but opposed you when you cooperated with those who sought to isolate Egypt after the Suez attack. There is no doubt that Egypt loses much when Jordan is separated from her, but the loss to Jordan is much greater. We supported every Arab country in its struggle for freedom; the Palestine case was our motive for opposing the Baghdad Pact, it was our motive for purchasing arms from the Soviet bloc (breaking the arms monopoly), and our stand on Palestine was the reason for the tripartite armed aggression in 1956.[24] We have borne the major burden of supporting Algeria's struggle for freedom, and we supported the independence of Tunis, Morocco, Sudan, Iraq, Oman, the Arab South,[25] Lebanon, and even Jordan. This we do as our duty, for we believe that our people, as a result of its material and moral potentialities, was placed by fate at the head of the Arab struggle and forms its base. The role of the base is not domination but service.

Domestically we seek democracy, not only in general elections, but also including participation in a national economic revolution to increase production and achieve equality in distribution. We seek to equalize opportunities and to melt the differences between citizens. We plan to double the national income in ten years. To achieve equitable distribution, we have limited land ownership, nationalized the British, French, and Belgian monopolies, the banks, and the insurance companies. We have levied progressive taxes and established cooperatives.

We believe in Arab nationalism as a true and genuine current moving toward comprehensive Arab unity. We are not so much interested in its constitutional form as we are in the will of the Arab people.

Our policy is a reflection of our existence, an existence against which we cannot rebel. But this does not mean that we wish to impose that policy on other Arab states, for I know that each

Arab state is more capable than others in facing its special circumstances and has more right to have the last word regarding those circumstances. *There is no doubt that there are things about which we can differ, but let us face those in a spirit of brotherly forgiveness.*[26]

The letter, even in its abbreviated form, needs little commentary. Although admitting the special circumstances of Jordan, Nasser claims for the UAR, in a phrase reminiscent of Rimawi, by virtue of its material and moral potentialities, the leadership of the Arab struggle for comprehensive unity. The contradictions which characterize the Arab situation are not explained, but they are strongly hinted at in Nasser's statements on domestic policy and in the section on positive neutrality, which was omitted.

The letters show that the UAR prefers to maintain normal relations with its sister Arab states as a basis for achieving its aims. The violent attacks on Hussain were quite suddenly switched off at his first overture—an overture which implied no concessions. Hussain is surely the weaker of the two, but the UAR prefers to bide its time and to use the tactics of the sun rather than those of the wind.

Though this represents the present policy of the UAR with regard to pan-Arabism, it was not the original position of the Free Officers when they took power. Ideologically they were, perhaps, not opposed to comprehensive Arab unity, but they had no position on the matter at all. From the little we know of the contents of the manifestoes of the Free Officers group before the 1952 coup, it is clear that comprehensive unity was not in their program, though Arab solidarity was mentioned as one of their principles. In the past, Egyptians have not been so sure that they were Arabs, some preferring to see themselves as part of Europe or to draw their nationalist inspiration from Egypt's pharaonic past.

Some of this controversy has been described in an article by A. G. Chejne. He comes to the conclusion, despite Egypt's leadership in the formation of the Arab League in 1945, that Egypt was not committed to a vigorous Arab policy until 1954.[27] His conclusion is well sustained by an examination of Nasser's speeches, which do not address themselves importantly to Arab questions until 1955, that is, until the controversy over Iraq's adherence to the Baghdad Pact broke out in full fury. Since that time there have been many references to the imperialists' attempt to convince the Egyptians that they were not Arabs and to foster pharaonism as a kind of intellectual imperialism.[28]

But an analysis of Nasser's speeches further indicates that comprehensive unity did not loom large in Egyptian policy until after the union of Syria and Egypt, that is to say, until forced upon Egypt by the logic of events themselves. On March 28, 1955, Nasser first stated the six principles of the revolution: (1) ending imperialism, (2) eradicating feudalism, (3) breaking monopolies and the political domination of capital, (4) establishing social justice, (5) creating a powerful national army, and (6) establishing a truly democratic system.[29] As late as June 1, 1956, these same six principles formed the skeleton of a major address.[30] In that speech a vague reference to the progress of Arab nationalism was included in Nasser's discussion of a strong national army and its role in resisting the Baghdad Pact.[31] It appears that Egypt's Arab policy was forced upon it first by fear of the consequences of the Baghdad Pact and later by the apparently unexpected support of the Arab people at the time of the nationalization of the Suez Canal Company.

All the evidence seems to point to the Anglo-Egyptian treaty initialled in August 1954 as the most significant turning point in Egyptian policy, even as the events of March 1954 set up the internal political conditions for that turn. Those earlier events by which Nasser took over from Naguib are well enough known. It is clear that Nasser and his supporters had not yet consolidated their position when they signed the treaty providing for the evacuation of the British troops from the Canal Zone. Nasser's speeches of that period are full of rebuttals against his critics, who claimed, apparently, that the new treaty was no better than that of 1936, that it did not provide for immediate evacuation, that some Britishers would remain, that it provided for the return of the British army, that the provision for consultation in case of the threat of aggression was the equivalent of joining a Western defense pact, and that Nasser was a tool of the imperialists. The list of audiences to whom Nasser spoke during these months reads like a catalogue of important interest groups. There followed speeches to a great many units of the military and the air force.[32] The most consistently repeated theme was that Egypt had joined no pact and would not do so.

The date of the attempted assassination of Nasser was the height of the domestic crisis, after which he was able to assert full control. But externally, the launching of the Baghdad Pact threatened to isolate Egypt and compel Nasser into an agreement that would endanger his government all over again. The hoped for financial support from the United States in return for agreeing to the terms of the Anglo-Egyptian Treaty began to fade as this new issue arose.

Nasser could not join a Western-dominated pact even if he wanted to,[33] and the circumstances prevailing at the end of 1954 determined that the refusal to join defensive pacts with non-Arab states would became a fundamental principle of Egyptian foreign policy. Nasser doubtless felt that he had made the maximum of concessions to Britain and the United States in the treaty—it was in discussing this treaty that he described his action as "realistic," in the sense of compromising. If the first task of any government is to preserve itself, then the first task facing the leaders of the revolutionary government was to prove that the treaty was not a surrender to the West. To prove their sincerity and to fend off great external pressures, they had to oppose extension of the Baghdad Pact to Arab countries. These circumstances led Egypt into Arab politics in the immediate aftermath of the signing of the Anglo-Egyptian Treaty of 1954.

The first major address in which President Nasser appears to have laid special emphasis upon Arab nationalism as opposed to Egyptian nationalism took place on August 12, 1956. There he said:

Then the voices in the Arab world began to say that it is not the Suez Canal, but the Arab Canal. Arab nationalism began to appear in its best form and clearest meaning. Various kinds of support began to come from Arab kings and presidents and Arab peoples. Arab nationalism began to show its existence and its truth. I read an article on Arab nationalism in a foreign newspaper, and it said, "Arab nationalism became a danger after 1952 and after the writing of the Philosophy of the Revolution." Then I *thought we as Arabs must be a single nation. We must fight as for a single cause.*[34]

From that time on, Nasser's speeches show that pan-Arabism had become one of the major components of Egyptian policy. This turn was doubtless a part of the more general effort to win wide support against a possible armed attack after the nationalization. But after the attack, the responses of Arab nationalists outside of Egypt were compelling: Jordan and Iraq were both ripe for revolution, and the Syrian Ba'this had begun to advocate seriously the union of the two countries.[35] Pan-Arabism might then be called "Nasserism," even more particularly after the Lebanese troubles of 1958.

The moral of these events is easily drawn. The close interrelationship of the three levels of Egyptian policy—Arab policy, domestic policy, and foreign policy—is obvious. The rational intent behind the choices made and the role of situational factors in narrowing the range of choice appear to overshadow the role of the still diffuse ideological and psychological factors associated with the broad nationalistic movement. It is the series of policy positions which appear to control the definition of nationalist ideology. Though revolutionary slogans and ideological controversies appear to be matters more of political style and expression within Egypt, they are nevertheless more important where the sense of a national identity is not so secure. Finally and more specifically, it should be borne in mind that two crises, one of internal security at the end of 1954, and one of external security at the end of 1956, were both turning points in Egypt's Arab and foreign policies. For domestic policy, the turning points were in February-March 1954, when Nasser took authority and moved against the still active conservative politicians, and in 1957, when the government suddenly found itself owning a large number of former British and French firms in addition to the Suez Canal Company.

IV ARAB SOCIALISM

For many observers, the true nature of the political phenomenon known as "Nasserism" is to be understood in terms of the social change taking place in the Arab countries. Although the full explication of this view is extremely difficult, due to the absence of relevant empirical data and our limited understanding of the operative mechanism which relates social change to political protest and political protest to declared policy, it is nevertheless possible to elaborate on the idea itself. In its simplest form, the social change thesis holds that as a result of western European pressures—economic, political, and military—on the Ottoman Empire, the traditional structure of Islamic society grew weaker; new classes, rival elites, were created, which challenged the existing distribution of social, economic, and political values. Although this social movement was at first moderate in its demands, its radicalism increased with the increase in the ranks of the new classes and with the increasing awareness of the weakness and economic and technical backwardness of the Islamic countries. From seeking military and bureaucratic reform it moved to demanding a constitutional form of government, then to opposition to foreign influence, to popular sovereignty, to secularism, to land reform, and more recently to socialism. In the Arab countries under the Ottoman Empire, the constitutional phase was followed by demands for independence. These political demands with implications of opposition to the traditional military, the bureaucratic aristocracy, the ulama, the landowners, and foreign and minority groups were justified by a nationalist ideology.

The hard facts at our disposal are few, but what there are of them indicate that the dominant ideology among the new classes, and especially among the Sunni Arabs of these classes, is pan-Arabism—probably under the leadership of President Nasser. If we proceed further for non-evaluative data to help us understand these things, we may attempt to assess the interests of these classes and compare those interests with the policies of social reform being carried out in the UAR. As we may now expect, these policies have been formed in the crucible of events, having been but vaguely fixed in the minds of the leadership before the revolution. The general direction was there, as part of the explanation of pre-revolutionary reality, but the method of achieving these goals was not at all clear, as Nasser himself has said. When once we have been able to compare these interests and policies, should we find some hiatus between the two, we shall have some idea of the nature and strength of the ideological residuum.

The two most important of the groups bearing the new nationalist ideology are the military and the bureaucracy, but these are not the only ones to have been affected by the changes of the last century and a half. The peasantry has been disturbed by the sometimes amazing growth of its numbers, by changes in tax-farming procedures, by new title-settlement procedures, by the change to cash crops in many places, by new irrigation systems which have relieved the peasant of ownership or control over his water requirements, and by extension of the network of modern transport and mass media to some rural areas. Tribes have been settled, decimated, and moved to new areas; they have had their traditional leaders removed and their products replaced in the markets. Small merchants and artisans have been weakened by the competition of standardized manufacturing and a new class of importers and wholesale dealers; their guilds have been dissolved, the activities of their semireligious organizations have been restricted, their sources of credit have dwindled, and their dependence upon the bureaucracy has increased. The ulama have lost their independence of government and their financial independence, and have lost much influence and prestige at the same time. Whole new classes have come into being in the cities. There is a new and growing industrial labor group; a very large group in the lower services category—hawkers, porters, car-watchers, sweepers, doormen, garbage collectors, and domestics; a much smaller group engaged in finance, foreign trade, and industry; a new group of professionals—doctors, lawyers, accountants, engineers, professors, economists, and, at much lower levels, journalists, teachers, nurses, technicians, and artists.

But the earliest changes, deliberately instituted, were in the military and then in the bureaucracy, as means of coping with the military pressures exerted from Europe. Efforts to modernize the military are a century and a half old, but the armies of the Middle East still reflect the characteristic dichotomy of modernity and often squalid traditionality which renders every Middle Eastern city incomprehensible to foreigners and an irritant to its middle-class inhabitants. The officer corps, but not the ranks, belongs to the modern middle class, though whenever imperialism held sway, or whenever there were important minorities, the officer corps was not "nationalized" until recent times; and then it was nationalized only where patriarchal forms of government had all but disappeared. (Until 1936, for example, the Egyptian army officer corps was predominantly Turkish, Circassian, or otherwise aristocratic in social origin.) These armies have been expanded, yet not so much as to account for their great influence. Their influence in recent times is due not to their size, but to their modern weapons, to the political impotence of the bulk of the urban classes, to the gradual loss of religious legitimacy by traditional rulers, and to the lack of cohesiveness among middle-class urban groups.

Students are still largely embryonic civil servants, and civil servants of the lower ranks are vestigial students. In these two groups we find the largest part of the urban middle class, especially in the politically dominant capital city. These, together with the far fewer professionals, high and low,[36] create the climate of nationalist opinion; they read, listen, discuss political events, applaud or denounce government policy, and belong to political parties; but rarely do they create a government or bring one down. These are the ones described as educated, cultured, or belonging to the intelligentsia, and it is the climate of their opinion which has provided the military with an ideology, even though the military was the first to be exposed to Western learning.

Nevertheless, revolutionary governments dominated by the military, even when they have learned the extent of their dependence upon the bureaucracy, are not the exponents of bureaucratic interests, but more nearly the exponents of the middle-class ideology which was created to justify those interests. The distinction is important, because the justification is made in general nationalist and often socialist terms, in the interest of the inarticulate peasantry and the relatively small class of workers.[37] More emphasis is given to the interests which must be curbed than to those which must be benefited. The military, however, does not hesitate to include itself in this conception of the national interest. The six goals of the Egyptian revolution include the creation of a strong national army, along with statements of opposition to imperialism, feudalism, and monopoly capitalism. The other goals of establishing social justice and a truly democratic system are extremely vague in meaning, and we have already noted that the Free Officers were at a loss as to how to achieve these ends when they came into power.

It is by no means easy to reconstruct the desires of the urban middle classes at the time of the revolution, but we may hazard a few generalizations. There can be little doubt that most would as soon have had Farouk go, and no doubt that all except some in the Canal cities wanted the British army to leave Egypt. If we bear in mind that many of the professionals are actually government employees, we may easily conclude that there was a broad consensus that salaries and allowances had to be raised, the cost of living lowered, inflation stopped, the rules for the protection of civil servants expanded and adhered to closely, promotions given regularly according to the book, and political victimization stopped. Low-cost housing was needed, bribery and corruption in the bureaucracy were sources of complaint, and the extension of urban amenities to outlying quarters was demanded. The great influence of the land-owning class was felt by many to be the reason for the failure to realize these objectives and for the corruption of parliamentary democracy.

Another general aspiration existed, expressed as the need for industrialization or economic development, but perhaps just as often sensed in the discomfort or insecurity of life in an environment of immense social, economic, and cultural contrast. Doubtless, many feel that they will benefit directly from economic development and the spread of literacy and education; but many benefit at present from the easy availability of cheap menial services. More, however, fall into neither category but are ashamed of the squalor of the metropolis and feel that the economic and social conditions now prevailing do not afford the environment in which a respectable civil servant can live a moderately ostentatious bourgeois existence.

If the foregoing is a fair representation of the demands of the nationalist classes in Cairo, it is not unreasonable to suppose that the Free Officers were well aware of them. They are, after all, sprung from the same classes;[38] their families were spread throughout many occupations, not excluding agriculture. Nor is it true that they had no objectives whatsoever when they took power. The objectives they had were mainly those which had been adumbrated, but not realized, under the monarchy. In many ways the revolution is a more vigorous continuation of prerevolutionary tendencies.

Not only in international questions and in the issue of British occupation was the position of the Revolutionary Command Council similar to that of the Wafd. The proposal for the High Dam at Aswan already existed. There had been a number of efforts to restrict land ownership and regulate tenancy, most of which had failed. Cooperatives had been established but did not work too well. Various community-development projects for agricultural areas had been started but were not really off the ground. Food subsidies were granted on certain staples to ease the lot of the urban lower classes. Industrialization plans were being worked on. Expenditure on education was increasing yearly, and the right of labor to organize was recognized.

These facts have led some to argue that the revolution was "unnecessary," but a great many more feel that landowner domination of the parliament and the king constituted formidable roadblocks to progress. The Free Officers swept them out of the way and proceeded as vigorously as they might to realize those projects which were already on the order of the day. The army was, of course, a direct beneficiary of the new regime, and large landowners were hurt, but it is difficult to single out any other group as having been particularly favored or penalized. As the government's domestic policy developed, however, the position of some improved while that of others declined. And, it should be borne in mind, domestic, social, and economic policy is still evolving.

We have already had some suggestion of the present configuration of the social and economic policy of the UAR in President Nasser's letter to King Husain. No detailed elaboration can be made here, but some additional information may be helpful. Not only have all banks and insurance companies been nationalized, but most large industrial establishments are government controlled and managed through three organizations: the Economic Development Organization, the Nasr Organization, and the Misr Organization. Eighty-two per cent of all nonagricultural investment is currently being made by the "Public Sector." The national income of Egypt was about 1267 million pounds during 1960–1961, while the government planned to spend over 700 million pounds in the regular and development budgets. Indirect taxes still account for much more than any other source of revenue for the regular budget, while profits from the Suez Canal and from government-owned companies, especially the nationalized British, French, and now Belgian concerns, contribute to the development budget. As a consequence, development policy is almost entirely a government affair; private investment, except through the purchase of shares of government companies, is no longer encouraged, in fact. Even new enterprises requiring as little as 1000 pounds capital must receive the approval of the Ministry of Industries, and all obvious loopholes are stopped up by the usual austerity regulations on imports, building, currency, rents, foreign travel, and prices.

About 10 per cent of Egypt's agricultural land has been redistributed, and paternalistic cooperatives have been established in the villages of these areas, though it is hoped to expand the system to include all agricultural areas. Education and health, community development, agricultural extension, and labor exchange services have all been increased, some more and some less. New labor legislation has given some additional protection to industrial workers. Adequate supplies of staple foods have been assured, and fixed prices generally prevail in the markets.

Still, Egypt's problems are very great. Rural destitution remains the rule. Migration to the big city is unabated. The population continues to increase at a rate sufficient to counterbalance development. The universities turn out more graduates, B.A.'s, M.D.'s, social workers, and lawyers than can find employment. The regular service is overstaffed, yet continues to hire some new graduates; many new functions are being granted to specialized organizations working under their own regulations and hiring the graduates of special institutes, the Faculty of Commerce, or retired Army officers. The professional classes feel the squeeze as austerity is tightened and their clients become more circumspect about fees.

It is clear that the UAR is engaged in a difficult race against time and the birth rate. It has set itself a plan to double the na-

tional income in ten years, a plan which is heavily dependent on
foreign currency to pay for capital goods, and it hopes to avoid
all inflation during that period.

From the foregoing it would appear that the nationalist classes
are not much better off economically than they were before. Some
peasants are better off, as are some workers, some merchants, small
industrialists, contractors, army officers, technical experts, economists, engineers, apparently a small class of rural dignitaries of
moderate land holdings, and some of the higher ulama.

The variety of these groups indicates that the benefits they have
derived are not the result of a fixed policy of redistribution. The
peasants who are better off are those who have received land and
who have had their rents reduced. Agricultural policy was one of
the major foundations of the legitimization of the revolutionary
regime until recently. Labor groups remain closely controlled, but
the modest benefits they have received are the direct result of
their assistance to Nasser during the crisis of March 1954. The
other groups, all of whom are small, have benefited because of the
importance of their contribution to the policies of the UAR or
because development funds, jobs, or concessions aiming at administrative rationalization have been channelled in their direction.

If the conclusions of our analysis and our method are accepted,
it follows that (1) there is a substantial gap between the interests
of the nationalist classes and government policies, which is in a
small part explained by alienation and in a much larger part explained by interpretations of the government's purposes and expectations, that is, their ideology; and that (2) if government policy has been oriented to the ideology of the nationalist classes, it
it has not responded in its development to the demands of these
classes except in making some minor concessions.

Despite this gap between the expectations of the nationalist
classes and the performance of the government, they support the
present regime, even if not with rabid enthusiasm. In general, the
urban lower class believes that the revolution has benefited it by
giving it greater dignity and protection, legal and otherwise, against
the wealthier classes, the minorities, and foreigners. The government frequently resorts to organizing student and worker demonstrations, which do not appear to be taken seriously by the urban

middle class; but the latter, in turn, supports Nasser and his foreign policy especially. The nationalist classes, as earlier described, range in their views from complete support of the government and belief in its ability to raise standards of living and to achieve equality to the view that the government's preference for nation-building policies is ruining the country by ruining its educated elite.

The more usual attitude, however, is that the squeeze on the middle classes is justified in order to benefit the less fortunate, but that it is rather unpleasant medicine. About internal policy there is much complaining, but usually in a spirit of patriotic sacrifice, resignation, or good-natured and self-directed laughter. Some are fairly optimistic about the future. Many would like greater political freedom. Surprisingly few, however, draw any conclusions from domestic problems to foreign policy.

These attitudes are no more than evidence of a largely unexpressed ideology. We have already noted that one of the central problems of pan-Arabism, according to its literary exponents, is its lack of an agreed theory. Some, like Aflaq, argue that no theory is necessary;[39] others, like Rimawi, argue that the theory is to be found in the evolving policies of the UAR; but it is likely that many more, like Nusaibeh, believe that the theory is somewhere out there waiting to be discovered.[40] It is further evident that there is no ideology of social reform separate from Arab nationalism. That is to say, nearly all writers and speechmakers insist that the reform of Arab society is one integral part of the nationalist idea, that social reform is a necessary prelude to the full realization of Arab nationalism, and that (or but) Arab nationalism itself defines the nature of the required social reform or the nature of the genuine Arab society.

The details of this problem are complex, and the literature extensive, so that here we can give only a summary impression of the diffuse idea of the ideal society which apparently prevails among the nationalist classes. Four types of theory come to explain this ideology, and we assume that the authors, in this case, do reflect the sentiments of their public. All four types are concerned with what is called Arab socialism. The adherents of the first of these we shall call the scientific socialists; the second are the humanists; the third are the Labor Party socialists; and the fourth, the pragmatic étatistes.

The scientific socialists use Marxist terminology, are obviously well versed in Communist literature, and are mostly concerned to prove that Marxism does not apply to the Arabs. Most of these writers are Lebanese or Syrians. A good example of one of them is Afif al-Bahansi's *Introduction to Arab Socialism.*[41]

The humanists are not economists but more likely belletrists who find in socialism a reflection of the goodness and charity of the simple human being. As yet I have found only Egyptians writing in this tone, and it would appear that there is a good deal of nonpolitical literature expressed in the same nostalgic, almost banal, romantic manner. Abd al-Mon'im al-Sawi's *The Socialism of Our Country* illustrates the point only too well,[42] and the same viewpoint has been expressed by Ihsan Abd al-Quddus in various articles in *Rose al-Yusuf.*[43]

The Labor Party socialists are followers of Laski and sometimes graduates of the London School of Economics. The most prominent of this small group is Hatim, who has written only one pamphlet but has sponsored many others and has had translations made of Laski's, G. D. H. Cole's, and Rostow's works.[44] The leading pragmatic étatist is, of course, President Nasser. The Ba'this fall somewhere between the scientific socialists and the humanists.

On the basis of a preliminary examination of this literature, certain important common features can be found. Because they appear to reflect popular opinion we shall concentrate our attention upon them to the exclusion of the interesting differences among the exponents of Arab socialism. All of these tendencies reject the Marxist idea of the class struggle. If there is any conflict among classes it is subordinate to the national struggle against imperialism and foreign capitalism. The Arab socialist ideal is that of cooperation among all classes, or binding the classes together, or reducing the distance between them, or encouraging their mutually responsible interaction.[45]

After rejecting both Hegelian and Marxian dialectic and Sartre's lack of an absolute ethical purpose, al-Bahansi finds the answer in man's nature: Man has freedom to act as a dynamic being and he has consciousness (*wa'i*). These two forces work together and their confluence is called conscience (*wijdan*). The confluence of the individual and the external world is similarly necessary and is called cohesion (*ilti'am*).[46]

Al-Sawi tells the story of a village boy whose father dies and who discovers in his obligation to his younger brother that fatherhood belongs to all men in their relations to one another, and then learns from the considerateness of his fellow villagers that every man is his brother's keeper.[47]

> He began to understand (he was only ten years old) that disputes among the people of our country were but a kind of social supervision over the behavior of the individuals themselves, should they deviate or take a mind to transgress against whatever the society considered good. He began to discover good interpretations for whatever he saw and heard, and all these explanations led him to the conclusion that the society of our country has a powerful awareness, that it does not determine anything which is not right and good.[48]

And again, the village celebration "explained to him the socialism of our country as the most beautiful of possible humanist explanations of socialism, and social justice, and democracy, and cooperation." [49]

Hatim accepts the view, accredited to Strachey, that a broad political organization of all the people is necessary to realize socialism; but in rejecting Marxism he points out that Arab society is not like others, divided into two warring camps, but is made up of homogeneous groups. "Arab society became homogeneous after political parties . . . ceased to exist." [50] Ihsan Abd al-Quddus uses the example of the extended family of the village *umdah* of fifty years ago to demonstrate Arab socialism.[51]

As near as can be judged from our preliminary survey, Arab socialism is a kind of emotional extension of the nationalist idea to the problems resulting from the loosening of traditional social ties. As Nasser put it in 1961 in a speech at Damascus University, Arabs must now think of the whole nation as their family, and they should enjoy the same privileges and owe the same obligations as they do to their families. The Arab nation is one great *gemeinschaft*, and evidence for this assertion is found in the various traditional *gemeinschaftlich* customs prevalent within families or in village society.[52] Class harmony and mutual responsibility are part of the distinctive Arab character and Arab philosophy.

If Arab socialism is essentially an atavism, that did not prevent various writers from putting forward specific suggestions for its achievement. Hatim and Bahansi both do this, but the most remarkably portentous suggestions appeared in the Ba'th constitution.[53] In its broad outlines, the government of the UAR has followed the Ba'thi line. To fully grasp the paradox here we must note again that the Ba'this are under a cloud in the UAR, that there is not a shred of evidence that the Ba'th has influenced economic policy in Egypt (as opposed to Syria), and that ex-Ba'thi Rimawi has developed a theory which looks to the pragmatic solutions of the Egyptian government for its inspiration.

The government of the UAR followed the Ba'thi suggestions not because they were Ba'thi suggestions, nor because they represented the most plausible operative interpretation of the national-social ideal, but because, after failing for a long while to find a way out of its economic difficulties, a number of circumstances made them seem the most plausible response to the existing situation and the great pressure for development. Practical difficulties prevented further time-consuming study. The next step was to rationalize the new policy in terms of the prevalent ideology of social reform, and the result is the aim of establishing a socialist-cooperative-democracy.

In his early speeches, Nasser did not use the term "socialism." He spoke of the need to advance all classes of the people,[54] then of the need to close the gaps which separated the classes,[55] of the desire to create a society in which the rich will help the poor,[56] and of the government as a government of all classes which looked on Egypt as one big family.[57] The first time that Nasser used the term "socialism" was on May 19, 1955, after his return from Bandung.[58] He explained it then to mean closing the gap between classes, and shortly thereafter said, "This is the first Id (*al Fitr*) we have assembled together in which our efforts to create a strong socialist society have made some headway." [59] Socialism was to be the method of achieving social justice.[60]

The last explanation of socialism suggests that he had something more definite in mind than merely the cooperation of all classes. This suggestion is further supported by several attacks on capitalism during the same period, changing one of the six principles of the revolution from ending monopolies [61] to ending the rule of capitalism. This emphasis must be contrasted with his earlier speeches immediately after the events of March 1954. At that time he told a number of labor groups that both capital and labor had their rights and that both should cooperate in their mutual interest and in the interest of the nation.[62] Nasser now uses the phrase "socialist-cooperative-democratic society," but in a variety of ways: as a society without exploitation [63] and as a society of owners.[64] However, he also has used the term "socialism" to refer to the "public sector" of the UAR economy.

From an examination of Egyptian economic policy it becomes clear that what began as a vague idea of somehow deriving an ideal society out of the ideological remnants of traditional society has now become a determined effort on the part of the government to direct the economy; to prevent the creation of large and independent concentrations of economic power and to control existing ones; and to rely only on loans, grants, and profits from government enterprises, compulsory and voluntary sales of bonds, and taxes for the development capital which it needs.

This is essentially a development policy, and as yet it has not deeply affected Egyptian social structure or social values. Land reform did affect social structure, though not so much as power structure.

The reason for the lack of a severe social impact from recent development policies is not only due to the time lag in social change and the limited nature of present achievements; it is also due to the paternalistic form which these policies have taken and to the relative compartmentalization of the developing sector. Politically, paternalism has meant recognizing and working through existing social groups and occupational associations, but the more modern associations have been reduced to protective societies capable only of pressing for redress of individual grievances, for the most part. The difference between a traditional interest system and a highly bureaucratized and rationalized one is not so great, except for the number of groups recognized.

Development policy has not created a really new elite. The revolution itself removed the aristocratic landowners' monopoly on all positions of authority, but it did not exclude members of the former elite. The new elite is not comprised of "new" men, it is rather made up of families (not individuals) of substantial middle-class positions within the traditional social structure. These families have some agricultural connections, so that the idealization of village life is not all nostalgia, but most members of the family hold government posts in various ministries, and many have relatives in the armed services and perhaps even among the ulama. Those who have the best training and/or the best connections, or who have demonstrated both their loyalty and their ability to get things done, may be coopted into the outer circle of decision makers or may become direct beneficiaries of development policy.

Traditional family structure and the values that go with it have not been attacked; instead, the educated groups most imbued with these values have been strengthened. It is, therefore, not at all a foregone conclusion that increased national income will accelerate social change. On the other hand, the failure of the development plan may lead to more drastic measures, which will break down further the traditional structures. It is difficult, therefore, to state whether social protest in Egypt is against Europeanization or against traditional Islamic social values.

The compartmentalization of the development effort was not envisioned earlier and is clearly another occasion of the triumph of events over ideals. The original hope for the cooperation of private capital with the government was disappointed first by the unwillingness of foreign capital to invest in Egypt and then by the withholding of the large sums expected from the United States after Nasser had signed the Anglo-Egyptian Treaty of 1954. The dispute with the United States over the Baghdad Pact, prolonged by the arms deal with the Soviet Union, was moderated by the promise of assistance in constructing the High Dam, but burst forth with renewed vigor after this promise was withdrawn.

Throughout this period Egypt was getting most of its advice from American experts in attempting to draw up a development plan; but no real plan was completed, nor had local capital responded very much to the development needs of Egypt, by the time of the Suez invasion. That invasion brought about the nationalization of the British and French firms in Egypt, so that in 1957 the government suddenly found itself with the largest industrial establishment in the country. Indeed, with the exception of the Misr group, the government then controlled all big industrial establishments.[65] Together with the few earlier government projects, these firms were organized under the Economic Development Organization, and a five-year plan was hastily put together for immediate implementation. East European advice was now sought and granted, the National Planning Commission was set up, and, as obstacles arose, various enterprises were nationalized, as were all major sources of savings and investment funds. The suddenly developing situation of 1957 pointed the way in which planned development might proceed. With its hands partly untied, the government proceeded vigorously along the only path it saw clearly; thus the form of the development policy of the UAR was sealed.

The national plan purports to be a coordinated social and economic plan, but its social aspect is restricted to the provision of funds for welfare services and education. Industrialization and the High Dam are the two biggest aims of the plan, and no competing demands will be permitted to stand in their way. The impact of these programs on Egyptian society and politics is still anybody's guess—at least one expert does not believe that the labor force will be expanded, though this is one of the government's goals.[66] At any rate, the quality and quantity of social change will be the result of the direction of the development program; development will not be controlled by an ideological conception of the ideal society.

In the meantime, for the people of Egypt, and especially the nationalist classes, the hiatus between their demands and the ability of the government to supply them is filled by the belief that there is some direct connection between the government's economic policy and their vague social reform aspirations. As one goes up the economic scale, this belief probably becomes weaker; but even where it is weak there is the compensatory feeling of a new dignity and importance for Egyptians and all Arabs on the international political stage.

NOTES

1. For a detailed study based on this view, see my *Religion and Politics in Pakistan* (Berkeley, 1961).
2. Abd al-Qadir Hatim, *Hawl al-Nazriyyah al-Ishtirakiyyah* [*On the Theory of Socialism*] Kutub Qawmiyyah Series, No. 14 (Cairo, July 1959), p. 8.
3. Abd Allah al Rimawi, *Al Mantiq al-Thawri* [*The Revolutionary Logic*] (Cairo, 1961), p. 95.
4. *Ibid.*, pp. 55–56.
5. *Ibid.*, p. 32. On the Ba'th Party, see the works of Michel Aflaq and Salah al-Din al-Bitar cited below, and those of Munif al-Razzaz, etc. See also "The Constitution of the Arab Resurrection Socialist Party (Ba'th)," *Middle East Journal*, Vol. 13, no. 2 (Spring 1959), pp. 195–200.
6. Hatim, *op. cit.*, pp. 5–7.
7. *Ibid.*, p. 8.
8. See Rejwan, in W. Z. Laqueur, *The Middle East in Transition* (New York, 1958), and H. Z. Nusaibeh, *The Ideas of Arab Nationalism* (Ithaca, 1956).
9. Tharwat Ukasha, *Itihaduna Falsafah Khalqiyyah* [*Our Union Is a Moral Philosophy*] al-Maktabah al-Thaqafiyyah Series, No. 16 (Ministry of Culture and National Guidance, n.d.), pp. 3–4. The National Union is the mass popular organization which replaces political parties in the UAR.
10. Kamal al-Din Husain, "Introduction," in Gamal Abd al-Nasser, *Falsafat al-Thawrah* (n.p., n.d.). Introductory insert has no page numbers.
11. Nasser, *Falsafat al-Thawrah*, pp. 26, 27.
12. President Gamal Abd al-Nasser, *Khutub wa Tasrihat* [*Speeches and Interviews*], published in ten volumes in Arabic by the Editorial Committee of *Ikhtama Lak* [*We Have Chosen for You*]. Additional volumes published in English by the Information Administration, all at Cairo, without dates. Hereafter cited as *Nasser's Speeches* (Arabic or English). Here, English, 1959, p. 570.
13. *Ibid.*, p. 315.
14. Not entirely unfair, however, for President Nasser has described his country as an exporter of ideology. *Nasser's Speeches* (English) (1959), p. 524.
15. Rimawi, *op. cit.*, pp. 60–62.
16. See Chapter 1.
17. K. Deutsch, *et al.*, *The Political Community and the North Atlantic Area* (Princeton, 1957).
18. In 1957 Aflaq was of the opinion that Rightists and Leftists could coop-

erate during the anti-imperialist stage of the Arab struggle: *Fi Sabil al-Ba'th* (Beirut, 1959), p. 220.

19. *Al-Jaridah al-Rasmiyya [Official Gazette]* No. 157 (July 14, 1960), p. 1264.
20. This is Ukasha's central theme, *op. cit.*
21. *Nasser's Speeches* (English) (1959), pp. 282–83.
22. *Al-Ahram* (March 31, 1961); *Egyptian Mail* (April 1, 1961). (Italics added.)
23. Muhammad Mustafa al-Sha'bini, *al-Hiyad al-Ijabi [Positive Neutrality]*, Kitab al-Madfa'iyyah (Cairo, 1960), pp. 72–95.
24. The emphasis on Palestine is a rebuttal to Hussain's claim that Jordan bears the brunt of the common Arab struggle.
25. The Arab South is the current term for Aden and the Aden Protectorate.
26. *Al-Ahram, loc. cit.* (Italics added.)
27. Anwar G. Chejne, "Egyptian Attitudes Toward Pan-Arabism," *Middle East Journal,* Vol. XI, no. 3 (Summer 1957).
28. E.g., Ukasha, *op. cit.,* p. 61.
29. *Nasser's Speeches* (Arabic), Vol. 3, p. 679.
30. *Ibid.,* Vol. 6, pp. 1170f.
31. *Ibid.,* p. 1222f.
32. These audiences are at best indirect evidence, but they do throw some light on the identity of the groups which the Revolutionary Council considered to be powerful and influential. It appears that a good deal of political thinking went into the "nonconstitutional" treaty ratification campaign.
33. The limitations on Nasser's leadership are suggested in an editorial by Muhammad Hasanain Haikal in *al-Ahram* (January 27, 1961).
34. *Nasser's Speeches* (Arabic), Vol. 7, p. 1393.
35. Salah al-Din al-Bitar, *al-Siyasah al-Arabiyyah [The Arab Policy]* (Beirut, 1960), p. 48, advocated the union of Syria and Egypt as the first step to Arab unity in 1955. Michel Aflaq, *Ma'arakat al-Musir al-Wahid [Battle for a Single Destiny]*, 2nd ed. (Beirut, 1959), pp. 66–85.
36. Teachers are civil servants, it should be remembered.
37. This is true of the Egyptian revolution despite occasional vagueness of expression; e.g., on March 27, 1955, Nasser said that "this revolution arose to represent the middle class, it arose to represent the hope of the majority of this people." *Nasser's Speeches* (Arabic), Vol. 3, p. 685. His audience was a group of workers. The major tendency at the present time follows this theme of lumping all classes together, but there was a significant difference between the attitude of the revolutionary government in the spring of 1954 and its attitude in the summer of 1955, as judged from *Nasser's Speeches;* see Vol. 2, p. 238, on students; p. 270, on the lawyers' syndicate; p. 279, telling the civil servants to think of the peasants; p. 361, on the bad effects of university education before the revolution; compare this with an important speech made on July 22, 1955, Vol. 4, mentioning the benefits bestowed by the Revolution on the writers and the intelli-

gentsia, p. 867; doctors, p. 870; teachers, p. 875; journalists, actors, and movie makers, p. 879; civil servants, p. 880.
38. Ukasha, *op. cit.*, p. 23.
39. See "Radical-Reform Nationalism in Syria and Egypt," *The Muslim World* (April, July, 1959).
40. H. K. Nusaibeh, *op. cit.*
41. Afif al-Bahansi, *Madkhal ila al-Ishtirakiyyah al-Arabiyyah* (Damascus, 1957?).
42. Abd al-Mun'im al-Sawi, *Ishtirakiyyat Baladina*, al Maktabah al-Thaqa-fiyyah Series, No. 18, Ministry of Culture (Cairo, n.d.).
43. E.g., *Rose al-Yusuf*, February 13, 20, and 27 and March 13 and 20, 1961.
44. Hatim is Minister of State in charge of broadcasting and the Information Service. He is also on the editorial committee of the Ikhtarna Lak series.
45. The last view is that of Muhammad Hasanain Haikal. Nasser prefers to speak of closing the gap between classes.
46. Al-Bahansi, *op. cit.*, p. 50.
47. Al-Sawi, *op. cit.*, pp. 11, 34, *et passim.*
48. *Ibid.*, p. 34.
49. *Ibid.*, p. 58.
50. Hatim, *op. cit.*, p. 41.
51. *Rose al-Yusuf*, February 13, 1961, p. 6.
52. Ukasha, *op. cit.*, p. 111.
53. See Note 3.
54. *Nasser's Speeches* (Arabic), Vol. 1, p. 76.
55. *Ibid.*, p. 101.
56. *Ibid.*, p. 150.
57. *Ibid.*, Vol. 2, p. 424.
58. *Ibid.*, Vol. 4, p. 743.
59. *Ibid.*, p. 751.
60. *Ibid.*, p. 768.
61. *Ibid.*, Vol. 3, p. 724.
62. *Ibid.*, Vol. 2, pp. 242, 244, 257.
63. *Ibid.*, (English) (April–June 1960), p. 115.
64. *Ibid.*, p. 152.
65. The Misr group has now been taken over by the government.
66. F. Harbison and I. A. Ibrahim, *Human Resources for Egyptian Enterprise* (New York, 1958), p. 135.

8

EGYPT'S POSITIVE NEUTRALITY

I THE UNITED STATES AND THE UNITED ARAB REPUBLIC

To act with wisdom and moderation and with enlightened self-interest is the antithesis of revolution and extremist protest. It is this sort of behavior that we least expect from the leaders of revolutionary governments, but wisdom and restraint are expected of the developed countries. Lack of restraint can take many forms, as Mossadegh's stubborn refusal to deal with the Anglo-Iranian Oil Company and Nasser's truculent nationalization of the Suez Canal Company. The one approached an infantile suicidalism; the other courted a direct reprisal. But were these acts of irrationality or were they miscalculations? It is evident that Mossadegh was sure that he would break British-American solidarity eventually. He was wrong, not mad. Nasser has said that he weighed the possibility of a British attack, but he decided that there was a 75 per cent improbability of that occurring. Both gambled and lost, though Nasser did not lose much; and for both, the domestic consequences of refusing to gamble probably outweighed even the great risks taken.

In one of the newest and more recondite apologies for the policies of the United Arab Republic and President Nasser's leadership of the Pan-Arab movement, those who called for wisdom and realism [1] are described as the indefatigable "stooges of imperialism." The true revolutionary position, the author holds, stands on principle and refuses compromise. Yet, in the aftermath of the treaty arranging for the British evacuation of the Canal Zone, it was President Nasser himself who used that exact term ("realism") to describe his motives in agreeing to less than complete, immediate, and unconditional evacuation of Britain's 70,000 troops.[2] There are other examples, too, that help to illustrate the existence of some policy flexibility in the UAR: the agreement with the Sudan on the division of the Nile waters, the resumption of normal relations with Britain (despite the latter's unwillingness to permit the UAR to open consulates where they chose in colonial territories), the acceptance of King Hussain's friendly overtures, and even the relatively mild reaction to the implication of the United States in the Cuban rebellion of April 1961.[3]

For the time being, at least, the policy of the government of the UAR cannot be viewed as a closed book, determined a priori to take the most extreme and uncompromising position. It still enjoys a range of freedom of action. Understanding the bases of its policy is not a useless academic pursuit, because it may suggest ways in which we can educe more accommodating reactions. This is not to argue, however, that the interests of the United States and those of the UAR are potentially the same, for they are not.

The conflict between the United States and the UAR is one of interests and ideology, but it is not a conflict between rationality and irrationality. Though there may be many relatively constant determinants of foreign policy, such as geography, demography, and economy, understanding these factors in their relation to specific situations is always an ideological process. Hence, aside from the normal aspiration of human beings for increased material welfare, other preferences and the choice of means depend on beliefs about what is good and on cognitive efforts to find out what is possible. When the neutralist states are accused of irrationality, it is assumed that our view of world affairs is the only correct one, that the irresponsible neutral refuses to recognize the aggressiveness of the Soviet Union and derives a vicarious pleasure out of seeing the culturally haughty and economically superior West get kicked around. This accusation may be correct, but it does not explain UAR policy, nor does it accord with Arab explanations of the policy of positive neutrality.

A plausible explanation is not a justification. Indeed, we are living in a world in which other nations perversely refuse to see things our way because their situation—that is, their interests and objectives—is not ours. Another important aspect of this problem should be borne in mind. The right of national self-determination may be quite acceptable in the abstract, but, like all abstract absolutes, it becomes a matter of dispute when put into practical application. Even if there is an agreement to apply the principle in a particular case, and often there is not, the boundaries of self-determination are always unclear.

It is a standard assumption in the West that all states are interdependent, and from this assumption certain conclusions about the limits of self-determination are derived. Interdependence is not a constant either, and its implications appear to vary with the postulation of diverse international systems. What is good for a "balance of power" system with a First World War technology may not be good for a bipolar system with a Third World War technology.

But nationalist ideologies do not appear to adjust to the times as easily as do counterideologies. Self-determination is not the only demand of unsatisfied nationalism; equality, too, is insisted upon, regardless of the size and power of the state. We may strongly hold that we have special responsibilities by virtue of our size and power, but it is unlikely that Nasser will accept this view any more than King Hussain will accept the assertion that the UAR has special responsibilities among the Arab states because of its moral and material circumstances.

Despite the fact that the use of the slogan "positive neutrality" is of relatively recent vintage, the current opposition to nearly all international acts of the United States has roots that go deeper than either Arab policy or the social policy of the United Arab Republic. To take only the most obvious example, we must go back at least to 1941–1942, when Britain pressed Egypt to declare war upon the Axis powers. Both Farouk and his Premier Ali Maher temporized, with the result that the British forced Farouk to appoint Nahhas Pasha, who did the necessary. Farouk swore that he would never forget that outrage, but it was left to the revolutionary nationalists to carry out his word.

A similar anti-Western reaction followed the refusal of the Western powers to act on Egypt's plea for United Nations intervention in her bid to revise the treaty of 1936 with Britain, on the ground that the circumstances of 1936 (the threat of Italian aggression) had passed. The failure of this initiative, as well as the Palestine Resolution of November 29, 1947, were important factors in Egypt's decision not to support the United Nations' action in Korea.

Later, opposition to the West took the special form of opposing the establishment of any joint-defense organization in the Middle East and of preventing other Arab states from joining such a pact at the time the West proposed the establishment of a Middle East Command and later a Middle East Defense Organization. Not only did Egypt demand evacuation before discussing any such pact; she also initiated the Arab collective security treaty in the Arab League, to forestall the Western effort and strengthen her counterclaim that the defense of the area should be the responsibility of the area powers themselves. These events took place before the revolution of July 1952, and to a large extent set limits on the policy choices available to the new regime.

As might be expected, the governments which held office under Farouk from 1942 to 1952 were immobilist. Their position *vis à vis* the West, and especially Great Britain, was one of withholding support rather than seriously seeking some powerful international counterweight. This generalization holds true despite some short-lived pro-Axis feeling when it was thought that Rommel might sweep into Alexandria from the desert. But, as events demonstrated, Egypt had nothing to offer in return for Western compliance and in desperation turned first to an ill-prepared involvement in the Palestine War and then to guerrilla attacks in the Canal Zone.

The attitude which prevailed at the time is nicely put in a brief article written by Salah al-Din al-Bitar of the Syrian Ba'th Party in 1950. After discussing the horrors of atomic war, al-Bitar wrote that the bipolar split is to be abhorred quite as much as the domination of a single power. The Arabs are seeking new social and political forms, but they are not finding the answers they want in either the American or the Soviet systems. Moreover, Western imperialism divided the Arab homeland, maintained it in a divided condition, took away Palestine, drove out its people, made it Jewish, and continues in its efforts to make Arab lands Jewish. Thus, the Arab position must reflect an attitude toward the West which is in harmony with the lack of Western justice. It must strengthen the Arab case in the United Nations, so that the smaller nations will be astonished and ask why the Arabs so behave when *they are non-Communist states in the Western sphere.* When they learn the answer, the smaller states will press the United States, United Kingdom, and France to change their duplicitous policies.[4]

There is no evidence here, or in the action of Egyptian governments up to 1955, of attempts to exploit the bipolar division of power by bringing Soviet pressures to bear against the United States. During that period, none of the neutralist states had done anything of the kind except for Yugoslavia. In this special sense, it might be said truly that the United States was the leader of the free world (or non-Communist world) during the period in question.

In order to change this situation two factors were needed that were not previously present: the first was the willingness of the Soviet Union to accept neutralist overtures, and the second was a revolutionary leader ready to take the double chance of incurring the wrath of the West and getting involved with Russia. Mossadegh had already shown the way, but the Russians were not yet ready.

Nasser made his decision to take the chance after becoming embroiled with the United States over the Baghdad Pact and the refusal of the West to supply him with arms. There was no real precedent on which he could rely or which could help to explain his action. We do know, however, that he had not yet consolidated his hold on Egypt; he has insisted on the decisive importance of the Israeli attack on Gaza in 1955. The precise importance of that attack is still shrouded in the heavy obscurity of the so-called Lavon Affair, so that Israeli motivation is a matter of dispute. Domestically, at any rate, it appears that the attack may have weakened Nasser's efforts to win the confidence of some of the military.[5]

The internal pressure on Nasser may have been compelling in itself, but it is worthy of note that the arms deal with the Soviet Union did not take place until after the Bandung Conference. From Nasser's speeches it is clear that that conference had a profound effect on his thinking. There is no way that we can be sure of the precise nature of this effect, but we can guess that he was impressed by the respectability achieved by Communist China at the conference and perhaps surprised also to see Indonesia thus responding to the creation of SEATO. He was perhaps also impressed by the respectability accorded the term socialism, which he used only after returning from Bandung. Above all, he may have been impressed by the size of the gathering, its potentiality for representing "world opinion," and its support for Arab causes. It may also be noted that the conference followed the first great Western defeat in Indo-China.

Whatever were Nasser's calculations of the risk, he gambled and won. Not only was there no appreciable negative response from the West besides pained surprise, but the United States did not join the Baghdad Pact and no guarantees or substantial arms were given to Israel. Instead, Dulles proposed a plan for a solution of the Arab-Israeli dispute to be financed by the United States, and when that failed to advance matters, the United States reluctantly agreed to assist Egypt in building the High Dam at Aswan on the basis of the advice of the United States Ambassador in Cairo.

The withdrawal of this offer of assistance may be seen as a delayed reaction. Apparently the first American view was that the whole problem was tied up with the Arab-Israeli dispute: no dispute, no need for arms.

But the time for such an approach had passed with the break between the United States and Egypt over the Baghdad Pact. With the wisdom of hindsight it may now be said that substantial economic aid should have followed on the signature of the evacuation treaty. That is what Nasser expected and needed. The dispute with the Israelis was not then a barrier to good American-Egyptian relations; to seek a solution to that dispute in order to improve those relations after they had deteriorated puts the cart before the horse. After this series of errors, the United States reversed itself.

If the Arab-Israeli dispute could not be resolved, it was thought, then perhaps its effects on United States-Egyptian relations could be overcome by really generous economic assistance; but this reasonable approach was not followed through. When Nasser recognized Communist China, it appeared decided that he was unalterably opposed to accommodation with the West. It is likely that President Nasser did not appreciate the effect that this act, which had been performed by England, India, and Indonesia, might have during that period of delicate negotiations. But it is an open question as to who was the more perverse and irrational, Dulles or Nasser. Several reports suggest that Dulles seized this and other excuses for doing what he had wanted to do from the beginning anyway. For Nasser it may or may not have been the right price to pay for the sale of 10 million dollars worth of cotton.

From 1954 through the end of the Suez crisis, we may conclude, Nasser was primarily concerned with the domestic security of his regime of moderate revolution. If he were to hold power and have the support of the more radical military, he had to avoid political and military entanglements with the West, increase the social services and the number of available jobs, and build up the army. Doing the best that he could with limited resources, he opposed the Baghdad Pact with Pan-Arabism, got the Soviet Union to sell him arms, and used the arms deal to get United States financial support for the High Dam. In this manner was Nasser started on the road to neutralism, but obviously it was a rather special kind of neutralism. The personal fate of no other neutralist leader was so closely tied to the outcome of his dealings with the great powers. The nullification of the Baghdad Pact was a personal victory. The arms deal was a personal victory. The withdrawal of the American offer of assistance in building the High Dam was a personal insult, and the successful nationalization of the Suez Canal Company was a personal achievement.

At the end of the Suez crisis, Nasser was no longer under great personal pressure. For domestic purposes, in any case, he had proven that his administrative organization was capable of holding itself together, and the value of his propaganda apparatus externally was established. With the realization of these two achievements, Egypt discovered itself with concrete opportunities to fulfill some of the aspirations only dimly suggested in Nasser's *Philosophy of the Revolution*. We have noted elsewhere the manner in which the nationalization of British and French firms provided the basis for a new economic effort from 1957. We have seen how Nasser's need for Arab allies against the Baghdad Pact and the Arab nationalists' need for leadership combined to present Egypt with a Pan-Arab policy.

The early months of 1957, which saw the defeat of the Eisenhower Doctrine, can be singled out as the turning point for Egypt, both domestically and externally. The Ba'th's idea of comprehensive Arab unity suddenly became a realistic possibility as one watched the reaction to the Suez crisis in Jordan, Syria, Lebanon, and Iraq. Moreover, the importance of the fact that both the United States and the Soviet Union had supported Egypt during the crisis, in opposition to their support of the Palestine Resolution of 1947, was not lost on Nasser. Hence, it is from this date that we can note a new purposefulness in the UAR's pursuit of positive neutrality.

For Nasser the new opportunities presented themselves in the form of realizing the dream of a great Arab state stretching from the Ocean to the Gulf, with Egypt playing the role of Prussia and he the role of Bismarck. The investment capital to be derived from the revenues from Arab petroleum and the Middle Eastern and African markets for the expected surplus manufactures of an industrialized Egypt constituted possible solutions for immediate economic problems. Egyptian neutrality changed from a defense against Western pressures to a positive means of achieving those goals by either winning the support of the great powers or excluding them from the Egyptian sphere of interest.

This discussion will now permit us to draw certain conclusions about the various phases through which Egyptian neutrality has passed. At first neutralism was (1) a device to press the West for certain concessions; then it became (2) a means of seeking Afro-Asian support for Egyptian goals; thereafter it was used as (3) a justification for dealing with the Eastern bloc; and most recently it has been (4) identified with Arab nationalism and has been used in an effort to exclude Western influence from the Middle East. It was doubtless also used to combat Soviet influence in Syria and Iraq, but it is evident that such gains as the Soviet Union hoped to make in those countries were offset by the expectations of greater gains from supporting Egypt. Hence, it is with Soviet encouragement that the "activist" neutrality of Egypt has developed its newer distinctive characteristics. These characteristics go beyond revolutionary Arab propaganda and include (a) cooperation with the Soviet Union in return for continued Soviet support, (b) an attempt to assert leadership among the Afro-Asian countries, and (c) a moderately successful effort to organize the movement of positive neutrality into a third bloc.

Cooperation with the Soviet bloc takes the form of sustaining the Soviet claims to be the friend of neutrals, to offer aid without strings attached, and to be diligently seeking peaceful coexistence. Nasser's bid for leadership in the Afro-Asian bloc is manifested in the number of Afro-Asian conferences held in Cairo and in his speech before the General Assembly of the United Nations in 1960. The effort to organize the neutralist bloc is evidenced in the high degree of cooperation between the United Arab Republic and Yugoslavia, a somewhat lessened enthusiasm for India, the establishment of the Afro-Asian Solidarity Conference, and the follow-up work after the Casablanca Conference. The final bit of evidence of growing importance of positive neutralism for pan-Arabism is the growing body of ideological writing on the subject.

An examination of the speeches and press interviews of President Nasser generally supports the outline presented above. His early speeches record his attempts to press the West for concessions. On November 20, 1953, he made his first criticism of the "free world," that is, the United States, for its failure to grant Egypt any development loans in the fourteen months since the revolution.[6] On April 19, 1954, he made a thinly veiled threat that he might seek arms from the Eastern bloc if the West did not comply with his request.[7] On the second anniversary of the revolution he made one of his most revealing statements about Egyptian foreign policy and his grasp of the Cold War situation; he said that this was no longer the age of power politics, but an age in which the great powers were vying for the friendship of the lesser powers. Egypt, he announced, would withhold its friendship from those who did not cooperate with her.[8]

This statement is in accord with the passive nature of Egyptian foreign policy at the time, but Nasser went on to identify Egypt as part of the Afro-Asian bloc and reviewed the strategic and moral foundations which would one day permit Egypt to play a more significant role in world affairs.[9] After initialing the evacuation treaty, Nasser repeated the latter theme, stating that the evacuation would permit Egypt to fulfill its international mission: *Egypt would force the world to recognize its existence.*[10]

Despite these euphoric references to future glories, Nasser withheld from declaring Egypt to be neutral; in fact, Egypt preferred neutrality but was still tied to Britain by the provisions of the treaty of 1954. Nasser explained that neutrality required power: "The question is, shall I wait until the enemy burns my house?" But his ambivalence was quickly revealed when he added that he believed a Third World War unlikely because of the balance of terror.[11] Nasser was attempting to justify the arrangement whereby the British might return to Egypt within a period of seven years, while at the same time suggesting that such a return would be unlikely.

After the controversy with the West over the Baghdad Pact had fully emerged, he stated that there was no difference between the East and the West: Egypt wanted no military pacts.[12] Nasser then set out to attend the Bandung meetings, and in speeches in India, Indonesia, back in Cairo, and in Yugoslavia he stressed the attachment of Egypt to the idea of Afro-Asian cooperation to achieve peace. He frequently repeated the ten principles agreed upon at Bandung, most of which refer to the preservation of the independence of small states, their equality, and the importance of the principle of nonintervention.[13] In Yugoslavia he first made the point that Egypt's foreign policy was a reflection of the principles on which the domestic revolution was based.

Despite the strength of this new neutralist tendency, Nasser revealed some hesitation, or at least uncertainty, about the re-action of the West in an interview with a correspondent from the *Daily Herald* after the announcement of the arms deal with Czechoslovakia was made. When asked if Egypt had taken a neutralist position, Nasser answered,

> How can we be neutral when we are tied for seven years more by a treaty with Britain about the Suez Canal base? The question is not one of whether we are neutral, but it is a question of not submitting to the control of any foreign power.[14]

II POSITIVE NEUTRALITY

Nasser's first recorded use of the term "positive neutrality" was in September 1956, after the Brioni conference, at the height of the Suez controversy. The preferred terminology reflects the ill-repute of the word "neutrality" at the time, and with this simple reference to positive neutrality the words "positive peaceful co-existence" appear four times in the same short interview.[15] The context further shows that Nasser was primarily concerned with justifying his opposition to the Baghdad Pact and his arms deal with the East.

In March 1957, however, Nasser identified Egypt's policy with Arab nationalism and the effort to have all the Arabs maintain the policy of positive neutrality.[16] In December 1957, Nasser de-clared that "positive neutrality and nonalignment have appeared in the area, words in which every citizen believes . . . every citi-zen of the Arab area used to call for nonalignment, for positive neutrality. . . ." [17] Nasser was no longer begging for arms or loans, he was threatening to mobilize all the resources of the Middle East for the end he deemed correct for the Arab nation.

If Nasser's speeches reflect the gradual development of Egypt's neutral policy, most of the ideological material is retrospective and can be taken as justification of current UAR policy; but the Ba'this of Syria long preceded Egyptian spokesmen in their firm attachment to neutralism. Each of the authors whose writings have been examined has his own approach, and they vary greatly in ability and insight into the problem. The writings are, furthermore, disparate in that they range from books to simple editorials or speeches. One can expect that the number of tracts on positive neutrality will be augmented as the intelligentsia catches up with policy makers, but for the present we must be content with materials of uneven quality. The only really important effort is that by Clovis Maqsud, but it is original enough to make it a little less useful as a gloss on current policy than the others. As a consequence of these limitations, we have deemed it preferable to deal with all together as they relate to certain common themes.

As we have seen, the major element in the Arab conception of neutralism is neither peace nor international responsibility, but the primacy of national independence, self-determination, and nonintervention. Muhammad Hasanain Haikal holds that the word neutrality first appeared before the revolution as an expression of the struggle for complete independence in a world divided into two blocs.[18] For Rimawi, independence and the refusal to enter the sphere of influence of any bloc is the very definition of positive neutrality.[19] Al-Sha'bini holds that positive neutrality is the only foreign policy which guarantees the realization of all of the "basic motivations of human behavior." He equates the nation with the individual and asserts that both are motivated by a group of needs that are "dynamically organized in a pyramidal form." These are self-preservation and economic requirements, security, peace, freedom and independence, and self-esteem.[20] There can be no economic or political "awakening" without independence, so independence must precede the achievement of self-esteem.[21] He exemplifies the achievement of the last stage by quoting from one of Nasser's speeches about how he threatened to throw George Allen out of his office if he came to deliver a "warning" from Washington.[22] But the implication of this independence is not evenly balanced between the two blocs. Its primary meaning is anti-imperialism, in the classical use of that term.[23]

Just about every writer agrees that positive neutrality is the external manifestation of the Arab revolutionary ideal or of the revolutionary policies of Egypt. Haikal explains the development of positive neutrality without the benefit of ideology in this way. Al-Ashmuni writes that peace has a new meaning, it is economic as well as political. The search for economic development and independence within Egypt had its international expression in the Bandung meetings, which spread the ideas of the Egyptian revolution over a great part of the world.[24] Rimawi, Bitar, and Aflaq, all of them Ba'this of one sort or another, agree that positive neutralism is a manifestation of the socialist ideology of Arab nationalism. Rimawi insists that the Arab socialists have a new solution; Bitar and Aflaq simply call for the working out of a middle road between capitalism and Communism, but all three see positive neutralism as an answer to the ideological aspects of of the bipolar struggle.[25] Maqsud, more consistent than the rest, flatly states that positive neutrality is *not* organically related to the national movement. It did not simply appear overnight, either. Its attachment to the Arab movement is a long story, including the Palestine defeat, the absence of a modern leadership, the military coups, and later experiences with both East and West.[26]

Maqsud's dissent points up the core of the problem of neutralist ideology for Arab nationalists. Nearly all writers grasp the fact that positive neutrality is a response to bipolarity. As a dependent variable, it is difficult to view it as an inherent element of Arab nationalism; hence, most writers dutifully call positive neutrality a "stage" in the historical development of the Arab movement.[27] But if it is only a stage, is the policy it implies merely a tactical device to realize certain Arab interests? There are really two derivative issues that flow from this question: the first is the moral question of justifying positive neutrality as more than tactical balancing, and the second is the practical consideration of whether or not the policy can achieve the goals claimed for it.

The moral issue is resolved by the questionable assumption that the interests of Arab nationalism accord with the highest moral needs of the world at this time. We have already seen that positive neutralism is held to be the foreign policy which will complete the domestic revolution that offers a new social and political solution to the world; and it is also held that Arab unity [28] can be achieved through positive neutrality and, in more general terms, that neutralism accords with the interest [29] of the Arab people. Far from avoiding moral issues, positive neutrality involves taking a stand on international issues. It hopes to build an international stream which will offer solutions to all problems, reduce the possibility of aggression, and build peace.[30] For Maqsud, the positive aspect of positive neutrality arises when the major bloc exponent which takes the correct stand is rewarded by neutralist support; thus, positive neturality means no *permanent* commitment to either bloc but encourages temporary support.[31] Rimawi disagrees with Maqsud's balancing idea and writes instead that positive neutrality does not mean neutrality regarding matters of principle. The Arab approach to international problems is one which stems from their own third way.[32]

All agree, as might be expected, that the goal of positive neutrality is peace. Rimawi alone fails to relate peace to Arab "interests." For him the desire for peace is a matter of pure principles; but the Arabs will not accept peace at any price.[33] Haikal writes that the Arabs need peace in order to develop. Aflaq believes that it is not in the Arab interest that either of the major blocs collapse; hence, it is important to work for the lessening of tension between the two and to work toward permitting both to fulfill their promises of freedom and welfare to all peoples. Professor Butros-Ghali carefully distinguishes between positive neutrality and peaceful coexistence; the latter, he writes, is the slogan of those involved in the Cold War and is based on the balance of terror, while the former is idealist and spiritual and is the slogan of the nonindustrial, militarily weak states.[34] The aim of the neutralists is to disarm the two armed camps.

Obviously, the sort of peace that is referred to throughout these works is the absence of a thermonuclear war. The point is made quite explicitly by Bitar.[35]

In order to stress the positive moral aspect of their neutrality, these writers take great pains to distinguish positive neutrality from legal neutrality, the Swiss type of neutrality, and the Austrian example of neutralization (to which the Laos problem might be assimilated). All of these are referred to as types of negative neutrality.[36] At worst, such neutral states stand by in isolation, hoping that they will not be affected by any hostilities; at best, they can act as arbitrators in minor disputes. Neutralized states may serve to reduce tension, but the restrictions on their foreign policies would be too great a burden on the nationalist states of Asia and Africa, even if Austria and Germany could abide neutralization.[37]

Besides, negative neutrality is dependent upon an older type of weapons technology which would permit neutrals to stay clear of hostilities, while positive neutrality is not related to any weapons technology.[38]

This last view of Maqsud is especially surprising, since he is the only one who has seriously attempted to relate his discussion of the balancing role of neutrals to the problem of mutual deterrence, and he devotes himself to a refutation of Henry Kissinger's *Nuclear Weapons and Foreign Policy*.[39] Tactical balancing is generally held to be a "negative" policy. Butros-Ghali defines negative neutrality in this manner, but denies that positive neutrality tends to increase international tension or to exploit the great power conflict—for by definition its aim is peace. The major stage on which the neutrals can act for peace is the United Nations, but their neutrality will not thereby be affected since, in the Security Council, both the United States and the Soviet Union must agree before action is taken. There is no mention of action by the General Assembly, and the very weak argument is rounded out by a supreme contradiction when the author writes that the neutrals are better off in case a hot war starts because then they can choose whichever side will benefit them most, while those who are not neutral will have no choice.[40]

Sha'bini uses the term balancing, but he does not have the same thing in mind. For him positive neutrality is comprised of the positive elements already discussed plus legal neutrality, that is, giving no benefit to either bloc that is not given to both.[41] Aflaq, as we have seen, implies that neutralist balancing must aim at preventing either bloc from crushing the other, but he does not indicate how this can be done. Rimawi simply denies outright that positive neutrality is either tactical or strategic.[42]

As against these rather flimsy attempts to discuss positive neutrality in practical terms, Maqsud's little book stands out. His approach throughout is historical and materialistic and has an air of realism about it. He is concerned less with the positive moral aspects of neutrality than with its positive political aspects. Where Rimawi's historical dialectic leads him to emphasize support for the United Arab Republic above all else, Maqsud's is bent toward the application of positive neutrality as a practical device for achieving Arab ends. According to Maqsud, positive neutrality is not isolation from, or equally opposing, both blocs, as Nasser would put it, but is supporting each in limited fashion: guaranteeing the West's oil but agreeing to the East's demands that the West withdraw from its foreign bases. This kind of balancing must be directed at finding solutions to problems and reducing tension.

Some pages later, Maqsud turns to a discussion of the sources of influence of positive neutrality, a discussion which throws more light on his concept of balancing. The first source is moral, and it implies mobilizing world public opinion both among the neutrals and within the committed states. The second source arises from the situation of mutual deterrence prevailing between the two blocs. Both bloc leaders tend to be moderate because of the great strain of the balance of terror. The greatest gain which has been realized through their moderation is their willingness to accept the neutrality of certain states.[43] Thus, the United States acted to end the aggression of its secondary bloc members in Egypt in 1956 and Soviet Russia tried to improve Indian-Chinese relations after the Chinese aggression on the Indian border. But when the United States and the Soviet Union met directly, they resorted to conventional warfare, which led to the development of the Kissinger thesis concerning the possibility of limited nuclear warfare. This notion, writes Maqsud, was based on misinformation about Soviet scientific achievements; hence the nuclear standoff still dominates East-West relations.[44]

The neutrals can take advantage of mutual deterrence to extend the area of peace. This is not opportunism, for politics is the art of the possible, and the possible at this stage of international tension lies in taking the initiative in straightening out the difficulties of mankind and harnessing technology to the purposes of peace. To this end the neutrals must: (1) keep the balance by working for disarmament, (2) encourage competitive peaceful coexistence, (3) work to establish an effective supervision over weapons production, (4) strengthen the United Nations, and (5) *avoid the making of any kind of agreement at the summit,* because (a) this will reduce the chances *for the neutrals to profit* and (b) it will create hopes that cannot be fulfilled.[45]

It remains for us to complete our juxtaposition of contemporary Arab neutralist theory with the political practice of the UAR by searching for interpretations of two of the more recent policy trends. These trends are efforts to build an organized bloc of neutrals and to win the leadership of the bloc. Most writers are silent on the question of a neutralist bloc. Sha'bini, whose views are about the most innocuous, denied that the goal is a third bloc. The neutralists should achieve their joint ends by strengthening their mutual relations and influencing world public opinion.[46] The aim of positive neutrality is to substitute collective security for bloc alliances and to revive the concept of the just war.[47] And again in discussing the 1956 Brioni meetings of Tito, Nehru, and Nasser, Sha'bini quotes *al-Ahram* as reporting that the Yugoslav authorities were astonished when reporters said that the basis for a new neutralist bloc had been laid, and those authorities declared that the best name for the policies of the three countries was "positive peaceful coexistence," not neutrality.[48]

The growing attractiveness of the idea of an organized neutralist bloc may be illustrated by the comparison of two statements of Salah al-Din al-Bitar, the first in 1955 just after Nasser's first visit to Yugoslavia and the second in 1957 after the Suez crisis. In 1955 al-Bitar simply reported that Nehru was the leader of the positive neutrals and that he was opposed to the formation of a bloc because he felt it would result in the tightening of the other blocs.[49] In 1957 he called for the unity of all the Arabs who supported nonalignment and neutrality as a basis for unifying all the Arab peoples.[50]

Maqsud's views on the matter are much more in keeping with the policy of the UAR after the Casablanca Conference. He denies that the neutrals desire to comprise a third nuclear force.[51] Their power is derived from their cooperation and moral influence, but they must be better organized.[52] Later he deplores the fact that the neutrals can take no direct initiative in the two-sided disarmament talks because they are not organized. Needless to say, Soviet insistence upon a three man triumvirate for the United Nations Secretariat, as well as for the disarmament supervision organization, plays right into the hands of those who would organize the neutrals. The question is, after all, which neutrals and how would they be appointed? Would they have to be acceptable to both the United States and the Soviet Union, or would they represent a neutralist bloc?

The fact that there are differences among the neutrals is noticed only by Maqsud. He notes that India refuses to use the term "positive neutrality" but ascribes this to the unpleasant connotation of the word "neutrality" in English, which is the language of the Indian elite.[53] He implies that there is no important difference between the policies of India and Egypt, though the West has treated them differently, especially since 1956.[54] There is no essential difference in their policies, nor can any difference be ascribed to the differences in national character. The differences are due to geographical circumstances. India has a secondary strategic position, so her neutrality is accepted, whereas the Arabs are in an area of critically strategic importance. The West will not, therefore, accept the neutrality of the Arabs.[55]

The arguments of those who support Nasser's candidacy for leadership of the neutralist bloc fall into two groups: they claim that Nasser initiated the term or the policy and that he has been its foremost exponent. Ashmuni blandly asserts that the Bandung resolutions reflected Egypt's revolutionary principles, and that Nehru followed in Nasser's footsteps.[56] He finds the origin of positive neutrality at Bandung. Butros-Ghali finds its roots in the Pantcha Sila, first recorded in the preamble of the Sino-Indian treaty of 1954.[57] Sha'bini insists that the meaning of positive neutrality has stemmed from the UAR and that it first appeared at the meeting of the Arab heads of state which issued its joint communiqué on February 27, 1957.[58] (The date is significant in view of the conclusion that the UAR altered its policies after the Suez invasion.) Rimawi does not call for the formation of a bloc, nor does he insist on Egypt's leadership of the neutralist bloc, but he does argue that the practical application of positive neutrality is to be found in the policy of the UAR, thus rendering all further theoretical discussion useless.[59]

As limited as they are, these tracts do provide us with some insight into the Arab idea of neutrality. Clearly, the Arabs are not primarily concerned with the Cold War and its peaceful demise. They are aware of the destructiveness which will result from a thermonuclear war and agree that a peaceful solution must be sought. However, they do not put agreement between the United States and the Soviet Union above their own aspirations. Positive neutrality means pursuing an independent policy in accord with the Arab national interest, which is further defined in terms of the Pan-Arab aspiration and in building Arab socialism.

Even though tactical balancing is admitted to be immoral, nearly all writers accept it in one form or another. The purpose of balancing is agreed to be peace and ending the Cold War, but this is to be achieved by dissolving the blocs, persuading the great powers to help strengthen the smaller powers, and by the gradual adjustment of the Soviet and American political systems until they meet at some point in the middle. The Arabs tend to disregard the differences between the Eastern and Western blocs except insofar as these two follow diverse but equally misguided ideologies. The Arabs also see the United States as their major opponent in achieving their nationalist goals, but they acknowledge that the Soviet Union's recognition of Arab neutrality is probably only a tactical device.

There is no evidence that the Arabs believe that irresponsible action on their part can turn the Cold War into a hot war, lose the Cold War for one side, or bring the Soviet Union into the Middle East. In working for their own ends, Arab neutralists are inevitably working for peace in their view. But such typical nationalist logic barely conceals their determination to turn the present international situation to advantage. Finally, these tracts not only sustain our analysis of the UAR's neutrality, they strongly suggest that the UAR will not be tightly bound by ideological considerations in the future any more than in the past. All agree that positive neutrality requires maneuverability and flexibility, even if not merely self-interested.

III RESPONSIBLE NEUTRALITY

Neutralism has become a generic term for the common features of the response of many underdeveloped countries to the bipolarization of international power. But neutralism in this broad sense is only a lowest common denominator. The basic neutralist position is a defensive one, and it is often aimed against Western assumptions or long-established positions which could not be borne in the face of domestic extremist opposition. Some neutrals remain in this defensive posture: India, Burma, Ceylon, Iraq, Lebanon, Sudan, Yugoslavia; some modified their defensive posture by seeking limited irredenta and accepting Soviet arms— Indonesia and Morocco are examples; others find themselves with new opportunities to play important international roles or to increase in power, influence, and territory: Egypt, Ghana, and possibly Cuba seem to fit in here. Some of those who have retained the defensive posture are more worried about aggression or subversion from other neutralist states, and these tend to be "neutralist pro-West." Those who have the most to gain from neutralism, not because of bipolarity but because of the structure of the subordinate or "area" international systems in which they are located, tend to be "neutralist pro-Soviet," as revisionists states might be expected to be. The latter also tend to be more pragmatic and less idealistic in their foreign policies, if only because they have specific goals; and they are for the same reason more committed to the idea of an organized neutralist bloc that can be counted on to respond in the right way at the right time.

Egypt's neutrality is not a copy of the Indian or Yugoslav policies; it derives special benefits from its position in the Middle East, including its relative lack of exposure to Soviet aggression and the aid policies of the Soviet Union. Another characteristic of the positive neutrality of the UAR is that although its beginning was essentially defensive, it has now become an active means of achieving revisionist ends. The UAR, alone in the Middle East, shares this ability to derive special international benefits from the pursuit of positive neutrality with certain African states. These are the two areas of the most significant "pan-nationalist" movements, and at the present moment the Pan-Arab movement appears to be the more vigorous. Hence, the UAR stands to be the greatest beneficiary of the strengthening of positive neutrality in the international arena, unless perhaps the benefits of the Soviet Union prove in the end to be greater.

Egypt and the Soviet Union have not been without their own

disputes—witness the union with Syria in 1958 and the Iraqi revolt of the same year. Some hard words were passed at the time, but it would appear that the Soviet Union has decided to let Nasser have his way in the Middle East in return for support elsewhere. If this assumption is correct, then the Soviet Union will not intervene in UAR relations with Iraq and Syria, and, as we have seen in Laos, the Berlin issue, and the problem of nuclear testing, the UAR will not lend support to a vigorous neutralist position in Cold War issues. The Congo issue appears to be an extension of the same sort of arrangement to Africa, with Nkrumah as the major beneficiary.

The United States stands to lose a great deal if the UAR succeeds in achieving its goals by its present methods. We will lose a good many friends whom we still retain and find them replaced by a power committed to hostility toward us. Nasser's Pan-Arabism does not now allow for compromise; it calls for the unification of armies, for a common market, and for popular organizations, but not for federal constitutions and political safeguards. Governments which resist these overtures, and even those who withhold their delegates from the numerous pan-Arab meetings held in Cairo, are accused not of disbelief in the ultimate truth of Arab nationalism, but of serving the interests of the United States. Whether we would or not, we are being compelled to play the devil in the piece.

We shall lose more than friends, of course. We shall lose our influence over important petroleum resources and our access to an important strategic area. We shall run the risk of seeing both Turkey and Iran subjected to pressure from the south as well as the north and may well fear the hostile manipulation of the entire neutralist bloc against us.

In the final analysis, it may be this "activist" neutralism of the UAR which most threatens American security. If the outcome of the Cold War depends upon the resolution of a series of Laos-like issues, the new responsibilities of the neutralist states have become manifest. The neutrals might have helped to establish a truly neutral government in Laos, but none was willing to incur the wrath of the Soviet Union. It is apparent that the neutrals cannot get together on a Cold War issue; their unity is limited to issues between themselves and individual Western powers. Neither is this limitation a perverse psychological reaction to the memory of imperialism; rather, it is due to the loose structure of the Western bloc, which permits some members to be flouted while others are courted. If the Russo-Chinese split hardens and China can find resources, the same game may be played with the Communist bloc.

At one time neutralism was no more than a tactical refusal to side openly with the West. It was a weak form of pressure, at a time when political and economic benefits were expected from the West alone and Western values were tacitly accepted. Our greatest loss in the Cold War has not been territory, but the loss of our unique position as the sole source of both material and ideological assistance in the developing states. Those who have accepted Soviet assistance as a challenge to this Western position, and who have sought to exploit what they too naïvely believed to be a fixed balance of deterrence, have also accepted the *a priori* political reasoning of neo-Marxism. Like the Soviet Union, these activist neutrals are ambitious revisionist powers with a new sense of their ability to control events. At the present time neither they nor we can say exactly what limits may be set upon the expansion of neutralist power by the nature of the dominant bipolar system —with the result that a series of small changes in the developing areas may destroy the balance of the system rather than relegate both superpowers to impotence, as the exponents of positive neutrality suggest.

It is useless to suppose that we can restore the earlier kind of neutralism, but it is worth noting that our earlier criticism of "negative" neutralism had some ideological impact. Proceding on the basis of this experience, it appears that we might well take the activist neutralists at their word: if positive neutrality is to be judged pragmatically by its ability to bring the Cold War to a peaceful conclusion, then let us so judge it. A *priori* assumptions about the necessary relationship between this function and the realization of the "interests" of the neutral states may be put to the same tests. For the rest, we can only try to use our material resources in such a way as to prove that responsible neutrality and enlightened self-interest do go together.

NOTES

1. Abd Allah al-Rimawi, *al Mantiq al-Thawri* [*The Revolutionary Logic*] (Cairo, 1961), p. 99.

2. President Gamal Abd al-Nasser, *Khutub wa Tasrihat* [*Speeches and Interviews*]. Published in ten volumes in Arabic by the Editorial Committee of *Ikhtarna Lak* [*We Have Chosen For You*]. Additional volumes published in English by the Information Administration. All at Cairo, without dates. Hereafter to be cited as *Nasser's Speeches* (Arabic or English), Vol. 3 (August 21, 1954), p. 487.

3. *Rose al-Yusuf*, May 1, 1961, p. 13, reported that the UAR Foreign Ministry threatened the United States chargé that his government could not guarantee the safety of the Embassy building and staff during the forthcoming demonstration unless the United States Embassy withheld from publishing its government's views on the Cuban affair.

4. Al-Bitar, *al-Siyasa, al-Arabiyyah* (Beirut, 1960), pp. 23–27.

5. *Nasser's Speeches* (Arabic) Vol. 3, pp. 686–688. From November 10, 1954 until December 2, 1954, Nasser addressed twelve military groups in the thirteen speeches made during the period; Vol. 3, pp. 598–634. In these speeches, Nasser recorded his gratitude for the role played by the Signal Corps officers (p. 598) and the Air Corps (p. 612) during the crisis of the previous February and March.

6. *Ibid.*, Vol. 1, p. 173.

7. *Ibid.*, Vol. 2, p. 275.

8. *Ibid.*, Vol. 1, p. 173.

9. *Ibid.*, pp. 420–421.

10. *Ibid.*, p. 477 (Italics added).

11. *Ibid.*, Vol. 3, p. 493.

12. *Ibid.*, p. 655.

13. *Ibid.*, pp. 718, 723, 726; Vol. 4, pp. 828, 848–849, 908f.

14. *Ibid.*, Vol. 5, p. 1032.

15. *Ibid.*, Vol. 7, pp. 1449–1450.

16. *Ibid.*, Vol. 8, p. 1572.

17. *Ibid.*, Vol. 10, p. 1804.

18. Muhammad Hasanain Haikal, *Al-Ahram* (January 27, 1961).

19. Rimawi, *al-Mantiq al-Thawri* (Cairo, 1961), pp. 98, 275.

20. Al-Sha'bini, *al-Hiyad al-Ijabi* (Cairo, 1960), p. 133.

21. *Ibid.*, p. 143.

22. *Ibid.*, pp. 146–149.

23. *Ibid.*, pp. 47, 102, 134; al-Bitar, *op. cit.*, pp. 68–69, 98.

24. Hasan al-Ashmuni, *Duwwal al-Hiyad*, Kutub Qawmiyyah, No. 85 (Cairo, December 20, 1960), pp. 6–7.

25. Rimawi, *op. cit.*, pp. 19–21, 52; Bitar, *op. cit.*, p. 32; Aflaq, *Ma'arakat al-Musir al-Wahid* (Beirut, 1949), p. 216.

26. Clovis Maqsud, *Ma'ana al-Hiyad al-Ijabi* [*The Meaning of Positive Neutrality*] (Beirut, 1960), p. 102f.
27. Haikal, *loc. cit.*; Maqsud, *op. cit.*, pp. 7, 101f.; Aflaq, *op. cit.*, 217.
28. Sha'bini, *op. cit.*, p. 13; Rimawi, *op. cit.*, p. 34; Maqsud, *op. cit.*, p. 102.
29. Bitar, *op. cit.*, p. 71; Rimawi, *op. cit.*, pp. 280–281; Aflaq, p. 216.
30. Haikal, *loc. cit.*
31. Maqsud, *op. cit.*, pp. 57, 87f.
32. Rimawi, *op. cit.*, pp. 277–278.
33. *Ibid.*, pp. 280–281.
34. Butros Butros-Ghali, *Dirasat fi al-Siyasah al-Duwwaliyyah* [*Studies in International Relations*] (Cairo, 1961), pp. 35–37.
35. Bitar, *op. cit.*, p. 67.
36. Sha'bini, *op. cit.*, pp. 47f., 59, 63; Maqsud, *op. cit.*, pp. 28f., 49–50; Haikal, *loc. cit.*
37. Maqsud, *op. cit.*, pp. 31, 49–51.
38. *Ibid.*, p. 109.
39. *Ibid.*, p. 121f.
40. Butros-Ghali, *op. cit.*, pp. 19–22.
41. Sha'bini, *op. cit.*, pp. 58–59.
42. Rimawi, *op. cit.*, p. 275.
43. Maqsud, *op. cit.*, p. 128.
44. *Ibid.*, p. 135.
45. *Ibid.*, p. 137.
46. Sha'bini, *op. cit.*, p. 60.
47. *Ibid.*, pp. 58, 100.
48. *Ibid.*, p. 94.
49. Bitar, *op. cit.*, p. 66.
50. *Ibid.*, p. 91.
51. There is some confusion here because the Arabic word for force (as in "third force") is the same as the word for power (as in "nuclear power").
52. Maqsud, *op. cit.*, p. 98.
53. *Ibid.*, p. 86.
54. *Ibid.*, p. 77.
55. *Ibid.*, pp. 94–95.
56. Ashmuni, *op. cit.*, pp. 7, 8.
57. Butros-Ghali, *op. cit.*, p. 6.
58. Sha'bini, *op. cit.*, p. 91.
59. Rimawi, *op. cit.*, p. 53.

9

THE MIDDLE EAST

AS A SUBORDINATE

INTERNATIONAL SYSTEM

I

Recent developments in the study of international politics reflect two major emphases. One comprises a variety of attempts at systematization and stresses the "frame of reference" approach;[1] the other seeks specific knowledge of national policies in greater detail and stresses the "area studies" approach.[2] Theoretically, the first explains international politics in terms of broad generalizations applicable to all international actors insofar as they conform to an ideal model or depart therefrom in a calculable manner. The second seeks to understand international politics in terms of the relationship of foreign policy to the total social and historical context from which it emerges.[3]

The variety of attempts at systematization are in the main derivations from or modifications of balance-of-power theories, but contemporary interest has focused primarily upon the notion of power rather than balance.[4] There is another tendency to substitute patterns of interrelationship of varying degrees of intricacy for the notion of balance.[5] Implied in this theoretical approach is the hypothesis that such patterns of interrelationship (sometimes called "system") are a function of the distribution of power among states (sometimes called "structure").[6] While system/structure theories are an improvement upon the crude notion of multilateral power maximization through a restricted number of diplomatic-military gambits, they lack the refinements necessary for dealing with "aberrant" action unrelated to power. One of the reasons for this lack of refinement is overemphasis upon US–USSR relations, an overemphasis usually summed up in the loose term "bipolarity."

An underlying assumption of most such approaches is that international politics is total and global. This assumption is based upon the possible character of modern warfare, and is therefore potential rather than actual. Insofar as the security considerations of the United States and the USSR have no territorial limit, international politics is global and total for these states. But the great-power view of world politics is not necessarily reciprocated by the lesser powers. While neither the great-power nor the smaller-power view tells the whole story, the view of the smaller powers is sustained by the development of a situation of mutual deterrence. Insofar as a situation of mutual deterrence obstructs great-power intervention, the smaller powers are free to act. Hence international politics is not global or necessarily total for the lesser powers.

The consequence of the nonglobal character of international politics for system/structure theories is clear. Any system or pattern of scientific rules which adequately describes US-USSR relations must fail to explain the politics of the uncommitted states. All that such theories may do for politics that are not oriented to the Cold War is to define the conditions under which they exist. In fact, we are confronted not with a single global international system, but with several, in a variety of relationships.

The substantive problem which concerns us here is the inapplicability of the theory of bipolarity to Middle Eastern international politics. The term "bipolarity" has been defined above as characterizing an international system in which there are only two actors. To this definition must be added the qualification that the persistence of the system is due to the roughly equal power of both actors.[7] In what sense may bipolarity characterize a universal system? I.e., in what sense can bipolarity explain the international politics of the Middle East? Two possible meanings of bipolarity present themselves, the first emphasizing structure and the second emphasizing system: (1) where the power of the United States and the USSR is in each case very much greater than the power of all other states, and where we are unable to ascertain whether or by how much the power of one exceeds the other, and where our estimates of power in each case may err in either direction by the same amount, and where the difference between actual and estimated power is greater than the sum of all uncommitted power;[8] (2) where the dominant factors of international relations are the very great power of the United States and the USSR and their rivalry, which leads each to attempt to counter every action of the other regardless of its locus or circumstances, and where the inferiority in power or the disunity of the uncommitted states renders them unable to resist effectively this pattern of great-power action.[9]

The systematic consequence of the first conception of bipolarity is the ability of the great powers to disregard the uncommitted states; it suggests that any attempt of one of the great powers to secure a foothold in an uncommitted state is a manifestation of a gratuitous imperialism. The structural consequence of the second conception is that the approximate equality of the power of the United States and the USSR is precarious, and so the uncommitted states may not be ignored.[10] Neither conception is fully explanatory of recent great-power policies in the Middle East, and if the second seems more accurate at present, it does not explain the success or failure of particular great-power actions.

From the point of view of the uncommitted states, neither of these conceptions represents a desideratum: their goal is to break bipolarity, or to insulate their own affairs against its effects, or to make use of it to gain their own ends.[11] This final alternative suggests the temporary reversal of the subordinate relationship of the Middle Eastern system, but our preferred explanation is that bipolarity characterizes only US-USSR relations and not their relations with third powers.

II

While historically minded persons will find no difficulty in tracing the evolution of Russian interests and aspirations in the general area of the straits and the Persian Gulf, they will be unable to explain the comparative inactivity of the Soviet Union in the Middle East from, say, the end of 1948 until mid-1955.[12] As evidence of American interest in the Middle East, the historian must be satisfied with the activities of a few devoted missionaries until the middle of World War II.[13] From 1945 on, the United States took an increasingly keen interest in the area. Since 1950 the United States has concentrated on organizing the defense of the Middle East, while renewed Soviet activity seems to have developed only after the initial and limited American success in bringing the Baghdad Pact into existence.

Soviet action in the Middle East to the end of 1948 was apparently aimed at deriving the maximum of territorial gain and political influence during the disorganized circumstances following the war. Subsequent American efforts to organize the defense of the area were rationalized by reference to aggressive Soviet behavior during the preceding period, but such efforts could also be related to the goal of sustaining British influence in the Middle East to the maximum possible degree, or to the principle of collective self-defense outside of the United Nations. Against a background of Soviet inaction and wide acceptance of the notion of bipolarity, American rationalizations have been unconvincing. We cannot know the reason for Soviet inaction until 1955, though several possibilities present themselves. The Soviets, no less than we, were concerned elsewhere, in Europe and in the Far East. The Soviets may have considered the Middle East of little importance. They may have judged the Middle East quite unready for the nationalistic *cum* Communist ideological offensive which worked so well elsewhere in Asia. Or they may simply have preferred to rely on the anti-imperialistic attitude of Middle Eastern leaders as sufficient to preclude the success of Western efforts.

Of more importance than the reason for Soviet inaction in the Middle East until mid-1955 is the circumstance under which Soviet activity was resumed with great intensity. The limited success achieved by the United States in the signing of the Baghdad Pact has already been mentioned. Aside from a series of dire warnings, the initial Soviet reaction was nil.[14] What elicited a far stronger reaction was the development of an important breach in Arab unity over the Pact. Thus, the Soviet Union was encouraged to act in the Middle East not primarily as a consequence of an American success, but as the result of the provision of favorable intra-area circumstances.[15] These circumstances—i.e., the Egyptian-Iraqi dispute—were the indirect result of wholly indigenous conditions characterizing the Middle Eastern international system.

More recent action by the United States in Jordan and with regard to Syria has tended to fall into the same pattern.[16] This tendency has not been complete, however, as exemplified by the Eisenhower Doctrine. The Doctrine was a reaction to a Soviet success, but its implementation was not at all suited to the circumstances provided by the indigenous system of Middle Eastern relations. The Doctrine was directed against a hypothetical act of Soviet aggression, so that adherence to its goals by some Middle Eastern states may be likened to an act of pure devotion. For those who saw no threat of overt Soviet aggression, and who accepted the general idea of bipolarity, the Doctrine was interpreted as an act of imperialism.

If overt Soviet aggression was considered unlikely in the Middle East, intra-area aggression and subversion had become more likely, if only because the Suez invasion nullified the Tri-partite Declaration of 1950, destroyed the Anglo-Egyptian Treaty of 1954,[17] and gravely weakened the Anglo-Iraqi arrangement under the Baghdad Pact. Unilateral American support for the Tri-partite Declaration was both unconvincing and inadequate.[18] Developments in Jordan, however, presented the United States with its first opportunity for limited but effective action aimed not at "constitutional" change of the Middle Eastern structure, but at its preservation. Support of King Hussain of Jordan by all manner of unconventional means, without eliciting any formal declaration from his government and without obtruding our disproportionately great power in the area, was at least temporarily successful.

This successful example of playing the Middle Eastern game by its own rules was followed by a perhaps typical example of American exaggeration. The temporary stabilization of the Hashimite Jordan regime was accompanied by some revulsion of Saudi feeling against too close association with Egypt. After a long cold war of their own, the Hashimite and Saudi houses began to discover a common interest in the institution of kingship and the aristocratic orientation of their regimes. When the extent of the Syrian commitment to the Soviet Union became better known (and perhaps increased as a result of frustrations in Jordan), the United States attempted a vigorous counteraction. The idea was ineptly phrased as a "quarantine" of Syria by neighboring states, but the slogan was never defined.[19] In spite of the wide popularity of the notion of Arab unity, publicity was given to a policy of dividing the Arab world while an American representative was canvassing support in the area. In view of subsequent events, especially the Syrian rejection of King Saud's offer to mediate the Syro-Turkish dispute, it would seem that the "quarantine" policy was out of keeping not with the inclination of Middle Eastern governmental relationships, but with their capabilities.

It is risky to generalize from so few examples, but certain suggestions present themselves for further study. From these examples it seems that initiative must be left to Middle Eastern states themselves. It would also seem that great-power involvement within the Middle Eastern system must be as unobtrusive as possible if it is to be successful. And, as might be expected in view of the low level of power in the area, action to maintain the *status quo* will be more successful than revisionism.

At least two cases of American intervention in Middle Eastern politics should be tested against these generalizations. These two cases are the landing of American troops in the Lebanon in 1958 and the involvement of the United States in the Egyptian-Yemeni-Saudi dispute which developed after the 1962 revolution in the

Yemen. In the first of these cases, American intervention was both obtrusive and successful, in the sense that the independence of the Lebanon was maintained and provision made for the reestablishment of normal government. Despite these contradictions of the general principles put forward, it should be noted that the invitation which brought in American troops was an act of final self-discreditation by Chamoun. The situation in Lebanon was stabilized by the election of a politically neutral President who then appointed a cabinet dominated by the opposition leaders. As a consequence of the crisis, all Lebanese came to a deeper appreciation of the imminent possibility of the demise of the Lebanon as an independent state. For some this was a pleasant prospect and for others this possibility meant little short of disaster. Regardless of these preferences, the area-international consequences of internal political squabbling became manifest in an immediate sense. From these events it may be possible to conclude that the United States will be willing to act again to preserve Lebanese independence, but it is also possible to conclude that American power alone cannot preserve Lebanese independence. At the time of the American intervention, the newly formed United Arab Republic of Egypt and Syria was but a few months old. The new revolutionary regime in Iraq was, in the summer of 1958, apparently well disposed toward the UAR. But that regime was threatened with intervention from Turkey. Under the circumstances, Egypt was not willing to become even more deeply embroiled with what was then a relatively hostile United States. Pan-Arab pressure on Lebanon has not abated, and it is only the dispute between Nasser and the Ba'thi leaders of Syria and Iraq after the 1963 coups in both those countries that has prevented this pressure from shaking the Lebanese government more severely. It is apparent that, even though the United States is willing to use its power to preserve the Lebanon, that power can only be used if the Lebanon is threatened from the outside or if there is again a prolonged and indecisive domestic dispute. The reason for the prolonged indecisiveness of the 1958 dispute was that issues of greater political moment than had been anticipated intruded upon what was essentially a hitch in the succession process in a modern constitutional system being run by a traditional oligarchy. The Lebanese case does not fit the rule nor yet does it invalidate the rule. The Yemeni case, which is still not finally resolved, does fit the rule and is another case of relatively successful intervention by the United States. In this case the initiative was again left to the area powers. Only after both Egypt and Saudi-Arabia were involved did the United States come into the picture. By this time American relations with Egypt had much improved. American action was also unobtrusive, and in due course involved sharing responsibilities for disengaging Egypt and Saudi-Arabia with the UN. Furthermore, the situation was helped toward resolution by the overcommitment of both area powers. The Yemen is still in a turmoil but the *status quo* between Egypt and Saudi-Arabia has been maintained. American action, essentially a limited support of Egypt in this case, might have had different and far more serious consequences for Saudi-Arabia had the new UAR of Egypt, Syria, and Iraq been firmly established. The new UAR has not been fully consummated politically, and Egypt may be more completely disengaged from the Yemen when and if it does become consummated, but the relationship between the two situations and the possibly self-defeating consequences of our own intervention point up the small extent to which we are in control of political developments in the Middle East.

Domestic politics in the Middle East, as elsewhere, are of great importance in determining the nature of its system. Here, however, the nature of domestic political issues is distinctive, and their bearing on international developments unique. It is fairly well known that the foreign policies of various Middle Eastern countries are designed to have a maximum of impact upon the domestic affairs of target countries within the system. Political and constitutional instability, coupled with the attraction of Islam and Arabism as political symbols, make the direct interventionist appeal a rewarding circumvention of the frequently inadequate or inefficient diplomatic process. However, the degree to which non-area states may engage in these tactics is strictly limited by the anti-imperialist bias of Middle Eastern political leadership. Furthermore, what may be done in the name of Islam or Arabism may not be done in the name of Western security or even Middle Eastern security. If the withdrawal of aid for the Aswan High Dam project was directed at weakening the Nasser regime domestically,[20] the move clearly backfired and demonstrated the limitations upon nonarea states attempting to play by Middle Eastern rules.

It would appear that the existence of a bipolar system, or the counterbalancing of the United States and the Soviet Union, cannot explain all post-Second World War developments in the Middle East. The fact is that the most vigorous of American efforts were pressed at the very time of the most complete Soviet inaction. The failure of American policy was due not to Soviet counteraction, but to indigenous circumstances militating against the acceptance of American overtures at their face value. These same circumstances explain why King Saud could accept American aid, could attempt to construct an anti-Egyptian Arab alignment, could welcome—if not accept—the Eisenhower Doctrine, and yet support Syria against the United States and Turkey at the United Nations. These same circumstances explain why Israel may act against structural change in the Middle East, and Turkey may not. And, on the brighter side, they explain why Communist arms sales to Egypt and Syria probably will not lead to the incorporation of these states in the Soviet bloc.

It is erroneous to look upon the Middle East as being in the "middle" between the United States and the Soviet Union. It is clear that the great-power relationship has an important bearing on Middle Eastern affairs, but the latter may not be understood wholly or even primarily in terms of the major international system. If power were to be likened to rays of light, we might say that extra-area power is "refracted" when projected into the Middle Eastern element. If we are ever successful in quantifying power for purposes of international political analysis, we shall have to give that power separate coefficients in each system. The concept of subordinate system complicates the problem of quantifying power, but it also complicates the problem of reducing the international system to a set of rules. Progress toward the latter goal, if it is at all attainable, must first depend upon identifying the unique characteristics of each system.

III

A preliminary and perennial problem is that of defining the area of the Middle East. Official definitions such as that of a foreign ministry or a United Nations body are arbitrary and meaningless in terms of a disciplinary approach. Possible criteria for delimitation of the area in terms of the study of international affairs might be the existence of regional organizations or defense pacts, but this is to neglect the close interrelationship of domestic and international politics, to take no account of power, and to fail to reflect conflicting intra-area policies. Elsewhere the existence of a religious alternative to nationalism has been cited by the present writer as a criterion for delimiting the Middle East in terms of the study of comparative government, and this characteristic was supplemented by reference to the shorter colonial experience of Middle Eastern states.[21] Hence, the most important characteristic setting apart the Middle East as a subordinate international system is the ideological context of its politics, both domestic and external. On this basis the Middle East proper stretches from Libya to Iran, with fringe areas including Afghanistan, Pakistan, and the Maghrib, and a core area including the Arab states and Israel. This definition may be allowed to stand for present purposes, with some refinement to be added in terms of the applicability throughout this area of the characteristics to be discussed.

With the exception of Iran, all parts of the Middle East proper —the Arab states, Israel, and modern Turkey—were once part of the Ottoman Empire. They share disparate elements of the formerly common Ottoman legal system, and vestiges of the old millet system. Wherever a landed aristocracy exists, it can usually trace its roots back to Ottoman times. All of these states have a common administrative tradition from which they have only partially departed. Except for Israel and, to a lesser extent, Lebanon, all are susceptible to a common Pan-Islamic ideal. Because of the location of Mecca and Medina within Saudi Arabia, that state may perhaps most advantageously manipulate the symbols of Islam. Pan-Arabism ties all these states, except for Turkey and

Israel. Because of the middle-class appeal of Pan-Arabism, the monarchical states are at a disadvantage in using the symbols of Arab nationalism in their foreign policies. Until the recent imposition of political boundaries upon the area, communication was comparatively unobstructed for those who desired or were compelled to travel or maintain commercial contacts throughout the empire. Despite administrative divisions and varying degrees of autonomy in outlying or inaccessible districts, the clergy of each faith comprised a single cohesive group.

The political boundaries which have been established in the area have little historical significance and frequently less ethnic validity. Moreover, these boundaries are often associated with imperialist intervention and consequently lack legitimacy. The existence of such boundaries over a relatively short period of time has tended to fix them in a legal and political sense for the present, but they must be recognized as inherently unstable. If they are to be retained for any purposeful reason, such policy will require positive action.

A phenomenon which may be directly related to the common political-territorial heritage of all these states is that nearly all are in some degree revisionist. Those that are not—Libya, the Sudan, and the Lebanon—are relatively unimportant or inactive; while Iran, like Turkey the residuum of a once great empire, is at least potentially revisionist. Nearly universal revisionism has resulted from the usual incongruity of nation and territorial state, from the persistent conception of certain parts of the area—the Gezira, the south Syrian Desert, Palestine, "geographical" Syria—as territorial units, and from the fact that none of the Middle Eastern states was a "winner" in the partition of the Ottoman Empire. Under these circumstances, diplomatic relations are more than usually tense and suspicious. Alliance is impossible except where states have no common border (Egypt and Syria) or an unimportant one (Iraq and Jordan, Egypt and Saudi Arabia). The Turco-Iraqi alliance of 1955 is therefore an exception to be explained in terms of the provision of a wider framework involving the major system, and in terms of the peculiar domestic political position in Iraq. The only other basis for alliance is a wide one, involving mutual self-denial through acceptance of the *status quo*. The Arab

League Pact was diverted to this purpose by Egyptian policy, and thereby earned general Arab support and even the capacity to recruit noncharter members. The negative character of the alliance was demonstrated in the lack of Arab concert during the Palestine War.

In view of this nearly universal revisionism, alliances with non-area powers are extremely suspect and highly unstable, because area interests generally receive a higher priority than nonarea interests. It would seem that any attempt by an extra-area state to establish close relations with two or more Middle Eastern states which have themselves been unable or unwilling to establish a bilateral alliance will be doomed to failure. Such seems to have been the fate of the proposed Middle East Defense Organization. Insofar as Iraq was concerned, despite the affinity of Nuri al-Sa'id and the palace for Turkey, the Baghdad Pact was more important as a revision of Anglo-Iraqi relations than as establishing close Turkish-Iraqi relations.

Another consequence of the former political unity of the area is the ease with which domestic politics may affect affairs in neighboring countries. Recently even Iran has grown closer to former Ottoman territories in this regard. The policies of Mossadegh undoubtedly affected the Egyptian position on the Suez Canal, while the fate of Farouk had its implications for the Shah of Iran. Turkish nationalist policies have had a tremendous impact throughout the Middle East, and not least in Iran. The fate of Islam in Turkey will elicit responses in all Muslim countries, as did the suppression of the Muslim Brethren in Egypt. Among the Arab states, it is well understood that an Egyptian editorial will threaten the stability of the Jordanian government, while a Syrian military coup will encourage Iraqi revolutionaries or terrify Lebanese leaders. In the confrontation of Israel and the Arab states this characteristic is less well defined, but domestic power shifts that portend alterations in the Middle Eastern international structure have an immediate effect on Israeli policy, as the treatment of Jews throughout the area affects domestic Israeli affairs.

With only partial exceptions, the power structure of the area must be reckoned in terms of population and foreign aid. Generally speaking, the entire area is characterized by profound weakness, governmental instability, and administrative inefficiency. The general lack of resources, low level of economic development, and low level of education are the fundamental causes of this weakness. Turkey, which is best endowed in regard to nearly all of these factors, has about the largest population in the area and has received the largest amounts of foreign military and economic aid.[22] Turkey is the strongest Middle Eastern power. Egypt, because of the size of its population (about equal to that of Turkey), would be of comparable power were it better endowed with mineral resources, were its population better educated and in better health, and were it the recipient of larger amounts of foreign aid and technical assistance. Israel has a small population, but has the best-educated population, a fairly efficient administration, and a relatively stable government. Israel has the highest standard of living in the area and has been the recipient of the largest per capita amounts of foreign aid. Israeli industry and technology are relatively advanced for this area as well. Israel probably stands next to Turkey in power. The population of Iran is the third largest in the Middle East (excluding Pakistan), but this population is spread over the largest land area and is characterized by much disunity. The Iranian situation is much the same as that of Egypt, except that it has a smaller population and has received larger amounts of foreign aid. Iraq, with a somewhat larger population than Syria, and having always enjoyed greater military and technical assistance, is the more powerful. More recently the expansion of Iraq's petroleum production has provided an adequate financial basis for economic development, so that Iraq may grow rapidly in power given internal political stability. Jordan has a small population, but, until recently, its power could be measured in terms of the British-trained, -led, -equipped, and -subsidized Arab Legion. The efficiency of this organization has probably fallen since its last test in 1948, so that it may be considered a sufficient achievement if the Legion can keep order in Jordan and sustain King Husain.

If it is granted that foreign aid and population are the key elements in the Middle Eastern power structure, then it follows that the scope of foreign intervention in the area is wide. Given the general weakness of the area, relatively large amounts of both material and technical aid can develop a temporary superiority of power even in such a state as Jordan. If such power could be turned to the purposes of an extra-area state, it might disrupt the entire Middle Eastern system. On the other hand, no Middle Eastern government need become the instrument of an extra-area state, because extra-area power may not be transmitted at full strength from the dominant bipolar system; nor can it become such an instrument, because of the ideological orientation of domestic Middle Eastern politics. In other words, it is possible for an extra-area state to help a Middle Eastern state achieve its own ends, but unlikely that an extra-area state can compel a Middle Eastern state to serve extra-area interests. Moreover, even in helping Middle Eastern states to achieve their own goals when these coincide with extra-area goals, the scope of foreign intervention is limited by the greater ease in maintaining the *status quo* than in changing it.

If the Suez invasion illustrates anything besides poor military execution and even worse political direction of the military, it illustrates the limited ability of extra-area states to commit power to the Middle East and the limited period during which such a commitment may be maintained. The time limit may be important, for its determines that, in the long run, the crucial power factor will be population (and possibly petroleum) rather than foreign aid. But this eventuality would require the complete insulation of the Middle Eastern system from all external influence— and such a situation is hardly conceivable at present. A more immediate consequence of the wide, if nevertheless limited, scope of external influence is the near equality of the role of each Middle Eastern state within the subordinate system, limited only by domestic political circumstances. These factors add up to an inherent instability of system, suggesting further that, should external vigilance be relaxed or a domestic (and therefore inaccessible) upheaval take place, violent changes will occur throughout the area. It is more than likely that extra-area states will be unable to control or direct these changes, because of the negative character of their influence and because in some cases there may be no widely accepted political authority through whom such influence may be channelled.

National security may be the irreducible minimum goal of any foreign policy, but the nature of the security problem in the Middle East is only vaguely related to the security problem in the major international system. Certainly, the concept of security in a nuclear war is so far beyond the scope of Middle Eastern governments as to be nearly meaningless. Even among the members of the CENTO, only Turkey seems to have given the problem some thought. In a more concrete if less humane approach to "nuclear security," we may say that the nature of the security problem in the Middle East differs from that in the major international system because of the relatively low public capital investment in these countries and the small portion of the population resident in urban centers. Middle Eastern countries do not make good targets for nuclear missiles.

To be meaningful for purposes of analyzing the international relations of the Middle East, the dominant security consideration must be related to actual foreign policies and hence to "local" problems. The Middle Eastern security consideration must be predicated upon the continuance of the present system. That is to say, national security in the Middle East means the security of existing individual states, and not the security of the free world or of Islam or of Arabdom.

There are some who argue for an Arab national interest in terms of an Arab nationalist ideology.[23] This argument suggests either that the interest of the Arab peoples is opposed to that of their governments in most cases or that an ideal is in some manner an interest, and that an interest may exist quite apart from benefiting any specific group of individuals. However that may be, the notion of an Arab national interest, insofar as it insists upon the political unity of the Arab states and possible territorial expansion at the expense of Israel, Turkey, and Iran, is a threat to rather than a substitute for the security interest of all existing states in the Middle East.

By relating the security consideration to existing states and by distinguishing it from at least one constitutionally transcendent ideology, it is a simple matter further to relate that consideration to the interest of a ruling elite. While the popular support for existing governments varies from state to state, it is clear that those governments, politicians, administrators, military officers, and allied groups have the greatest stake in continued independence. If this point of view is pressed far enough, we may find in some cases that the threat to the security of the state is as much internal as it is external. This seems to be the case in Iran and most of the Arab states.

The domestic political process in these states has an important bearing on the manner in which this kind of security is pursued.[24] The dominant characteristics of this process are the stringent limits upon access to or participation in decision making and the erratic, uncontrolled progress of social mobilization. The latter characteristic results in short-lived and disoriented political or interest organization and correlative erraticism in political action, frequently punctuated by disjointed acts of violence.[25] Lacking popular support in most cases, and often lacking reliable information, Middle Eastern governments are at a loss to provide against sudden upheavals. One of the greatest weaknesses of these governments in the last analysis is the lack of means to satisfy increasing demands for jobs and higher standards of living, or demands by the military for better equipment and a larger establishment, or both of these at the same time. Problems such as these induce Middle Eastern governments to accept foreign aid, not primarily as a means of strengthening or developing their country, or as a means of guaranteeing their security against extra-area aggression, but as a means of staying in power.

IV

Within the Arab core of the Middle East the preceding generalizations apply with the greatest relevance. The overlapping of domestic and foreign politics, the relative equality of all international actors, and the paradoxical inadequacy of the diplomatic process are all enhanced by the common ideal of Pan-Arabism. While certain developments permitted us to talk of groupings of Arab states—the Three Kings group and the Cairo-Damascus entente—subsequent events have demonstrated that such groupings have not basically altered the Middle Eastern system.

It is among the Arab states that the equality of role of each participant is most out of keeping with the facts of international power. How else can we explain the rivalry of Egypt, with its 26 million people, and Iraq with only 5 million? How else can we explain the threat that King Abdallah posed for Syria? The posture of individual Arab states may change: Jordan, from Abdallah's aggressiveness to Hussain's defensiveness; Iraq, from Kassim's isolation to Arif's attempts at wider Arab unity; Saudi Arabia, from close association with Egypt to the support of traditional Yemeni authorities, and from financial support of Syria to financial support of Jordan; but all remain as though fixed in place, because of domestic political circumstances, because of extra-area influence, and because Israel exists in their midst. Intra-Arab rivalries have, therefore, an air of unreality about them, and many an ingenious diplomatic program has been cast on the trash heap.[26]

There is another sense in which four of the Arab states are equal. Egypt, Syria, Iraq, and Saudi Arabia can each make an impressive claim to be the political nucleus about which the future inclusive Arab nation-state will form. Egypt's claims are based upon its larger population, more important contemporary cultural achievements, and recent international successes. Syria can assert its conception and early nurturing of the Arab movement, its provision of a throne for King Faisal ibn Hussain, and its historical position as the locus of the "Arab" caliphate. Iraq's claims stem from its early achievement of independence, its superior power in the Fertile Crescent, its initiation of political Pan-Arabism after World War I, and its not inglorious history as the center of the Abassid Caliphate. Saudi Arabia is, however, the original Arab homeland, the seat of the "Rightly Guided" Caliphate, and the center of the Islamic religion. Even King Hussain of Jordan claims leadership in the Arab struggle, as a consequence of his great-grandfather's leadership of the Arab revolt of 1916. Neither Lebanon, nor Libya, nor the Sudan can make similar claims, but all are quite content with the coexistence of these rival aspirations.

Despite the rough equality of role among the Arab states, the pattern of their interaction is marked both by variations in intensity and by incomplete multilateralism. The greatest intensity exists in the relations of the Fertile Crescent countries. Egypt has become a full participant in this intense pattern as a result of the conflict with Israel and Israel's logical choice of Egypt rather than Jordan as the country to defeat, as a result of the disagreement with Jordan over the future of the Arab portions of Palestine, and as a result of the three year union of Syria and Egypt. The source of the greater intensity of Fertile Crescent relations is the more extreme applicability of the earlier generalizations on boundaries, revisionism, domestic politics, and Pan-Arabism. These same factors determine that the intensity of relationship is almost completely multilateral in character. Libya and the Sudan participate in this system only through their relations with Egypt, and these relations are for the most part bilateral.

Saudi Arabian policy among the Arab states has been marked by both astute caution and a curiously anachronistic element. Saudi caution is based upon the inability of the Saudi government to project its power beyond its own borders, and upon the extreme vulnerability of the existing social and political structure of that country to the influences of middle-class Arab leadership in the more "modern" states. The anachronistic element enters in the tendency of the King to utilize internationally the quasi-diplomatic methods which have served the House of Saud so well domestically. The domestic success of these methods is due to the combination of dignity, honesty, and power maintained by the King; but their lack of international success is due to the absence of international power. Saudi Arabia is, of course, vitally interested in the Fertile Crescent, and for a time its foreign policy was dominated by the dynastic feud between the houses of Hashim and Saud. But the intensity of Saudi action internationally has been notably less than that of the others (except for Libya, the Sudan, and the Yemen), first because the Hashimite states were dominated by the common British ally, later because Egypt was better able to accomplish Saudi purposes in maintaining the division of the Fertile Crescent, and more recently because of the recognition of common interests with the Hashimite states. Developments in Syria in 1957–1958 and in Yemen in 1962, perhaps coupled with some pressure from the United States, have prodded King Saud to attempt too much.

The preceding analysis suggests that Egypt is the hub of Arab relations, and the essential element in the success or failure of extra-area policy.

Turkey, Iran, and Israel stand in a special relationship to the Arab "core" of the Middle East. Turkey retains the aspect of a former imperialist overlord, an aspect which is enhanced by Turkey's insistence upon its European status. Prevalent anti-Western attitudes involving the use of the slogans of neutralism and anti-imperialism may be applied against Turkey with little shifting of ideological gears. Turkish membership in NATO and the secularism of the state are further distinguishing characteristics. The total effect of these special features has been to hamstring the operation of dominant Turkish power in Middle Eastern affairs.

During the postwar period, the Turkish government has made several overtures to the Arab states, with a view to engaging them in closer relations. For a long while the United States hoped to use Turkey as the cohesive element in organizing the area for defense. Except for Iraq, which had always been somewhat more favorably inclined toward Turkey, the response of the Arab states has been negative. And well it might be, for a continuing Middle Eastern problem is how to prevent renewed Turkish domination of or intervention in Arab affairs. The global problem of security against the Soviet Union runs a poor second to this local structural problem.

The systematic tendency of the Arab states has been to exclude Turkish influence, and this was matched earlier by Turkish aloofness from Arab problems, Turkish recognition of Israel, and the relation of Turkish security to that of Western Europe. The change in Turkish policy was due to American predilection, and was based upon calculations related to the global conflict in the major system and not the peculiar characteristics of the subordinate Middle Eastern system. Obviously, this policy failed, and for good reason, but it established the special role of Turkey in the Middle East. That special role is one of bridging the gap between the major and the subordinate systems, for the position of Turkey has a good deal of ambiguity. The imperialist epithet may be applicable to Turkey in an historical sense, but not in terms of the immediate post-World War I policies of nationalist Turkey. Turkey, too, can be seen as a new nation-state pointing the way to a successful political renaissance for other new non-European states. It is the latter aspect of Turkish history that would have to be stressed for Turkey to play a more effective role in Middle Eastern affairs.

Iran also has a special relationship to the Arab states, and it, too, tends to bridge the gap between the major and the minor systems. There is no tendency for Iranian policies to be construed as imperialist; usually Iran has been the most abject of those suffering imperialist intervention. The particularly unfortunate position of Iran was that of being coveted by both Britain and Russia while being allied to neither. But for rather special circumstances, the fate of Iran might have been that of nineteenth-century Poland. To escape from this position Iran has recently sought to emulate the part of Turkey in alliance with the West, a possibility opened to Iran only by the decline of British power in the Middle East.

Iran is separated from the Arab states by the divergence of its sectarian Islam and by the historical effect of a four-century-old political boundary. Despite the vagueness or shifting character of this boundary, it has had a persistence which has served to prevent the complete cultural and political assimilation of Iran and Iraq. On the other hand, the existence of important Shi'i holy places in Iraq exemplifies the usual Middle Eastern overflow of domestic into international politics. The competitive Iranian oil industry rivals that of neighboring Arab states, but it is not a truly divisive factor. While Iran may benefit from the disruption of oil production in the Arab states, as those states benefited from the interruption of Iranian oil production, such competition implies a close interrelationship rather than a disinterested lack of relationship.

Despite its adherence to the Baghdad Pact, Iran has a close relationship to the Arab states in many ways. The sense of unfulfilled nationalism in Iran is familiar and makes Iran a member of the new-nation international. While Iran, or the Shah, has preferred an alliance with the West to the equal pressure of both East and West, it is clear that the highest good for Iranians is the absence of all pressure. In this sense Iran joins with most neutral states in desiring to break bipolarity. The pressure of the

Soviet Union is so great, however, and the domestic position of the Shah would be so weak in the absence of external aid, that it is unfeasible for Iran to act upon this favored policy.

Because of its non-Arab character, Iran cannot interfere in inter-Arab relations; but because of its history as a victim of imperialist exploitation, Iran more than Turkey dignified the Baghdad Pact with a sincerity which had some appeal in the Middle East. Under Mossadegh some effort was made to win Arab support against the British, and it seemed as though a close relationship might develop between Egypt and Iran. Nothing came of these beginnings because of the extreme disparity in the kinds of problems faced by each country, and because neither had the power to help the other. With Mossadegh's fall, the two countries grew apart until Iran's rerecognition of Israel resulted in a complete break of diplomatic relations between Egypt and Iran. Furthermore, Iran's typical response to pressure is to confound the outsider by a demonstration of weakness and anarchy rather than strength and defiance. A strategy of this kind does not encourage alliance, nor does it produce international leadership.

Should Iranian power increase, and should the pressure from the north abate, it may be expected that Iran will return to more aggressive policies abandoned over a century ago. A truly strong and stable Iran might willingly attempt to involve itself in the diplomatic maneuvering among the Arab states, and might be better able to lend support to the government of Iraq should that state become isolated from other Arab states.

Israel, like Turkey and Iran, is another link connecting the Middle Eastern and the major global system, but it is the weakest systematic link of the three. Its function in this regard is largely negative. Since the Arab states cannot themselves cope with what they consider to be a disruptive element in their region, the role of the great powers in confirming the partition of Palestine has had a continuing impact on the Middle East. The existence of Israel, not yet accepted by the Arab states, lends constant validity to the dependence of the Middle Eastern structure upon the major bipolar structure. This situation tends to foster the notion that the Palestine question may be solved to the satisfaction of the Arab states only if the influence of the great powers is entirely withdrawn. Since the Soviet Union did in fact withdraw from the Middle East after 1948, emphasis was placed upon the withdrawal of the Western powers. Lately the Soviet Union has been invited into the area to counterbalance American influence—an example of members of the subordinate system attempting to exploit the possibilities of the major bipolar system.

Within the Middle Eastern system itself, the place of Israel is important; but again it functions in a largely negative manner. Israel has functioned as a stabilizing influence in inter-Arab affairs by preventing important structural shifts and diverting the energies of the Arab nations from their own disagreements or internal difficulties. If, in time, peaceable political unity ever comes to the Fertile Crescent, its success would seem to depend upon Israel's continuing to moderate the application of Egyptian pressures on Syria and Jordan. The demise of the Kingdom of Jordan will probably be delayed more by the presence of Israel than by external financial aid and military support.

The state of Israel was established at least as much by military action as by resolution of the General Assembly, and this fact has tended to focus attention in and around Israel on the question of armaments. The continued state of quasi-belligerency has perpetuated this tendency, not only because of recurrent border incidents, but also because of the diplomatic boycott of Israel. The diplomatic boycott has compelled Israel, in seeking to exert its structural weight in the area, to participate in the Middle Eastern system by the measured use of force. The tendency to stress armaments diverts scarce resources from economic development, and thus has a deleterious effect on all concerned that external intervention has been unable to prevent.

V

The preceding discussion of the special characteristics of the Middle Eastern international system, though far from providing a manageable group of systematic rules, should serve to illustrate its distinctive nature. If bipolarity is a useful term in describing certain contemporary aspects of international politics, it is clear that it is inadequate to describe either relations within the Middle East or between the major bipolar system itself and this subordinate system.

It is much more difficult to derive policy suggestions from this kind of preliminary analysis, but one point does stand out. It seems clear that policies based upon the assumption of global bipolarity will be unsuccessful in the Middle East. It may be further suggested that policies derived from the assumption or reality of a situation of "mutual deterrence" in the major system will effect no progress toward the solution of disputed problems in the subordinate system. If the mutually deterrent system is to work in the subordinate area, each of the great powers must indicate its willingness to fight over the most minor issue, while the indigenous states must act in so responsible a manner as not to change mutual deterrence into mutual destruction. Since Middle Eastern states are neither responsible nor keenly aware of the relationship between the major and minor systems, it does not seem likely that they will act to sustain the situation of mutual deterrence. It is far more likely that the Middle Eastern states will feel compelled to act in terms of their own complex system so as to preserve their individual positions within the Middle Eastern structure, and that they may feel that mutual deterrence is a condition which exists independently of their action, i.e., that the United States and the Soviet Union will, in the last analysis, not react to the moves of third parties in the Middle East if such action would entail a global nuclear war. In this sense Middle Eastern states, and the Arab states in particular, may believe that there is more room for maneuver along the brink than actually exists.

NOTES

1. For a discussion of some of the issues involved, see Fred A. Sondermann, "The Study of International Relations," *World Politics*, **X**, No. 1 (October 1957), p. 102; and Kenneth W. Thompson, "Toward a New Theory of International Relations," *American Political Science Review*, **XLIX**, No. 3 (September 1955), pp. 733–746.
2. Despite Sondermann's views it seems to me that a strong rationale for this approach is presented in Ernst B. Haas and Allen S. Whiting, *The Dynamics of International Relations* (New York, 1956).

3. To be distinguished from Sondermann's "freight car" category.
4. Especially Hans J. Morgenthau, *Politics Among Nations* (New York, 1948).
5. Especially and most recently, Morton A. Kaplan, *System and Process in International Relations* (New York, 1957).
6. See William Reitzel, Morton A. Kaplan, and Constance G. Coblenz, *United States Foreign Policy, 1945-1955* (Washington, D.C., 1956), especially Chapter xvi.
7. See Kaplan, *op. cit.*, p. 40 (the fourth "condition").
8. This is similar to Kaplan's "tight bipolar system," *ibid.*, p. 43f.
9. Similar to, but not quite the same as, Kaplan's "loose bipolar system," *ibid.*, p. 36.
10. *Ibid.*, p. 40 (the fifth "condition").
11. The final alternative contradicts Kaplan's fifth condition, cited above, as well as his rules 7, 9, and 10, *ibid.*, pp. 38-39. This difference is an additional reason for the present writer's preference for the concept of subordinate systems to that of "loose" bipolarity.
12. Walter Z. Laqueur, *Communism and Nationalism in the Middle East* (New York, 1956), p. 260f.
13. E. A. Speiser, *The United States and the Near East*, rev. ed. (Cambridge, Mass., 1950).
14. E.g., *Pravda* of March 8, 1955, cited in Committee on Foreign Relations, U.S. Senate, *Events in the Middle East* (Washington, D.C., 1957), p. 9.
15. See Guy Wint and Peter Calvocoressi, *Middle East Crisis* (Penguin Special, 1957), pp. 52-53.
16. Re Jordan: Department of State, *US Policy in the Middle East*, September 1956-June 1957 (Documents), p. 69, "News Conference of Secretary of State Dulles, April 23, 1957." See also note 63, *Ibid*. On April 30, 1957, six US naval vessels of an amphibious force visited Beirut: "Developments of the Quarter," *Middle East Journal*, XI, No. 3 (Summer 1957), p. 286. Re Syria: see *New York Times*, August 17, 1957, *et seq.*, especially August 21 dispatch by D. A. Schmidt, ". . . the US by itself cannot do anything. . . . It is up to the governments of the Middle East. . . ." (p. 1 in nearly all cases).
17. The British government still insists that the treaty is valid.
18. The latest reaffirmation of the Tri-partite Declaration stressed its applicability to the Israeli-Arab dispute only; Department of State, *op. cit.*, p. 65, "News Conference Statement by President Eisenhower, April 17, 1957."
19. *New York Times*, August 23, 1957, p. 1, dispatch from Washington by D. A. Schmidt, in which the term "isolation of Syria" is used. "Quarantine" was the revised version of this phrase.
20. Wint and Calvocoressi, *op. cit.*, p. 69.
21. "Prolegomena to the Comparative Study of Middle East Governments," *American Political Science Review*, LI, No. 3 (September 1957), pp. 651-652.

22. "United States Aid to the Middle East, 1945–1957," *Middle Eastern Affairs*, VIII, No. 11 (November 1957), p. 385f.
23. H. Z. Nusaibeh, *The Ideas of Arab Nationalism* (Ithaca, N.Y., 1956), p. 84f.
24. See Dankwart A. Rustow, *Politics and Westernization in the Near East* (Princeton, 1956).
25. See George McT. Kahin, Guy J. Pauker, and Lucian W. Pye, "Comparative Politics of Non-Western Countries," *American Political Science Review*, XLIX, No. 4 (December 1955), pp. 1024–1027.
26. E.g., Egyptian-Syrian-Saudi Joint Command, announced March 6, 1955; Five-Year Egyptian-Saudi Defense Treaty, announced October 27, 1955; Jordan-Saudi-Syrian-Egyptian "Unified Frontier" plan, announced March 23, 1956; Egyptian-Saudi-Yemeni Five-Year Defense Pact, announced April 21, 1956; Lebanese-Jordanian coordinated Defense Pact, announced May 21, 1956; similar Jordanian-Syrian arrangement of May 31, 1956; and the Egyptian-Saudi-Syrian agreement of January 19, 1957, to subsidize Jordan.

INDEX

Muslim names are to be found listed under the most familiar element of the name, usually the last element.

279